MW01434720

THE DESCENDANTS OF
ELISHA COLE

WHO CAME FROM CAPE COD TO WHAT IS NOW
PUTNAM COUNTY, NEW YORK, ABOUT 1745

COMPILED BY
JOSEPH O. CURTIS
NEW YORK

ILLUSTRATED

NEW YORK
TOBIAS A WRIGHT
1909

.C69
1909

ADDITIONS AND CORRECTIONS

PAGE 7. Simion Dakin should read Simon Dakin.

PAGE 27. Joshua, d Feb 3, 1826.

PAGE 33. Susannah Ogden, b June 25, 1755. She made application for a pension Dec, 1851, she being then 95 years old, and gave date of enlistment of her husband, Daniel Cole, as 1778, rank as sergeant, Cap Mead's Co., Col. Ludington's Regt, and that she was married to Daniel in 1771. Her claim was rejected, not enough evidence being given of his service. "N Y. in the Revolution" distinctly shows her claim was a just one. At that time (1851) Revolutionary State Papers were not as accessible as they are today

PAGE 33 No 42, Mary, b Nov. 26, 1781, d at home of her son-in-law, Caleb Hazen, at Penn Yan, N. Y., on Dec. 2, 1878

PAGE 38 No. 92 should read McKinstry.

PAGE 53. No 206, Mary Jane, should be Mary Ann

PAGE 55. No 226, date of marriage should be Nov, 1833.

PAGE 57. No. 49, Lydia, the 2d wife of Elisha J Cole, was a sister of George Frost, the husband of Mary Cole, No 42

PAGE 167. No. 42, Laura Frost, b. at Carmel, N. Y., Oct 30, 1808, m to Caleb Hazen, Jan 2, 1828, and d. at Penn Yann, Oct 30, 1889

   Harrison Frost d Dec. 29, 1815, aged 2 years.

   Sarah J. Frost, b 1815 d Feb. 23, 1896

PAGE 190. No 398, Minor Cole Taft, should be Miner Cole Taft.

PAGE 192. Phebe Huff, b. 1852; m. 1878

   Charles Huff, b 1854, m 1877.

   Minnie Huff, b. 1856, m 1877.

   Alida Huff, b 1858, m 1878

PAGE 196. No. 554 should be 555.

INTRODUCTORY

The Cole name in the United States is variously written Cole, Coles, Coal, Coale and Cowles

It was brought here by three distinct families

About the year 1625, Jacob Kool came from Holland to New Amsterdam, now New York, under the auspices of the West India Company, and from this man sprang a race of Coles that located at Tarrytown on the east bank of the Hudson and along the west side from its mouth to Kingston They were distinctly Hollanders, and maintained their national customs and names more or less for over a hundred years.

The ship *Hercules* from Sandwich, England, arrived at Plymouth in 1634 Among the passengers were James Cole of Sandwich, carpenter, wife Joan and two children.

After their arrival, four other children are on record as born to them:

    Abraham, b Oct. 3, 1636,
    Isaac, b. 1637, d. June 10, 1674,
    Mary, b Jan. 20, 1639,
    Sarah, b Boston, Nov (?) 15, 1641,

About 1633, three brothers, Job, John and Daniel Cole, appear in the annals of Plymouth Colony Daniel being the ancestor of Elisha, who settled in what was then Dutchess County, N Y, and is now town of Kent, Putnam County

All the lines from, and most of the descendants of Elisha Cole, are given in this book. Only one accustomed to work of this kind can understand the discouragements attending it. The descendants are scattered in nearly every State in the Union Some have shown an indifference to the work that has prevented securing a complete record of their line, and many letters to those who could help remain unanswered

Many have helped, however, and especially am I indebted to Miss Harriet N Cole, of Caramel, N. Y, Mrs E D Cole, of Addison, Mich, Mrs Austin La Fever, of Corning, N Y., and Otis, son of the late Joseph G. Cole, who gave me all of his father's records At the time these records were collected (1866-1875) there was living a number of persons who had a personal acquaintance with Elisha or his children, among them being John Cole, grandson of Elisha, Joseph Hopkins, who married a grand daughter, and Naomi Ballard, who married a grandson Included in this work will be found records of Colonial families that intermarried with the Coles, together with Colonial and Revolutionary items of interest. Where age at death is given in years, months and days, it is mostly taken from tombstones. Some names may be misspelled, and I have changed such names as Sally to Sarah, Polly to Mary, Peggy to Margaret, etc

Numerous members of the family have added an initial letter to their name A man christened John Cole would call himself John W Cole, etc Children who died young are not indexed

In the annals of this country the Cole family is old It has been seen and participated in everything of moment from Puritan days to the present time. In the records of great achievement it is not particularly noted, but, as a race, the Coles have proved themselves sturdy, courageous, self reliant and independent. Theirs seems to have been the story of fair intelligence, solid respectability, innate piety and consistent mediocrity To be sure, they have produced good soldiers, prominent lawyers, fairly eminent divines and accomplished physicians, but the "even tenor of their way" seems to have been mostly in the field of pioneer agriculture. Nevertheless, they have had no criminals and very few drunkards They have clung to the sturdy religious principles and hard-working habits of their Puritan ancestry, and throughout the length and breadth of America have spread the example and gospel of the sturdier virtues which go to make a nation great This book does not claim to be perfect The editor has simply tried in a modest way to jot down the record as far as the limited resources at his command would permit

The usual abbreviations are used. b for born, m for married; d. for died, d y for died young, d. unm for died unmarried, etc

During the Revolution the militia was called out when wanted, kept as long as wanted and soldiers then sent to their homes

Sometimes a regiment, or a part of a regiment, would be called out half a dozen times in the course of a year, and for a week or so at a time In New York, the militia were in many hotly contested fights. Many men undoubtedly performed splendid service in the militia and then returned to their homes, leaving no record of their services that can now be found

The Colonel of each militia regiment was requested to see that each member present himself when "warned," each soldier to be equipped with a blanket, flint-lock rifle or musket, powder horn and a flint, and often a tomahawk A private received per month, a pound of sugar, 2 ounces of tea and some tobacco Their pay was six and two-thirds dollars a month As late as April 27, 1784, a majority of the soldiers had not been paid On this date the Legislature passed an act for such payments, and the State Treasurer was required to issue to persons to whom payment was due, or their legal representatives, certificates of indebtedness bearing 5 per cent interest Such certificates could be received in payment of taxes, purchase of forfeited estates, etc

In Dutchess County there were seven regiments of militia One regiment, the "Associated Exempts," composed of men between 50 and 60 years of age, were to be called out only "in time of invasion." One regiment of "Minute Men" and one company of 69 men called "Cooper's Rangers," commanded by Capt Ezekiel Cooper. The 7th Regiment, Dutchess County Militia, Col Henry Ludington, is the most interesting to descendants of Elisha Cole, as its members were principally residents of what is now the towns of Kent and Caramel. Among the members of the Cole family, or individuals who married into the Cole family, and who fought in the War of the Revolution, are the following, the original spelling being given Daniel Cole, Ebenezer Cole, Elisha Cole, Elisha Cole, Jr, Joseph Cole, and Reuben Cole, Ensign Caleb Hazen, Astin, Ager, Ballard, Barit, Berry, Bruster, Carver, Chase, Crosby, Drew, Ganog, Ganong, Ganoung, Ganung, Green, Hasin, Holmes, Hopkins, Horten, How, Howes, Hughson, Huson, Keley, Kerley, Killey, Knapp, Merick,

Marick, Myrick, Odal, Odel, Odle, Odall, Ogden, Sloot, Slat, Small, Smally, Smith, Sprage, Spreg, Townsend, Weeks, Wixsom, Wood

During the summer of 1907, the writer, while seeking material for this genealogy, had occasion to consult the records of the Carmel Baptist Church. To his surprise he found that the earliest records was that of "The Church of Christ in Frederickstown," dated Oct ye 16, 1790, and is the commencement of book 1 of records Following this date is a list of those "received in fellowship," mostly undated, but doubtless received previously to 1827, as the book closes with an account of a meeting held Saturday, Aug 25, 1827. The records, with the exception of the above list of names, contains nothing of interest to either an historian or genealogist They contain no records of births, marriages or deaths, being composed of accounts of the meetings held, which are without interest to those of the present time. Further research confirmed my suspicions that the Caramel Church was not the original Church, but an offshoot from it

The Baptist Church of Millerton is undoubtedly the parent church, as the following from its records will show

"Historical Sketch of the Baptist Church in North East Town" (Now Millerton)

"This church was constituted about the time of the remarkable revival under Whitefield A number of members from a Presbyterian church in a place then called South Precinct, Dutchess county, New York, now Franklin, Putnam Co, withdrew and joined one of the Congregational order that held to open communion Among them were Simon Dakin and others, who afterwards embraced the Baptist sentiment, and a church was constituted on Phillips patent, Nov 6, 1753, composed of nine members Elder Dakin was ordained about this time and continued in Pastoral care over it until his death on Sep. 19, 1803, in his 83d year In Sep 1771 the number of members was 67 The church removed to this town in May 1773. The cause of their coming was in consequence of a mob that arose and made considerable disturbance on the patent, together with local privileges they hoped to enjoy The members not removing were by their own request, constituted into a church by themselves. Mr Nathan Cole, a licentiate from this church May 2, 1772 afterwards became their pastor."

The above is a copy of an ancient document among the church records, written about a hundred years ago by the then pastor, Thomas Winter

The church, of which not a vestage now remains, was located where is now the old graveyard at Spencer's Corners, about two miles from the present Millerton Among those buried there is Hannah, daughter of Elisha Cole and wife of Freeman Hopkins.

The first book of records of the Millerton church commences as follows·

"Y^e book of records of the Church of Christ in Phillips Pattant This church was constituted in Nov , about the 16, A D., 1751 and our members were nine."

Then follows the list of members, all before Jan 3, 1761, the first nine being undoubtedly the original members·

Simion Dakin, Elijah Calkin, Josiah Baker, Recompense Thomas, Matthew Rowlee, Reuben Close, Barzillai King, Elisha Cole, Heman King, Joseph Baker, Robert Fuller, Nathan Cole, Jonathan Hayes, Elisha Smith, Isaiah Robinson, Edmond Baker, Hezekiah Eastman, David Carter. Joseph Rundel, Samuel Beebe Obed Harvey, Obed Harvey, Jr., Jesse Smith, Thomas Knapp, Martin Elmer, Amos Hanchet, Joshua Dakin, Susannah Burch, Obedience Bobbet, Rebecca Dakin, Elizabeth Willkon (?), Sarah Chichester, Jemima Stewart, Sarah Calkin, Eunice Hays, Eleanor ———, Amai Robinson, Eunice Barber, Mehitable Cole, Mercy Harvey, Ann Roe, Eunice Brownel, Anna Rogers, "Liddey" Smith, Mary Rundle, Alice Willoughby, Ruth Case, Mary Smith, Anna ———, Joseph D. Eastman, Zeruiah Newbury

"August ye 1st 1772.

Mahitibel Cole gave a relation of her experiance of the work of God in her soul " (This was the wife of Nathan Cole)

"Nov ye 5 1774

Petition from members of the church in Phillips Pattent, viz, Joseph Barber, Eunice Barber, Sarah Newbury and Susannah

Parker, for dismissal from this church and recommendation to Elder Nathan Koles"

"Oblong April 1, 1775

The church agrees to send to the church at Dover, Batmans Pattant, Philips Pattant and Pittsfield under the care of Elder Samuel Waldo Elder John Larrance, Elder Nathan Cole and Elder Valantine Rathbun."

COLONIAL FAMILIES INTO WHICH THE COLES HAVE MARRIED

BREWSTER—PRINCE—FREEMAN.

William Brewster, b. England Came to New England in the *Mayflower* in 1620 with his wife, Mary, and children She died and he married for his second wife a Mrs Southworth on Aug 14, 1623 He d in April 1644 He was the first Governor of Plymouth Colony

His daughter, Patience Brewster, was b in England and followed her family to New England in 1623 in the ship *Ann*. She m. Aug 5, 1624, Thomas, b 1600, son of Thomas Prince (Prence), of Lechlade, Gloucestershire, England She d. in 1634, and he married (2) April 1, 1635, Mary, dau. of William Collier He d at Plymouth, March 29, 1673, "leaving widow Mary" She d Dec. 9, 1695, buried Dec. 12 in what is now North Dennis.

He was one of the appraisers of Gov William Brewster's estate. He came to New England in the ship *Fortune* in 1621, being then in his 22nd year He was chosen Governor in 1634, and again in 1638 In 1657 he was living at Eastham and was chosen Governor. The law required that the Governor should live at Plymouth, but the court granted a dispensation and he continued, while holding office, to reside in Eastham In 1665 he removed to Plymouth, where he resided until his death His salary as Governor was £50 a year He left seven daughters, all of whom married His marriage to Patience Brewster was the ninth in the colony, the first being that on May 12, 1621, between Edward Winslow, of the *Mayflower,* and Anne (Fuller) White She was the mother of Peregrine and widow of William. She had been a widow seven weeks, he a widower less than three months

The third child of Thomas and Patience (Brewster) Prince was Mercy, b, Plymouth, 1630-1 She m, Eastham, Feb. 13, 1649-50, John Freeman, of Sandwich, Cape Cod He d Oct 28, 1719, age 98. She d Eastham, Sept 28, 1711, aged 80.

Their third child was Deacon Thomas Freeman, b , Eastham, Sept , 1653. He m there, Dec. 31, 1673, Rebecca, b Oct 30, 1655, dau of Jonathan and Rebecca (Bangs) Sparrow He d. Feb 9, 1715-16, in 62nd year She d Feb 17, 1740, in 86th year Their tombstones in Harwick He was elected Deacon of the First Church of Harwick on Nov 28, 1700 He was also Town Clerk, Selectman, etc

Their fifth child was Capt Joseph Freeman, b , Eastham, Feb 10, 1682-3 He m there, Oct 13, 1709, Lydia, b. there 1685, dau of Jonathan and Lydia (Gorham) Thatcher She d at Harwick, Sep 3, 1724, aged 39 (from tombstone), and he m. (2) Sept 9, 1736, Mrs Mary Freeman, wid of Nathaniel, who d Aug 2, 1735. She was b 1688, the dau of Elkanah Watson, of Plymouth Cap Joseph d. at Harwick, March, 1756 His will, dated March 10, 1756, proved March 18, 1756 He was Selectman, Justice of the Peace, Captain Train Band, etc

The fifth child of Capt. Joseph and Lydia (Thatcher) Freeman was Rebecca Freeman, b , Eastham, March 20, 1720 She m there, Oct 4, 1744, Jonathan Hopkins.

HOPKINS.

Stephen Hopkins, b in England in 1585 Nothing known of his first wife. He had two children by her, Giles and Constance He m (2) St Mary's Church, Whitechapel, London, March, 1617, Elizabeth Fisher. He came over with his family in the *Mayflower* He was an Assistant, 1633-1636. He d at Plymouth between June 16 and July 27, 1644. She d. at Plymouth between 1640-1644 He was a member of the Council of War, 1642-1644 He also owned the first horse in the colony His will, exhibited at Court, Aug , 1644, shows lands, "15 cattle including a yearling heifer without a tail. A mare, two pigs and chickens. Four silver spoons, iron pot, brass pot, a great kittle, a less kittle, a small kittle and another kittle," and also mentions son "Gyles" and his son Stephen

Giles, oldest son of Stephen Hopkins, was b in England about 1608. He m , Yarmouth, Cape Cod, Oct 9, 1639, "Catorne," dau. of Gabriel "Whelden" He d , Eastham, in 1690, before April 26 She d , Eastham, after March 15, 1689 They had:

THE DESCENDANTS OF ELISHA COLE 11

Joshua, who m Mary, the dau of Daniel Cole. This was the first of many marriages between the Cole and Hopkins families. Giles and "Catorne" had Stephen, second child and oldest son, b, Yarmouth, Sept., 1642. He m, May 23, 1667, Mary, b. Nov. 4, 1650, dau of Ensign William and Rebecca (———) "Myrick" He d Oct. 10, 1718, aged 76 She d 1700-1. They both d. in what is now Brewster, Mass

Stephen and Mary (Myrick) Hopkins had Joseph (seventh child), b, Eastham, 1688, m there April 17, 1712, Mary, b. Oct 26, 1694, dau of John and Hannah (Freeman) Mayo He d, Harwick, April 24, 1771, aged 83 years She d, Harwick, Jan 15, 1771, aged 76 years Tombstones both standing there.

Joseph and Mary (Mayo) Hopkins had eleven children. Two of them only are of interest in this work Joseph, the second child, b, Harwick, May 10, 1715, and Jonathan, the fourth child, b, Harwick, Dec 17, 1719-20. He was bap. by Rev. Nathaniel Stone, Oct 11, 1724 He m, Eastham, Oct 4, 1744, Rebecca, dau of Capt Joseph and Lydia (Thatcher) Freeman. He d. ———. She d, Carmel, Jan 15, 1801, aged 81.

About 1755 he, with his family, removed to the "Oblong," now a part of Putnam County, N Y The records of the first church of Harwick show they were dismissed "to yᵉ church in or near the Oblong. Aug 1, 1756 under the pastoral care of Rev Mr. Kniblow" (Niblo) They had Edmund, b. Oct. 18, 1745, Lydia, b. July 30, 1747, m Nov 3, 1774, Samuel King, Mary, b. about April 6, 1748, at Brewster, Mass, formerly Harwick; Joseph, b. April 6, 1751; Freeman, b. 1753, m Hannah, dau. of Elisha Cole; Thatcher, b 1754, m Eleanor, b, Pawling, Nov. 7, 1754, dau of Thomas and Deborah (Benedict) Ragan She d March 24, 1786, aged 30 years (buried Gilead). He m. (2) Mary ———. He d July 7, 1830, aged 76 years She d. Feb 17, 1839, aged 84 years 8 months Hillside Cemetery, Peekskill. He was a tanner and shoemaker.

Jonathan, b. May 27, 1756, m Deborah ———. She was his second wife and the mother of all his children Name of first wife not known. He d. Dec 12, 1836, aged 80 years. She d Aug. 20, 1826, aged 68 years, 8 months.

Thomas, settled Covert, N Y Dau. m. Abner Bangs. Dau. m Leverton Thomas.

Joseph, son of Jonathan and Rebecca (Freeman) Hopkins, m. Elizabeth Townsend They lived at Phillipstown He d Jan. 31, 1833, aged 81 years She d Dec 16, 1837, aged 82 years. They had (names of these children obtained from Louise (Cole) Denison, a dau of Sally, but not in order of birth) ·

> Jane, d. y.,
> Jane.
> Rebecca, b. Dec 7, 1779; m Elisha Cole 3rd;
> Sally, b. Sept. 10, 1781, m. Daniel Cole;
> Nancy, m. Joshua Cole,
> Chloe,
> Lizzie,
> Asenath,
> Adilla.
> Jonathan,
> Alvah,
> Leonard

Joseph, the second child of Joseph and Mary (Mayo) Hopkins, m. at Harwick, Sept. 16, 1736, Mary, or Mercy, Berry. Both joined the church Aug 29, 1742 They dismissed to church in Oblong, care Rev. Elisha Kent, Sept. 3, 1849-50 They probably removed a year or two previously He d Jan, 1762, she d Dec, 1798. They had:

> Solomon, b May 31, 1739,
> Isaiah,
> Edward,
> Berry,
> Joseph,
> Mary,
> Hannah, bap April 17, 1757,
> Eli

The first child, Solomon, m Elizabeth Crosby. He was a Captain in the Revolution He d Sept. 29, 1792, aged 54 years. She d Jan 6, 1804, aged 62 years Both tombstones in Gilead cemetery. They had

Jeremiah, b Aug. 16, 1762,
Bethia,
Reuben, b 1767, d July 22, 1798, aged 31 years,
Sarah, m Philip Spencer, Aug 20, 1788,
Mary,
Elizabeth

Jeremiah, son of Solomon, m, about 1783, Thankful Stone. He d Oct. 17, 1829, aged 67 years She d. April 18, 1833, aged 70 years He was a Major of Militia Both buried in Gilead They had:

Joseph,
Solomon,
Enos, b Mar 1, 1789, m Cynthia, dau of Joseph Cole;
Naomi,
Hannah,
Abraham,
Mirah,
Nathaniel, b Jan 26, 1797, m Theresa Travis
Jeremiah,
Reuben, d. aged 31 years
Thomas

The earliest will of record shows that another branch of the Hopkins family settled in Dutchess County. It is that of Stephen Hopkins, of Crumelboro Precinct, Dutchess County, N Y, and dated March 9, 1758; probated April 20, 1767 He was probably Stephen,[4] Stephen,[3] Giles,[2] Stephen,[1] and a brother of Joseph Hopkins, who m Mary Mayo He d Feb 8, 1767, aged 61 years She d ———. Both buried in Amenia burying ground The will mentions wife "Jemina" and following children

Noah, m Mary ———,
Roswell, "one of his Majesty's Justice of Peace for County of Dutchess "
Capt. "Michal." m Mehitabel, dau of Rev William and Temperance Worthington, of Saybrook, Conn, he d Nov 17, 1773, aged 39 years, she d. July 14, 1771, aged 34 years,

Wright,
Stephen, m. Jemima Bronson,
Benjamin, m , Apr. 10, 1766, Zerush Rudd,
"Ruban "

HAZEN

The first mention of the name which has been found is in the records of Rowley, Mass : "Elizabeth ye wife Edward Hassen was buried 1649, Sept. ye 18th "

Edward Hazen probably came over with the Rev. Ezekiel Rogers and colony who settled at Rowley, Mass , in 1639 He had eleven children, all born there He m (2), March 2, 1650, Hannah, dau of Thomas and Hannah (———) Grant He was buried at Rowley. July 22, 1683 His wid m , March 17, 1684, George Browne, of Haverhill, who, Sept 9, 1893, adopted her youngest son, Richard, as sole heir to his large estate He d Oct 31, 1699, aged 76 years She d Feb , 1715-16

Edward Hazen was Judge, Selectman, etc , 1650-54-60-61-65-66-68-69

His fourth child was Thomas, b Feb 29, 1657, m., Jan 1, 1682-83, Mary, dau of Thomas Hewlet, whose father was Sergt Thomas Hewlet, one of the first settlers in Agawam, now Ipswich, in 1632-33 He was a farmer in Rowley at the time of his father's death He removed to Boxford, Mass , before March 22, 1689, when he was made freeman In 1711 he removed to Norwich, Conn , and lived in that part then called West Farms, but now Franklin In 1716 he and his three sons were petitioners for its incorporation as a parish He d April 12, 1735 She d Oct. 24, 1727, aged 65 years They had eleven children, the third being

John, b March 23, 1688, m Mercy (bap at Topsfield, Mass , June 2, 1689), dau of John and Sarah (Perkins) Bradstreet and grand dau. of Gov Simon Bradstreet, who was b. in Hambling England, 1603, and came to America in the *Arbella* with Gov. Winthrop in 1630 He m Anna, dau of Gov Thomas Dudley He lived at Salem and d March 27, 1697 Mercy d at Norwich, Conn , Nov 22, 1725, and he m (2), May 31, 1726, Elizabeth, probably the dau. of Daniel and Elizabeth (Douglass)

Dart He d. at Norwich, 1729, leaving seven children, five having died Of his sons—

Caleb, b. April 4, 1720, in Norwich, m there, 1739-40, Sarah, b at Barnstable, Mass., March 16, 1721, dau of Eleazer and Sarah (Sears) Hamblin He d at Carmel March 5, 1777. She d there Dec, 1814 Both tombstones in old Gilead cemetery Caleb came from Norwich in 1740 and settled upon what is called Hazen Hill, in the present town of Carmel He was a farmer, and also had a furnace for smelting iron and a forge (The biographical history of Putnam County states that Caleb and his father-in-law came to Putnam County. This is not so, for Eleazer Hamblin d at Sharon, Conn, Oct 31, 1771, aged 76 years, and is buried there, as is also his wife, Sarah Sears, who d Feb 6, 1785, aged 88 years) They had:

> Sarah, b 1742, m. Isaac Merrick,
> Charity, b 1744, m in 1763 Elisha Cole,
> Caleb, b Nov 7, 1749, m Ruth Wright, he d. March 31, 1806; she d Dec 18, 1828, aged 77;
> Aaron, d y,
> Mercy, m Abner Mead,
> Capt Eleazer, b 1755, m Oct 14, 1784, Huldah "Rowlee", he d Sept 20, 1893;
> Moses, b Feb, 1758, m Mary Caldwell, he d. Jan 20, 1834,
> Abigail, b Aug 21, 1765, m Abel Smith.

Of the above, Aaron, Caleb and Moses were privates in the 7th Regt, Dutchess County Militia, in the Revolution, and the father was Ensign in the same regiment

DENISON

William Denison was b in England about 1586 He m in Bishop's Stortford, Nov 7, 1603, Margaret Chandler They came to America in 1631 They lived at Roxbury, Mass, where he d Jan 25, 1653-4 She d there Feb. 3, 1645-6

They brought three children with them to America·

Daniel, b about 1612, who settled at Boston and was made freeman there April 1, 1634. He d in 1682

Edward, who settled at Roxbury

George, bap at Bishop's Strotford, England, Dec 10, 1620 He m at Roxbury, Mass, Bridget, dau of John Thompson She d. 1643 He returned to England and fought under Cromwell in the battles of York, Marston Moor and Naseby, rising to the rank of Captain He was wounded at Naseby and carried to the farmhouse of John Borodel, where he met his dau Ann, who later became his wife They came to America and settled at Stonington, Conn He d at Hartford, Oct 23, 1694 She d at Stonington, Sept 26, 1712, aged 97 years

Their 2nd son, George, b. about 1653, m Mercy, b at Barnstable, Mass, daughter of John and Desire (Howland) Gorham He d at Westerly, R I, Dec 27, 1711 She d there Sept 24, 1725

John Howland, of the *Mayflower*, m Elizabeth, dau of John Tilley They had

Desire, who m John Gorham John was wounded in King Phillip's War and d two months later

George and Mercy (Gorham) Denison had:

Samuel, bap at Westerly, Sept 26, 1686, m (probably) Mary Minor. He settled in Saybrook, Conn, in 1716, and was probably m. there Had

Christopher, b. about 1720, m, March, 1742, Elizabeth Kelley. He was a member of the "Royal Americans" under Wolfe at Quebec and was killed there They had·

Christopher, who was in the Revolution and received a pension He lived at Hudson, N Y, and d in 1839, aged 96 years

John, youngest son, b Dec 2, 1744, in Saybrook, Conn; m Lydia Piatt in 1766 He was with his father at Quebec. He d in Chenango County, N Y, April 25, 1825 She d Sept 15, 1787, aged 43 years They had:

Beckwith, b in Saybrook, Nov. 22, 1780; m. June 5, 1816, Mary, b Jan 31, 1785, dau of Caleb Leete and Mary (Griswold) Hurd She was his second wife She d at Covert, N Y, March 10, 1826, and he m (3), Oct 10, 1826, Desire Wixom He d at Covert, Sept 15, 1859. She d. there Oct 15, 1859.

(Items regarding Wolfe and John and Christopher Denison were told by Beckwith Denison to his son, James H , the brother-in-law of Ira H Cole) They had

Mary Caroline Denison, who m Ira H. Cole.

LEETE.

Thomas Leete, of Oakington, Cambridgeshire, England, buried there July 9, 1564   Had.

Thomas, m Nov 12, 1548; d Feb 4, 1582. Had:

Thomas, of Oakington, m , June 2, 1574, Maria, dau of Edward Slade, of Rushton, Northampton   He d Nov. 12, 1616   She d. Sept. 25, 1610   They had

John, of Dodington, Hunts, bap May 13, 1575, in Oakington, m Ann, dau of Robert Shute, one of the Justices of the King's Bench   He d in 1648. They had:

William, named in Visitations of Hunts in 1613   He m his first wife, Anne, dau of Rev John Paine, in the Parish church of Hail Weston   The record of the church reads . "Guilielmus Leete uxorem duxit Annam Pain primo die Augusti Anno Dom 1636."

They came to America in 1639 and were among the first settlers of Guilford, Conn   His wife d Sept 1, 1668, and he m. (2) Apr. 7, 1670, Sarah, wid of Henry Rutherford   She d Feb 10, 1673, and he m (3) Mary, wid of the Rev. Nicholas Street   He d. at Hartford, Conn , April 16, 1683, and is buried there   She d Dec 13, 1683. He was Colonial Governor of Connecticut for forty years   He had nine children, the second being

Andrew, b 1643, m in Guilford, June 1, 1669, Elizabeth, dau. of Thomas and Dorothy Jordan   He d at Guilford, Oct 31, 1702 She d there March 4, 1702   He was made Assistant to Colony (Senator) in 1667 and served until his death   They had six children, the second being

Caleb, b Dec 10, 1672, m at Guilford, Nov 4, 1697, Mary, b. Feb 16, 1676, dau of Daniel and Elizabeth (Jordan) Hubbard   She d April 22, 1719, aged 43 years, and he m (2) May 10, 1721, Abigail, the wid of Matthew Caldwell   He d at

18   THE DESCENDANTS OF ELISHA COLE

Guilford, Dec 3, 1760, aged 87 years   She d there Nov. 10, 1755

(Daniel Hubbard lived in Guilford and m Elizabeth Jordan, Nov 17, 1664.) Caleb and Mary had

Dorothy Leete, b Aug. 2, 1712, m Dec 17, 1750 (being his second wife), Daniel, b 1696, the oldest child of Ebenezer Hurd Daniel Hurd's first wife was named Smith, and by her he had three sons and three daughters   He d. at Clinton, Conn, Jan. 1, 1763 or 1766   No record of her death has been found.

Ebenezer Hurd was b Nov 1668, at Stratford, Conn   He went to Waterbury, and from there to Killingworth   He m. at Stratford, Sarah, b there Feb 24, 1666-7, dau of Robert and Sarah (Picket) Lance

Daniel Hurd—Dorothy Leete had:

Dorothy, d ———, aged 20 years

Caleb Leete, b Jan 22, 1753, m., 1775, Mary Griswold, who was b 1754   He d 1827, aged 74 years   She d 1819

The Leete family were prominent in Connecticut, the members being better educated than the majority of the people, and were endowed with a strong tinge of aristocracy ; it being a tradition that their ancestors were of the English nobility   Caleb Leete Hurd being the only son of Dorothy Leete, inherited the old homestead   He was an easy going man, and having a large family, did not add to his inheritance, and his children had to make their own way in life   Caleb Leete Hurd and Mary had:

       Dolly, b. Feb 12, 1776; d Aug 31, 1779,
       Daniel, b April 12, 1777, d. March 4, 1827;
       William, b Oct 1, 1778; d Aug, 1803,
       Elias, b April 6, 1780, d Nov 25, 1840,
       Leete, b Nov 25, 1781, d Nov, 1880
       Achilles, b Jan 20, 1783, d May 14, 1864,
       Mary (Polly), b Jan 31, 1785; d March 10, 1826, m Beckwith Denison in Covert, N. Y ; their son James Hervey Denison, m Louise, dau of Daniel Cole, their daughter, Mary Caroline Denison, m Ira Hazen, son of Daniel Cole, Mary Hurd Denison was an exceptionally intelligent woman for her day and generation,

The Descendants of Elisha Cole 19

Dolly, b Oct 27, 1786, d. Oct 7, 1874;
Ethlinda, b July 4, 1788, d Oct 18, 1865;
James Hervey, b May 31, 1791, d Jan 18, 1857,
Samuel, b Nov. 13, 1792, d. Nov 17, 1792,
Aaron, b Sept. 10, 1794, d July 27, 1885;
Laura Ann, b Aug 3, 1796, d Sept 17, 1870.

Of the above, Elias was a sea captain and the father of two daughters and a son William Hurd was a carpenter and lived at Burdett, N. Y Leete was the best off of his family and represented the aristocratic part Dolly m a Hamlin and lived at Naples, N Y James H. was a cabinet maker and undertaker and lived at Dryden, N. Y His seven or eight children all died young except Laura, the last child, who m. a Griswold and lived near Dryden Aaron lived on the homestead. Laura m a Methodist minister while on a visit to the family of Daniel Cole at Covert in 1825 They settled in Richmond County, Ohio

COLE FAMILY

About 1633 three brothers, Job, John and Daniel Cole, appear in the records of Plymouth Colony.

Job removed to Yarmouth in 1642 and his name is on the list of able-bodied men there in 1643 In 1648 he removed to Eastham and was Deputy from there in 1654 His name appears on the list of freemen in 1670, but not on that of 1695, so he must have died between those dates He m , March or May 16, 1634, Rebecca, dau of William Collier "Rebecca Cole ye widow of Job dyed twentie ninth of Decr 1698 being about 88 "

William Collier, of London, came over in 1633, having been for several years a "merchant adventurer." His four daughters of "excellent character" came over with him. He was Assistant for twenty-eight years between 1634 and 1665, and one of the plenipotentiaries of the United Colonies in 1643 His daughter Sarah m , May 15, 1634, Love Brewster, son of Elder William Brewster, of the *Mayflower* Rebecca m. Job Cole, as above stated. Mary m , April 1, 1635, Thomas Prince, who was afterwards Governor. The fourth daughter, Elizabeth, m Nov 2, 1637, Constant Southworth, whose widowed mother was the second wife of Gov William Brewster, who she m Aug 14, 1623

Job and Rebecca had .

> John, who m Elizabeth Keiler, Nov. 21, 1667,
> Job and Rebecca (twins), b , Eastham, Aug 26, 1654.

John Cole, the second brother, never m , and d. at Plymouth in Dec., 1637. In his will, proved Jan 2, 1638, he mentions his brothers Job and Daniel and sister Rebecca, wife of Job, and his brothers-in-law Edward, Joseph and John Collier

Daniel, the third brother, and ancestor of Elisha Cole, of Putnam County, N. Y , was granted fifty acres April 6, 1640 He was an able-bodied man, Yarmouth, 1643; freeman, 1645 , Deputy from Eastham, 1652-54-57-61 and until 1674, Selectman for nine years from 1667; Inspector of Shot and Lead in 1662 "Every Township in the Govern^t shall provide a barrel of powder and leade or bulletts answerable to be kept by some trusty man in every towne that it may be ready for defence in tyme of neede and danger" June 10, 1661, Daniel Cole, of Eastham, licensed to retail "wine and strong waters." He was a member of Yarmouth County Train Band in 1643. He m Ruth Chester.

"Daniel Cole Dyed ye one and twentyeth day of Decr in the yeare 1694 in ye Eightyeith y^r of his age Ruthy ye wife Daniel Cole dyed ye 15th of Decr in ye year 1694 in ye Sixte Seaventh ye of her age" Eastham records.

Daniel and Ruth had:

+1 John, b. July 15, 1644.
2 Timothy, b. Sept. 15, 1646. He was one of the East grantees of Narragansett township.
3 Hepzeibah, b. April 16, 1649, m George Crisp. He d. and she m. (2) Daniel, b Plymouth, Mass, 1636-37, son of Deacon John and Abigail Doane. He settled at Eastham, 1645 Prominent man and large land owner. He d Dec. 20, 1712 in 76th year. No record of her death.
4 Ruth, b. Apr 15, 1651, m John, b Plymouth, Nov. 16, 1649, son of John and Abigail Youngs He d and she m. (2), 1720, for his third wife, Capt Jonathan, son of Edward and Rebecca Bangs He d at Brewster, Cape Cod, Nov. 19, 1728
+5 Israel, b. Jan 8, 1653.
6 "James Cole ye sonne of Danyel borne in Decr in ye yeare 1655"
7 Mary, b March 10, 1658; m. May 26, 1681, Joshua, b 1657, the seventh child of Giles and Catharine (Whelden) Hopkins. This was the first of many marriages between these two families He was "the most opulent man of the time." She d March 1, 1734; buried at Orleans, Mass
+8 William, b Sept 15, 1663
9 Daniel, b Sept. 1666; m. Mercy, dau. of the Rev Samuel and Elizabeth Fuller He d Eastham,

June 15, 1736, in his 70th year. She d. Sept 25, 1735, in her 63rd year.

1

JOHN, m at Eastham, Dec 12, 1666, Ruth, probably the dau of Lieut Joseph Snow. He d Eastham, Jan 6, 1724-25 She d. there Jan 27, 1716-17. Children:

- 10 Ruth, b Mar 11, 1667-8; m March 26, 1689, William Twining. He was probably a son of the Wm. "Twying" who was a member of the Yarmouth Company in the expedition against the Narragansetts, Aug. 18, 1645
- +11 John, b. March 6, 1669-70
- 12 "Hephzibah," b June 20, 1672
- 13 Hannah, b March 27, 1675; d. June, 1677
- 14 Joseph, b June 11, 1677; m Oct 6, 1715, Mercy Hinkley
- 15 Mary, b Oct 22, 1679
- 16 Sarah, b. June 10, 1682

5

ISRAEL, m April 24, 1674 or 1679, Mary Rogers He was a representative to General Court of Massachusetts at Boston from Eastham, 1698 Selectman 1694 for 5 years He was one of the proprietors of Truro, Mass., June 18, 1701 He d. before 1730 Children·

- 17 Hannah, b. June 28, 1681
- 18 Israel, b June 28, 1685 (Probably others.)

8

WILLIAM, m at Eastham, Dec 2, 1686, Hannah, b. there Jan 2, 1667, daughter of Stephen and Mrs Susanna (Dean) Snow At the time of Susanna's marriage to Stephen she was the wid of Joseph Rogers and dau of Stephen and Elizabeth (Ring) Deane They lived at Eastham and she d there June 23, 1737 Children

+19 Elisha, b. Jan 26, 1688-89
20 David or Daniel, b Oct. 4, 1691.
21 Hannah, b Dec 15, 1693
22 Jane, b. Jan 4, 1695

11

JOHN, m Mary ———, lived at Eastham He d Dec 13, 1746 She d Feb. 17, 1731. Children

23 Jonathan, b. Oct 4, 1694
24 John, b Oct. 14, 1696.
25 Mary, b. Aug 25, 1698
26 James, b. Oct 23, 1700.
27 Nathan, b. Jan 21, 1702-03.
28 Joshua, b. Mar 20, 1704.
29 Moses, b July 22, 1707
30 Phebe, b Oct 29, 1709
31 Thankful, b. Oct. 20, 1712; d.y.
32 Joseph, b Oct. 13, 1714.
33 Thankful, b Oct. 19, 1716.

19

ELISHA, m. Anne. Record of them is very incomplete There is no published record of their marriage, nor have I been able to ascertain her family name or date of their death The only way we know that a marriage took place is from the fact that the birth of children is recorded in Eastham records as "of Elisha and Anne Cole" Children.

34 "Joshua Cole, the son of Elisha and Anne Cole, was b at Eastham Oct 9, 1715"
35 Eunice, b Nov 24, 1717.
36 Mary, b ———
37 Elisha, b ———, 1719 He was the settler in Dutchess, now Putnam County Tradition in and published records of Putnam County give his wife's name as Hannah Smalley, as also do records of Jos G Cole, who obtained them partly

from grand children of Elisha She must have been a second wife and the mother of most of his children Eastham records under date of Sept 4, 1739, state that, "Then entered the intention of Elisha Cole Jr. and Priscilla Smalee, both of Eastham to proceed in marriage " And again, under date Dec 13, 1739, "Then Elisha Cole Jr and Priscilla Smally, both of Eastham, were married in Eastham by me
                              Isiah Lewes, Minister'
Priscilla was probably a dau of Joseph "Smale," who m , 1717, Priscilla Young, of Eastham.

Priscilla (Smalley) Cole probably d. a few years after marriage, and Elisha then m. Hannah, who may have been a sister or cousin of Priscilla's Elisha's first child, Joshua, did not come to Putnam County He may have been the only one by Priscilla, and on Elisha's removal with second wife and family he was left with relatives

ELISHA COLE

Elisha Cole and wife Hannah Smalley came to Putnam County, N. Y, then called Fredericksburgh, Dutchess County, from Harwick, Cape Cod, in the Autumn of 1746 or Spring of 1747 and built a log house near the stream that is the outlet of Barrett's Pond in the present town of Kent In 1748 he built a grist mill on the outlet, and it was called Cole's Mill, and since that time a mill has been in operation on or near the site of the first mill and owned by a member of the Cole family until 1888, when New York City purchased the water rights for reservoir purposes. This stream is the west branch of the Croton River and supplies Reservoir D The reservoir was commenced Aug 27, 1890, and completed in 1896 There appears to be no picture of the mill in existence The following description of the property appears in the condemnation proceedings: House, one story and attic; barn, 21 x 32; carding mill, 36 x 20, saw mill, 13 x 46; grist mill, 21 x 22

The father of Hannah Smalley and his family moved to this section about two years before Elisha and family came At the time of the arrival of Elisha and wife they had four children. Joshua, the eldest, never came here Why, cannot now be ascertained, but he married and left issue. Elisha was a Baptist preacher An unmarried sister of Elisha's, named Mary, came with him from Cape Cod She afterward m a man by the name of Barber or Barbour, and d at an advanced age Elisha was partly paralyzed and somewhat demented before his death, which took place about 1801 Hannah's mental powers gave way, while physically she was very strong She d in 1811

The land upon which Elisha settled and built his mill belonged to Roger Morris. son-in-law of Frederick Phillipse This property was confiscated by the State and was sold to Elisha by the Commissioners of Forfeiture, June 11, 1782 "The parcel containing 396 acres, more or less, consideration £234 9-1"

The Descendants of Elisha Cole

There is hardly an old family in Putnam County that have not intermarried with the Coles, and the marriage of first and second cousins have been frequent, and in one instance a Cole became, by marriage, the aunt of her own cousins

Elisha was one of the original nine members of the Baptist church, Nov 16, 1751 He was an elder in Carmel church, preaching in open air in the Summer and in private houses during the winter, the society having no building until about 1780.

He was a member of the 7th Regt, Dutchess County Militia, Col Henry Ludenton, in the Revolution.

Elisha and Hannah had

1 Joshua, b. ———.
+2 Elisha, b. Jan. 26, 1743
+3 Nathan, b ———, 1744
+4 Joseph, b Jan 11, 1746.
5 Eunice, b Jan 1748, m Hackaliah, son of Joseph Merritt. He d and she m (2) Nathan Crosby. He d Oct 27, 1805, aged 72 years. She d. Jan 17, 1821, aged 73 years.

He was a private, 3rd Regt, Dutchess County Militia, in Revolution. Hackaliah and Nathan were widowers at the time of their marriage to Eunice, Nathan having five children by his first wife.

+6 Daniel, b Nov 26, 1749
7 Hannah, b 1751, m Freeman, b 1754, son of Jonathan and Rebecca (Freeman) Hopkins. He d. March 31, 1830, aged 76 years. She d March 31, 1802, aged 51 years

He was a member of the 7th Dutchess County Militia in Revolution Later a Baptist preacher

8 Naomi, b 1753, m. Jesse Smith He d 1825 She d. 1794.

He was b Putnam County and was a member of the 7th Regt, Dutchess County Militia, during Revolution, and was present at the capture of Stony Point by Anthony Wayne His son, Chas. G. Smith, m Margaret, dau of Ebenezer Cole

+9 Ebenezer, b. ———, 1754
10 Priscilla Ann, b ———, 1756, m Gen James Townsend, b. 1756, son of Charles Townsend. He d. Carmel, March 13, 1832, in his 76th year. She d there June 11, 1839, in her 83rd year

He was a grandson of Elisha Townsend, who was b. at Oyster Bay, August, 1704, and d North Salem, July, 1805

James was a prominent man and was a member of the 7th Regt., Dutchess County Militia, in Revolution He was a Lieutenant, 1786; Captain of Infantry 1793, Lieutenant Colonel, 6th Regt., Dutchess County Militia, 1812, and on Nov 9, 1812, Brigadier General, 30th Brigade, Infantry of Dutchess County, and until Feb 3, 1817, when he resigned

11 Mercy, b ———, 1757, m. Tracy, b Sept 8, 1756, son of ——— and Mary (Tracy) Ballard He d. Carmel, Jan. 4, 1829, aged 72 years. She d Feb. 8, 1826, aged 69 years He was a private, 7th Regt, Dutchess County Militia, in Revolution

+12 John, b Oct 6, 1761

2

ELISHA (Elisha), m 1763, Charity, b ———, 1744, dau of Caleb and Sarah (Hamblin) Hazen. He d. Feb 3, 1826, aged 83 years, 5 days. She d ———, 1811

He bought from Committee of Forfeiture, Aug 30, 1788, a farm of 513 acres in Phillip's patent This land is near Long Pond in the present town of Carmel, Putnam County, N. Y., and is still owned by the Coles Elisha and wife are buried in the family plot on this farm. Elisha was a private, 7th Regt, Dutchess County Militia, Col. Henry Ludenton His father-in-law, Caleb Hazen, was Ensign Elisha's father, three brothers and a son of his also served in this regiment during the Revolution. (See N. Y. in the Revolution, Vol. I., p 150)

THE DESCENDANTS OF ELISHA COLE

"June the 17 1786
"Cornel ludenton sir be pleased to pay unto the barer hear of Joseph Cole the wages due to me and you will oblige
your friend
Elisha Cole Junr "

(Manuscripts of State of N Y in Revolution, Vol. 8, p 250 Vol. 8, p 233 Received Certificate no 42500 amounting to £1 7s 3d for services performed in Col. Henry Ludington's Dutchess County Regiment. Said certificate delivered to Joseph Cole June 17, 1786.

Elisha and Charity had:

13 Sarah, b ———, 1763, m. for his second wife, Barnabas, b. 1761, son of Timothy Carver He d. Aug 29, 1831 She d Dec 4, 1851, aged 88 years. No issue. His first wife was Hannah, dau. of Gen. James and Priscilla (Cole) Townsend

Barnabas Carver was descended in the sixth generation from John Carver, of the *Mayflower* He and his father were privates, 7th Regt , Dutchess County Militia, in Revolution. He was Member of Assembly, 1806, Major, 61st Regt , Dutchess County Militia, 1812, and for years Judge of Common Pleas

+14 Reuben, b. ———, 1765
+15 David, b. ———, 1768.
+16 Eleazer, b May 17, 1770
+17 Obed, b Aug 17, 1772
 18 Elizabeth, b June 15, 1774 , m William, son of Charles Agor (The name originally—"McGregor) He d March 16, 1848, aged 75 years, 18 days She d Feb 16, 1841, aged 66 years, 8 months. Lived at Red Mills, now Mahopac Falls.
+19 Elisha, b Aug 8, 1776.
 20 Hannah, b May 18, 1778, m Thaddeus, b July 7, 1771, son of Thomas and Phebe (Mabie) Bax-

ter. He d. Cold Spring, N Y, Aug. 14, 1847. She d. there Dec. 14, 1840.

+21 Daniel, b Dec. 22, 1779
+22 Joshua, b ———
+23 John, b. Feb 22, 1782.
 24 Naomi, b ———, d u m, aged 17 years

3

NATHAN (Elisha), m. Mehitable ——— He d Feb 6, 1803 She d. Aug 15, 1807, in 59th year

An exhaustive research has failed to discover her family name, and it will probably remain a genealogical puzzle Partial records of Nathan and family compiled some twenty-five years ago give her last name as "unknown" She might have been the Mehitabel, bapt Harwich, Cape Cod, March 18, 1749, dau of Lemuel and Lydia Berry. Lemuel and wife removed to "Oblong," in Dutchess County, about 1756, and it will be noted that Nathan and wife had a dau Lydia, the first of that name in the Cole family

Nathan lived in a house that stood where the Smalley house now stands in Carmel He left no will, but Abner Bangs was appointed administrator of his estate on Feb. 14, 1803, by consent of heirs who signed

He was licensed to preach by the Baptist church in Carmel, then Phillips patent, on May 2, 1772 On removal of the church in May, 1773, to North East Town, the members not removing were constituted into a church by themselves and Nathan Cole became their pastor Among those remaining were Elisha Cole, Heman King, Barzilla King, Robert Fuller, Josiah Baker, John Wright, Recompense Thomas, Edmund Baker. On Dec. 12, 1791, the church agreed to pay to Elder Nathan Cole £12 for the ensuing year He preached much of the time for thirty years, and d. after only one day's sickness

During the early part of the Revolutionary War the people in what now constitutes the counties of Putnam and Dutchess were very much divided in sentiment regarding the war, seriously dividing neighborhoods and in some instances families.

Soon after the news of the battle of Lexington reached the people in the vicinity of Putnam County, then Fredericksburg, they met in public meeting and adopted resolutions expressing their sentiments in the form of a pledge   The following is the
"June 1775
one adopted, and to which Nathan subscribed
"This may certify to all people whom it may concern, that I the subscriber, am willing to do what is just and right to secure the privileges of America both civil and sacred and to follow the advise of our reverred Congress so far as the word of God and the example of Jesus Christ and I hope in the grace of God no more will be required.
As witness my hand"

This section was "between the lines," and soon became infested with "cowboys," who made raids upon the property of the Whigs, so in order to protect themselves, the inhabitants organized into what was called the "minute men," subject to call at any moment   Elder Nathan was one of these until 1777, when he enlisted as a private in the regular army and was with Washington at White Plains and along the Hudson

This information was obtained from John Cole, a nephew of Elder Nathan, and from Mrs. Jane Hopkins, who lived near Nathan, and although but a young girl at the time, was intimately acquainted with him and his family.   Jane Hopkins, mentioned above was a dau. of Tracy and Mercy (Cole) Ballard, and wife of Joseph Hopkins.

Nathan's tombstone in the old graveyard at Carmel contains a quaint inscription in verse.   A copy will be sent to any subscriber to this book who may desire it.
Nathan and Mahitabel had (b at Carmel)

+25   Nathan, b. March 7, 1783.
 26   Mehitabel, b ———.
 27   Lydia, b ———, m. Nathan Crosby, Jr, son of Nathan Crosby and his first wife

4

JOSEPH (Elisha), m Rebecca, b Jan 21, 1752, dau Jabez Berry. She d Feb 15, 1801, aged 49 years, 24 days, and is buried on

Cole farm near Long Pond. He m. (2) Susan Berry, b. March 15, 1744, and wid. of Obediah Chase, who d July 4, 1799, 56 years. She was probably a sister of Joseph's first wife. At the time of the marriage of Joseph and Susan (Berry) Chase, they each had eleven children He d. Feb 24, 1814, aged 68 years, 1 month, 13 days She d 1836, aged 92 years.

Joseph Cole, Jabez Berry and Obediah Chase were members of the 7th Regt, Dutchess County Militia, in the Revolution Children by first marriage:

+28 Berry, b. Feb. 24, 1769.
29 William, b ———, 1771, d u m
30 Susannah, b. Sept. 23, 1773, m Henry, b. Reading, Conn, Dec 12, 1769, son of Josiah and Elizabeth (Bouton) Nichols They lived at Kent, Dutchess County, N Y He d Feb 10, 1849, aged 79 years, 1 month, 14 days She d Oct 2, 1856, aged 83 years, 2 months, 10 days.

Josiah Nichols was a cavalry officer in the Revolution

31 Anna, b. ———, 1775; m. Charles Green
+32 Joseph, b Oct 29, 1775
+33 Samuel, b. Dec 24, 1777
+34 Nathan, b Aug 17, 1780
35 Ruth, b Jan. 19, 1783, m Sept 12, 1801, Alvin, b Kent, Oct 4, 1778, son of Obediah and Susan (Berry) Chase She d April 17, 1832, in her 49th year, and he m (2) Sept 16, 1832, Martha Elizabeth, b Kent, 1789, dau. of David and Clara Northrup (Kelley) Dingee He d Feb 26, 1853, in Pawling, N Y She d Oct 23, 1857, in Fishkill, N. Y
+36 Asahel, b. May 31, 1786
37 Cynthia, b Sept. 4, 1788, m. Dec 6, 1809, Enos, b March 1, 1789, son of Jeremiah and Thankful (Stone) Hopkins He d March 23, 1859, aged 70 years, 22 days. She d April 1, 1864, aged 75 years, 6 months, 28 days. Three of their children m Coles Jeremiah Hopkins was a member

of 7th Regt., Dutchess County Militia, in Revolution.

+38 Levi Hall, b. July 1, 1791
+39 Ramah, b. Feb. 27, 1795

6

DANIEL (Elisha), m Susannah Ogden She was b June 25, 1775 Have been unable to discover who were her parents, but Daniel and his brothers, Ebenezer and John, married sisters He d Dec 10, 1834, aged 85 years, 1 month, 14 days She d Nov 3, 1857, aged 102 years, 4 months and 8 days

Daniel was a member 7th Regt., Dutchess County Militia, in Revolution He was b, m and d at Cole's Mills, in the town of Kent, which property was sold to the City of New York and is now ten feet under water, being part of the West Branch Reservoir He was ordained a deacon of the Baptist Church Nov 22, 1798, being the first man of record set apart as a deacon by ordination in the Carmel church. He was widely known as Deacon Cole Children

+40 John, b. Aug 29, 1775
41 Margaret, b ———, 1776; m Jan 1, 1795, Levi, b April 13, 1771, son of Caleb Hall He d near Sussex, N. J., Aug 31, 1821 She m (2) Asa Wilson He d ——— She d June 24, 1857, at the home of her daughter Susan Adams, Sussex, N. J

Rev. Levi Hall was licensed to preach by order of the Peekskill Baptist Church in 1793. He was ordained as pastor of the Baptist church at Pleasant Valley, N Y, Sept 9, 1794, by Elder Freeman Hopkins, of Patingtown, Elder Ebenezer Cole, of Phillipstown, and Deacon Cole, of Frederickstown He and family moved to Sussex, N. J, where he farmed and preached, being pastor First Baptist Church of Wantage from 1815 until his death

42 Mary, b ———, 1777, m George Frost He d June 28, 1815, aged 43 yrs

43 Eunice, b. 1781; m Elmer, b. Kent, Oct. 4, 1778, son of Obediah and Susan Berry Chase. They removed to Tompkins County, N. Y, then to Delaware County, Ohio

44 Sarah, b. 1783, m. Nathan Hall. His descendents, say he was a son of Caleb Hall, Jr, and nephew of Rev Levi Hall.

+45 Jesse, b. Sep. 10, 1784.

+46 Daniel H, b. Aug. 24, 1786.

47 Ivah, b. Sept 4, 1788, m Hosea, b 1785, son of Thomas and Rachel (Sunderlin) Townsend. He d June 24, 1833 in 48th year. She d. Apr 10, 1838, aged 49 years 7 months 6 days.

48 Henah, b. 1790, m Silvanus, son of Thomas and Rachel (Sunderlin) Townsend.

+49 Elisha J, b. Mar. 30, 1793.

50 Havilah, b. Oct 2, 1795, m. Charles B, b Dec 23, 1795, son of Issachar and Esther (Buckingham) Norton He d July 22, 1879. She d Mar. 11, 1861.

51 Hannah, b. Jan. 17, 1798; m Levi Hall, b July 1, 1791, son of Joseph and Rebecca (Berry) Cole

9

EBENEZER (Elisha), m (1) Mary Ogden. She d. Aug. 30, 1806, aged 44 years. He m. (2) Mrs Mary Wilson, widow of Thomas, who d Oct. 7, 1807, and dau. of Joseph Ogden He d Aug 18, 1815, aged 61 years She d Apr 16, 1825, aged 62 years, 11 months 27 days

Ebenezer lived and died in Philipstown. He was a private, 7th Regt Dutchess Co Militia in the Revolution He was deacon in the Baptist church and became pastor in 1802 at a yearly salary of $30. He performed the marriage ceremony for each of his twelve children His daughters, Vashti and Azubah were married at the same time Children

52 Azubah, b. ———. m. Silas, b. 1775, son of Gould John and Elizabeth (Miller) Selleck. Lived at

The Descendants of Elisha Cole

Putnam Valley, N Y He d Apr 6, 1830, aged 75 years She d Oct 2, 1853

53   Vashti, b ———, m. William Farrington Lived at Putnam Valley

54   Eliza, b ———; m. Ezra, son of John Kelley Settled in Iowa.

55   Annis, b ———, m Ira, son of John Kelley Settled in Iowa

+56   Nathaniel, b. Mar. 7, 1783.

+57   William, b ———.

+58   Ebenezer, b. Dec. 27, 1786.

+59   Joseph, b. Feb 25, 1789.

60   Naomi, b 1801, m. John, son John and Susan (Cronk) Odell. He d July 1, 1855, aged 54 years 10 months 8 days. She d Sept 1, 1880, aged 79 years, 9 months

61   Mary, b. Dec. 14, 1791; m Apr. 20, 1809, John, b. Oct 6, 1790, son of John and Martha (Barrett) Lickley. They lived at Putnam Valley. He d Jan. 11, 1843, aged 52 years 3 months 8 days. She d. July 18, 1876

She was well known and liked by her nephews and nieces and was always called "Aunt Pop Lickley." This name is variously spelled. Pellitreu has "Likely." On John's tombstone is "Lickly," and on his wife's, "Lickley"

62   Junia, b ———, d y.

63   Margaret (Aunt Peggy), b. Feb 4, 1794; m Chas. G, b Feb 13, 1789, son of Jesse and Naomi (Cole) Smith. They lived at Putnam Valley. He d. Apr. 5, 1875, aged 86 years 1 month 23 days She. d Nov. 18, 1871, aged 77 years 9 months 14 days No issue.

+64   James, b Feb. 3, 1803.

12

JOHN (Elisha), m. ——— Ogden He was one of the three brothers who married three sisters Their children were born at Carmel. They moved to "between the lakes" or Western New York He d. Sept 24, 1850.

The above Ogden marriage is from records of Jos G Cole and must be an error, for in the John Cole bible his wife's name is given as Mary Washburn, date of her birth as Feb 2, 1767, and date of m of John and Mary as Aug. 21, 1783 He was Ensign 1786, Lieut 1793, Capt. 1797, and Lieut Col Elijah Townsend's Regt of Dutchess County Children

+65 Lewis, b. Aug 1, 1785
66 Libbeus, b May 7, 1788 Drowned in Cayuga Lake, Mar. 4, 1810.
67 Cyrus, b May 17, 1791, m May 7, 1815 Hannah Kelley They settled in Ohio
68 Phebe, b. Feb 4, 1795, m Sept, 1814, David Thomas
69 Thurza, b. Sept 21, 1797, m. Sept, 1817, Lewis Porter, b Conn. May 24, 1786 She d at Covert, N. Y, Oct 20, 1867 She was his 2nd wife, his first being Samantha King, who d. Mar 21, 1817.
+70 Harvey, b Apr 9, 1800
71 Eliza, b Mar 21, 1803; m. Oct 29, 1836, Amial T. Wixom and had Ann Thurza, b Oct 15, 1837
+72 Ogden, b. Nov 4, 1805.
73 Lydia Ann, b Sept 5, 1811; d y.

14

REUBEN (Elisha, Elisha), m Elizabeth, b. Sept 1, 1766, dau. of Heman and Elizabeth (Cartright) King They lived at Carmel. He d Oct 30, 1840, in 75th year. She d Dec. 26, 1858, aged 91 years 3 months 26 days

Reuben was a member of 7th Regt. Dutchess Co Militia during the last years of the Revolution, and in 1806 was a captain in Lieut Colonel James Townsend's 61st Regt Dutchess Co Militia His father-in-law, Heman King, was also in the same regiment during the Revolution Children.

+74 Heman, b Sept 6, 1785

+75 Charles, b ———.
76 Hannah, b ———, 1788, m Eleazer Henry, b. 1784, son of Henry and Mary or Eliza (Sears) Baldwin. They lived at Mahopac He d Aug. 27, 1868, aged 84 years. She d Jan 7, 1874, aged 85 years. Henry Baldwin was a member of the 7th Regt Dutchess Co. Militia in Revolution.
77 Sarah, b 1790, m Frederick, son of John Knox. He was alive in 1842, d. at Lake Mahopac She d. Oct 10, 1854, aged 64 years.
+78 Ebenezer, b. Aug. 20, 1793
79 Zillah, b. Sept 16, 1795, d. u. m March 24, 1818, aged 22 years 6 months 8 days
80 John, b———, 1798, d u m, March 24, 1828, in his 30th year.
81 Adah, b ———, 1802; m Lewis, b Sept. 21, 1797, son of Henry and Susannah (Cole) Nichols. He d Jan. 5, 1888, in 91st year She d. Feb 27, 1868, in 66th year On her tombstone she is called "Adelia." In her father's will she is "Adah"
82 Elizabeth, d May 6, 1815, aged 9 years

15

DAVID (Elisha, Elisha), m Hannah Bangs They lived at Frederickstown, Dutchess Co, N Y. He was assessor there 1788-91 About 1800 he removed with his family to Edmeston, Otsego Co, N Y, where he died He was a farmer He d. Feb. 13, 1833. She was b June 10, 1779, d May 3, 1842 David and wife left Dutchess Co. for Columbus, Chenango Co Their son Eli was born on the journey In crossing the North (or Hudson) River their sleigh broke through the ice and they lost most of their effects Children·

+83 Eli, b Feb 14, 1796
84 Bethia, b Mar 28, 1798, m Columbus, N Y, Jan 30, 1817, Rev William, b Whitestone, N. Y., Jan 5, 1795, son of Israel and his 2nd wife

Ursula (Wood) Greenleaf They moved to Wisconsin and died there. He d Nov 12, 1850. She d. Apr 1, 1879

+85 Abner Bangs, b. Dec. 8, 1799.
86 Polly, b. Apr 28, 1801; d u m, at Edmeston May 3, 1842.
+87 Nathan, b. Sept. 7, 1803
88 David B, b Nov 7, 1805, at Columbus, Chenango Co, N. Y.
+89 Elisha, b Mar 2, 1807.
+90 John, b. Jan 26, 1809
+91 Chester, b. Oct. 18, 1810
92 Sarah Maria, b. Jan 15, 1813; m Friendship, N Y, Aug. 25, 1835, Rev William McKinstrey, b Windom Co., Vt., June 14, 1795. He d Minn Nov. 22, 1882 She survived him He removed with his parents in 1810 to Ontario Co., N Y. To Cattaraugus Co. in 1820 He was one of a family of twelve children He was ordained deacon of the Methodist church in 1834. Lived at Olean, N Y., and in 1867 removed to Minnesota.
93 Amorilla, b Apr 21, 1815; d. Apr 29, 1816
+94 Alonzo, b Sept 21, 1817.

16

ELEAZER (Elisha, Elisha); m June 30, 1793, Sarah Hitchcock She b. May 1, 1773, d Aug 30, 1826, aged 53 years 4 months. He m. (2) Elizabeth (Washburn) Cole, widow of his brother John He was a farmer. He d. May 29, 1838, aged 68 years 11 days She d. May 3, 1857, aged 71 years Her tombstone reads "Betsy wife of Eleazer Cole and formerly widow of John Cole. Children (1) marriage.

+95 Hiram, b. June 3, 1796.
96 Naomi, b Oct 5, 1799; m John Reynolds
97 Almon, b. Feb. 27, 1802; d u m. in the West.
+98 Eleazer H., b. May 4, 1804.
+99 David, b May 4, 1807, d. Sept 4, 1807.

David Cole family record

Children

Eli Cole   Feb. 14th 1796
Bethia   March 28th 1798
Abner B.   Dec. 5th 1799
Polly   April 21st 1801
Nathan   Sept. 7th 1803
David W.   Nov. [?] 1805
Elisha   March 2nd 1807
John   Jan. 28th 1808
Chester   Oct. 15th 1810
Sally M.   Jan. 10th 1813
Anderville   April 21st 1815
Alonzo Cole   Sept. 21st 1817

Deaths

Amos Cole   [?] 19th 1811
[?]   May 5th 1844
[?]   Feb. 15th 1833
Mother   May 5th 1842

THE DESCENDANTS OF ELISHA COLE 39

+100 Harrison, b. Sept. 23, 1808.
101 Sarah Jane, b Mar 23, 1811, m. Jesse, b Nov. 23, 1803, son of James and Abigail (Roberts) Hughson He d Feb 23, 1862. She d near Naples, Ontario Co, N. Y.
102 Harmon, b Apr 6, 1813, m Julia, b. Feb 28, 1817, daughter of Daniel H and Sarah (Tillott) Cole. No issue He d Mar 8, 1883, aged 69 years 11 months 2 days She d. Dec. 2, 1885, aged 68 years 9 months 5 days.
103 Laura, b May 4, 1815; m. at Carmel to Russell, b. Aug 29, 1805, son of James and Abigail (Roberts) Hughson She d Aug 8, 1832, aged 17 years, 3 months, 4 days, and he m. (2) Esther, b Nov —, 1820, in South East, N Y, daughter of Edmund and Sarah (Kent) Haines He d. Feb 3, 1881. She d Apr 26, 1879 Russell Rughson-Laura Cole had only·
George M., who married Mariette Townsend

Eleazer had by 2nd marriage, born at Carmel·

+104 Theron, b Oct 5, 1827
105 Theda, twin of above; she m at Carmel by Rev. Chas B. Keyes on Nov 28, 1848, to Erastus, b Carmel June 17, 1821, son of Enos and Cynthia (Cole) Hopkins. He d. June 9, 1902 She still lives at Brewster, N. Y.

17

OBED (Elisha, Elisha), m Nov 17, 1794, Lydia, b Jan. 23, 1775, daughter of Henry and his second wife Mary (Lounsbury) Baldwin He d Aug 26, 1841, aged 69 years She d Oct 23, 1858 Lived at Carmel He was probably baptized Obediah. Children:

106 Henry, b Apr 21, 1796, d Sept. 24, 1814, from disease contracted in the War of 1812.
107 Rachel, b July 27, 1798, m. Oct 1, 1817, Mentor W, b July 27, 1795, on Hazen Hill, Carmel, son

of Caleb and Ruth (Wright) Hazen He d Feb 16, 1881, aged 85 years, 6 months, 21 days She d. May 3, 1874, aged 75 years, 11 months, 11 days He served in the War of 1812 and was stationed at Harlem, N Y. City

108 Alanson, b May —, 1800, m (1) Oct 14, 1842, Naomi, b. 1808, dau. of John and Rachel (Sunderlin) Kelley. She d. Feb 16, 1867, having been a member of the Carmel Baptist church for 37 years. He m (2) Sept 9, 1868, Calista, b Lake Mahopac, dau of Joseph and Chloe (Pinckney) Ganong and wid. of Samuel Miller who d. Dec. 6, 1845. He was a farmer No issue by either marriage He d Sept 1, 1889, aged 84 years, 4 months She d. July 24, 1882, aged 68 years

109 Mary, b. Dec. 22, 1802, m Jan 25, 1827, Bailey Howes He b Mar. 20, 1798, d. Jan 19, 1872. She d. Jan. 3, 1867

+110 Alfred, b Jan 28, 1805.

111 Ansel, d Aug 20, 1808, aged 1 year.

112 Elizabeth, b. Oct. 19, 1810; m. Oct 4, 1835, Edson, b. Dec. 20, 1812, in Carmel, son of James and Mehitable (Warren) Sloat. She d Oct 6, 1843, aged 3' years, 5 months, 7 days, and he m (2) Apr 17, 1846, Jane, b. Jan. 14, 1820, in Carmel, dau. of Lewis and Martha (Ganong) Wright He d Patterson, N Y, Mar. 19, 1886 She d there July 21, 1886.

113 Minerva Ann, b Oct 13, 1815; m. Oct 30, 1842, William, b. Oct 19, 1812, son of ———— and Hannah (Baldwin) Clausen. He d. Napoli, Catt. Co, N. Y, Jan 13, 1857, and she m. (2) James M. Brown She d Jan 14, 1894. Had by 1st marriage:

Olan, b Oct 2, 1849; d. u m. Feb. 24, 1879.

No issue by 2nd marriage.

19

ELISHA (Elisha, Elisha); m Oct. 29, 1797, Rebecca, b Dec. 7, 1779, daughter of Joseph and Elizabeth (Townsend) Hopkins. He d. July 18, 1851, aged 74 years, 11 months, 11 days She d Dec. 31, 1862, aged 83 years 24 days. He was a farmer and bought, Feb. 1, 1830, upon the payment of $291 60, from Mary Gouverneur the daughter of Frederick Philipse, the north part of the Philipse farm, he having bought the south part from Frederick Philipse, Dec 2, 1828, having previously leased it at an annual rental of £7 Upon this farm is the Gilead burying ground in which is buried Enoch Crosby, the Revolutionary spy, who is the "Harvey Birch" of Cooper's novel The oldest inscription there is to Sarah, wife of Jesse Smith, d. Nov. 17, 1766, 62 years

On Nov. 9, 1812, Ensign Elisha Cole, Jr, of Lieut Colonel James Townsend's 61st Regt. of Dutchess Co Militia, was appointed lieutenant. Elisha's father-in-law, Joseph Hopkins, was a member 7th Regt Dutchess Co Militia in the Revolution. Children·

+114 Laban, b Sept. 17, 1798.
 115 Jacob, b Nov. 22, 1800, d. May 12, 1803.
 116 Eliza, b Jan. 25, 1803, m. Oct 12, 1822, Floyd, b Putnam Valley, son of Gilbert and Sarah (Field) Bailey. He d. Livonia, Livingston Co, N Y, July 21, 1865 She d there Nov. 28, 1876
+117 Jacob, b June 1, 1805.
+118 David, b Dec. 5, 1808.
 119 Son born and died Mar 7, 1810.
+120 Jonathan, b Feb 5, 1811.
 121 Chloe Ann, b Apr 26, 1814; d Carmel (unmarried), May 7, 1903, aged 89 years
 122 Huldah, b July 4, 1817, m. Dec 10, 1836, Harry, b South Salem, N. Y, Nov. 13, 1810, son of Lewis and Debra Ann (Webb) Hanford He d. Norwalk, Ohio, Jan 27, 1890 She d there Jan 30, 1892.
 123 Antoinette, b June 8, 1820, m. Dec 3, 1837, Isaac, b South East, Putnam Co, N Y, Dec 20, 1813,

son of Jesse and Eleanor (Foster) Kelley. He d Feb. 21, 1886, aged 72 years, 2 months She d Feb. 14, 1890, aged 71 years 6 months Isaac was a farmer, and in 1871, 110 acres of his land was taken for reservoir purposes by the city of New York

+124 Rufus, b. Apr. 26, 1823.
+125 Byron, b June 30, 1825.

21

DANIEL (Elisha, Elisha), m. Carmel, Jan 5, 1801, Sarah, b Carmel, Sept. 10, 1781, dau of Joseph and Elizabeth (Townsend) Hopkins. She d Covert, N Y., July 2, 1841. On her tombstone is 1842, but family Bible has the date as above He m (2) at Covert, Sept 15, 1845, Mrs. Mary Beadle, nee Osborn, b Lyons, N Y., 1803. He d Covert, Oct 12, 1848 She d Easton, Washington Co., N Y, about 1855.

He was a farmer and removed from Carmel to what is now Covert, N. Y, in 1808 He served for about three months in the War of 1812.

The name of his father-in-law, Joseph Hopkins, appears in New York State Manuscripts of the Revolution, Vol 8, page 235, as having received certificate 42,578 for £2 7s 1d. for services in Col Henry Ludenton's Dutchess County Regt Joseph's father, Jonathan Hopkins, and brother, Jonathan, Jr, also served in this regiment, as did Daniel's father and grandfather

"Daniel was 5 feet 10 inches in height, broad shoulders and robust frame Large blue eyes, dark brown hair. Quite passionate in early life, but later learned self control Fair education, quite a thinker and student and great Bible reader People of recent years have no idea of the poverty of reading matter that their grandparents endured Have heard mother say that all the books they had in her house were the Bible and 'Pilgrim's Progress' Mother was tall, weighed 160 pounds, black hair and eyes, broad forehead, nose medium, fair complexion and resolute disposition Her opportunities for education were very limited She could barely read and write, but

DANIEL COLE
No. 21

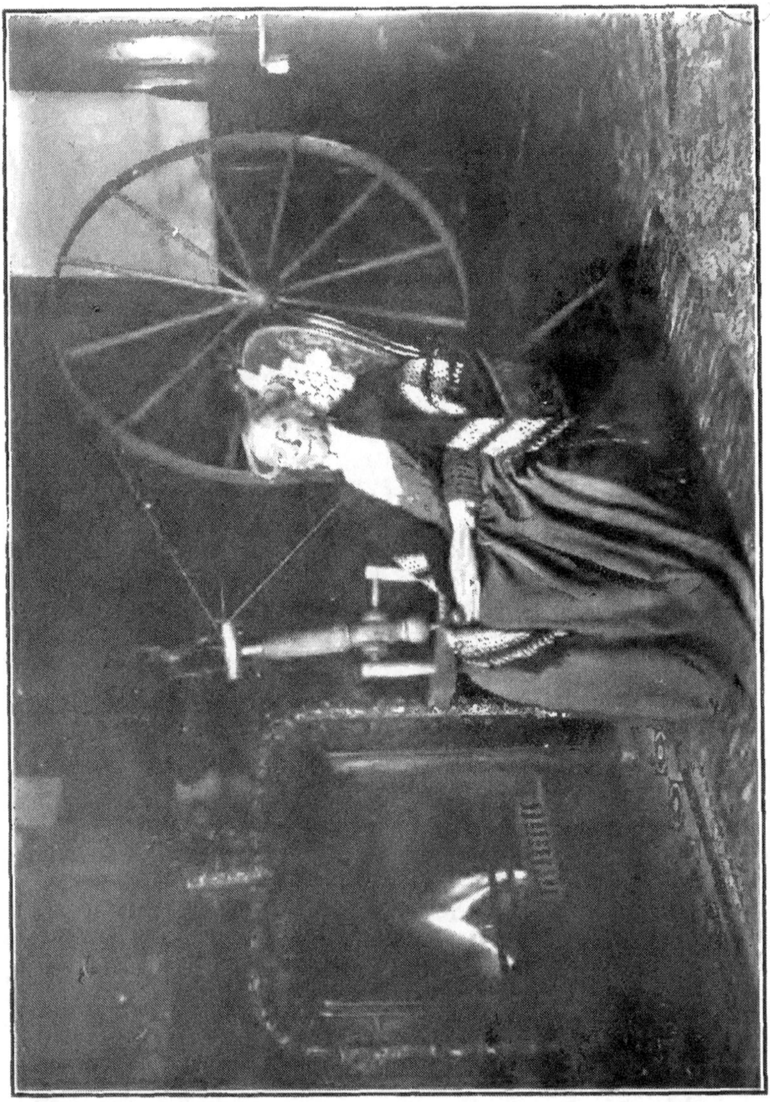

had a taste for picking up knowledge and a good memory and judgment."

(Above from their daughter, Mrs Louise Denison.)

In Daniel's family are the oldest living Coles, viz. Elizabeth Cole Terry, 98, Ira H Cole, 91, and a son-in-law, James H. Denison, 91 (Since this was written Mrs Terry has passed away) Children.

 126 Julia, b. Nov. 6, 1801; m Nov. 26, 1820, William, b. 1796, in New Jersey, son of Claudius Tunison. He d Lucas Co, Ohio, Apr. 2, 1850. She d. Weston, Mich, Aug 14, 1877.

 127 Anna, b July 10, 1803, m Mar 2, 1820, Thomas, b. New Jersey Aug 10, 1797, son of John P. and Elizabeth (Miller) Tunison He d Sept 30, 1886 She d at Fairfield, Mich, Mar 26, 1886 He was a shoemaker, then farmer They lived in Seneca and Schuyler counties in New York State, and in the fall of 1849 removed to Lucas Co, Ohio In 1868 they moved to Fairfield, Mich John P Tunison was born in New Jersey, 1762, and was in Revolution.

 128 Lydia, b Oct 8, 1805, m May 19, 1825, Charles, b Covert, June 17, 1806, son of Samuel and Anna (Tidd)) Ogden. She d. Covert, Oct. 1, 1825, and he m (2) Fanny Waddell He d. Covert, 23, 1894.

+129 Ezra, b Mar 30, 1808.

 130 Elizabeth, b Nov 10, 1810; m Aug. 28, 1831, John, b. River Head, R. I, 1805, son of Samuel and Irene (McClure) Terry. He d. Peru, Huron Co, Ohio, July 3, 1859 She d. Oct. 1, 1908, at Lawrence, Kansas.

  Great industry characterized her entire life, working constantly until her eyesight became poor. She was the champion spinner in all the country around her girlhood home. She left ten grandchildren and ten great-grandchildren

+131 Aaron Hazen, b. Feb 20, 1813

132 Minor Thomas, b Apr 26, 1815, d u m. Hector, N. Y, July 6, 1842.
+133 Ira Hazen, b July 26, 1817.
134 Adelia, b. Sept. 19, 1819, m Covert, N. Y., 1839, John Chapman, b. Putnam Co, N Y., Feb 1, 1808, son of John and Hannah (Chapman) Hall He d Covert, Dec. 21, 1882 She d Interlaken, N. Y., Feb. 25, 1897.
135 Sarah Roxanna, b Dec. 22, 1822, m. Covert, Sept, 1846, Pierpont, b Covert, Feb 21, 1818, son of Lemuel and Julia (Bennett) Bassett. He d Covert, Dec 18, 1881 She d. there Oct 14, 1851
136 Louise, b. Mar. 22, 1826; m Sept. 2, 1846, at Covert, to James Henry, b. Covert, June 13, 1817, son of Beckwith and Mary (Hurd) Denison. Removed to Sheboygan Falls, Wis., 1846 He is living there She d there Nov 13, 1902.

22

JOSHUA (Elisha, Elisha); m. Nancy, dau of Joseph and Elizabeth (Townsend) Hopkins, being the third brother to marry a daughter of Joseph Hopkins. He removed from Carmel and settled at Tecumseh, Mich He d ——— She d ———

Some correspondents give him as a son of Elder Nathan, but records of the late Joseph G Cole, compiled some thirty years ago, place him as above, and Ira H Cole, of Covert, (133) states that his father, Daniel, had a brother by the name of Joshua who went to Michigan At the time Mr Cole was collecting his records a number of aged people were living who were acquainted with Elder Nathan's family, and had he a son Joshua, they would have known of it. Children.

137 Adeline, b ———, m Morris, b ———, son of George and Mary (Cole) Frost He d ———. She d. ———.
138 Alvah, b. ———.
139 Ansel, b ———.

140 Annis, b ———.
141 Alzada (Azra), b. ———
142 Almeda, b ———, m ———

23

JOHN (Elisha, Elisha); m. Jan. 11, 1806, Betsey Washburn, b. Feb 5, 1786, dau. probably of Jonathan and Mary (Merritt) Washburn Mary Merritt was a dau of Hackaliah and Eunice (Cole) Merritt John lived on what is still the Cole farm near Long Pond, town of Carmel, and is buried in the family plot there. He d Feb 3, 1822, aged 39 years. His wid married his brother Eleazer Children

+143 Hymen, b. Oct 10, 1806
144 Son, b. Sept. 1, 1809; d Sept 2, 1809
145 Lydia, b Nov. 5, 1810, m. Elah, b Sept. 2, 1804, son of Joseph and Rachel (Wood) Ballard He d. Oct 10, 1844. She d. Mar 21, 1876. Had Susan, Mariette and Eliza Ann, who married Elah Hopkins
146 Susan, b. Mar 22, 1813, m Jan 29, 1840, Allen, son of Jesse and Mary (Organ) Cole
147 Son, b and d Feb, 1816
148 Henry, b May 11, 1817, d u. m, Nov 15, 1838, aged 21 years, 6 months, 4 days
+149 Jarvis Washburn, b. Apr. 30, 1819

25

NATHAN (Nathan, Elisha); m Franklin, Dutchess Co, N Y, Dec 24, 1803, Esther Northrup She d Ovid N Y., Aug 17, 1805, and he m (2) at Ovid, Oct 11, 1807, Sarah Scott, b Ridgefield, Conn, Nov 16, 1790 He d. Chester, Ill, June 8, 1840 She d there Apr 22, 1876

In 1820 Nathan went to St Louis, Mo. In 1821 his wife and six boys followed him, floating on a raft, with twelve other families from Olean Point, N Y, to Shawneetown, Ill, and from there across Illinois to St Louis in an ox-cart For several years he was engaged in the beef and pork packing business at East St Louis In 1837 he moved to Chester, Ill, bought land and started a saw mill, with a corn-stone attachment. In 1839 he built a flour mill with two run of four-foot stones He was succeeded by his third son, Hermon C, who operated the mill until 1855, when he built a new and up-to-date one. During a part of the time from 1840 to 1861 H C Cole's eldest brother, Abner B, was associated with him In 1868, H. C Cole admitted his sons Chas B. and Zachary T. as partners In 1888 the business was incorporated as the H. C. Cole Milling Company The mill now has a capacity of 700 barrels per day, with a trade that takes the full output.

For sixty-seven years the mill has been run continuously by three generations, and is so far as known, the oldest mill in the Mississippi Valley that has been conducted by the same family

The records of the "Council of Appointment of New York State" show. 1811 Seneca Co, Nathan Cole, Ensign Col. Hugh Graham's Regt 1815 Seneca Co., 38th Brigade Infantry, John Sayler, Adjutant, vice N Cole, promoted 1816 Seneca Co Nathan Cole, 2nd Brigade, Major and Inspector. 1821. Seneca Co 38th Brigade, Anthony Schuyler, vice Cole, removed Children (1) marriage:

150 Eli, b Aug 1, 1805, d Aug 23, 1805

Children of (2) marriage (born at Ovid, N Y.)

+151 Abner Bangs, b. May 8, 1809.
152 Burt Scott, b May 5, 1811, d u m, Chester, Ill., Aug. 13, 1855 He owned and operated a ferry across the Mississippi from Cole's Mills to a point directly opposite
+153 Hermon Camp, b. May 9, 1813
154 Oliver C., b Nov 3, 1815; m May, 1836, at Hannibal, Mo, to Louise Stowe He was an engineer and was killed by the blowing up of a steamboat on the Mississippi River near Alton, Ill, June 1, 1836 No issue She married (2) Harry Veech
155 James Monroe, b Dec 26, 1817; d u m, in Texas, Aug 29, 1839

PLANT OF H. C. COLE MILLING CO.

THE ORIGINAL OF THIS RECORD IS IN COLORS AND STILL IN THE POSSESSION OF A DESCENDANT OF BERRY COLE

+156 James Madison, b May 27, 1819.
+157 Nathan, b St Louis, July 26, 1825.

28

BERRY (Joseph, Elisha), m (1) Feb. 16, 1794, Hannah, b Feb. 21, 1777, dau. of Joseph and Sarah (Carpenter) Lewis She d. Dec 25, 1824, aged 47 years, 11 months, 2 days. He m. (2) Dec 25, 1825, Adah, dau. of ———— and Tamar (————) Carl. He d. Carmel, May 29, 1835, aged 66 years, 4 months, 5 days His wife, Adah, was dismissed from Carmel Baptist Church and with her three children removed to Central Illinois

Sarah Carpenter was the dau of John Carpenter, one of the oldest settlers of Dutchess Co.

Berry, like his grandfather, owned and operated a grist mill The mill was located on his farm in the town of Carmel. The motive power was water from the Long Pond outlet A short time before his death he moved to near Red Mills, now Mahopac Falls In his will he leaves "to daughter Harriet Jane, $91 and one feather bed and straw tick which is the remainder of her setting out." Children:

158 Melinda, b Sept. 24, 1795, m June 5, 1813, Selah, b Mar 24, 1792, son of Tracy and Mercy (Cole) Ballard He d. Carmel, May 2, 1870, aged 78 years, 1 month, 8 days She d there, Mar 18, 1873, aged 77 years, 5 months, 24 days.
159 Alveyson, b Oct 25, 1797, d Apr 9, 1811
160 Rebecca, b May 31, 1799, m May 1, 1816, Stephen, b South East, Dutchess Co, N Y, 1796, son of Jedediah and Abigail (Ganong) Wood. They lived near Penn Yan, N. Y She d. there Sept 15, 1848 He d at Painted Post, N. Y, Apr 28, 1878.

Jedediah's father was Nehemiah Wood who came to Dutchess County from Long Island before the Revolution. He d. 1857. His wife was also a Ganong.

161 Alzada, b Feb 26, 1801, m June 4. 1818, Zeba, b Feb 16, 1796, son of Tracy and Mercy (Cole)

Ballard. He d Mar 24, 1862, aged 66 years, 1 month, 8 days She d Mar. 11, 1859, aged 58 years, 11 months.

162 Neurissa, b Oct 15, 1802, m. Sept. 9, 1819, Ardalia, b Oct 26, 1801, son of James and Priscilla (Cole) Townsend They lived at Carmel He d. Oct 29, 1821, and she m (2) William, b Apr 11, 1816, son of Darius and Clarissa (Fairchild) Smith. He was a hatter He d Apr 2, 1859. She d Mar 10, 1860, aged 57 years, 4 months, 25 days.

163 Abiatha, b Sept 22, 1804, d July 12, 1825

+164 Ormond Hayes, b July 6, 1806

165 Clarinda, b Jan 6, 1809, m Jan. 31, 1821, Jonet, b. Carmel, June 6, 1808, son of Daniel and Adah (Ganong) Ganong He was a farmer Lived at Union Valley, and was one of the largest land owners in Putnam County He d Oct 3, 1888 She d May 15, 1885, aged 76 years, 4 months, 13 days

This name is mostly spelled Ganong, but also Gannong, Gannung, Ganoung, Ganun and Ga Nun The first emigrant of the name was Jean Guenon, who landed at New Amsterdam in 1657, and settled at Flushing, L I John, great-grandson of Jean was, in 1756, one of the signers to a call for a pastor to Westminster Congl Society in what is now Carmel He lived at Lake Mahopac. His will, dated Feb 12, 1786, in which his name is spelled Genung

John, Jacob, Marcus, Isaac and Reuben Ganong were privates 7th Regt Dutchess Co Militia in the Revolution

166 Uretta, b Sept 14, 1810; m Feb 10, 1831, Thomas, b Cold Spring, N. Y, Apr 28, 1806, son of Thaddeus and Hannah (Cole) Baxter He d Tarrytown, N. Y, Nov 17, 1884 She d Aug 27, 1867, aged 56 years, 11 months, 13 days

167 Amanda, b Apr 30, 1813, d Nov. 16, 1825

168 Hannah Jane, b Nov 22, 1815, m Nov 29, 1839, Hosea, b Sept 21, 1812, son of James and Sally

(Townsend) Carver They lived at Red Mills He d there Apr. 25, 1854 She d. there Nov. 27, 1890

    169 Adaline, b Nov 22, 1826, m John Thatcher No issue.
170 States G, b Apr 15, 1829; m Elizabeth, dau of Archibald Birdsall. No issue
171 Jordan J, b Apr. 16, 1833

32

JOSEPH (Joseph, Elisha), m. Carmel, Feb. 2, 1797, Phebe, b Jan 28, 1776, daughter of David and Sarah (Hyatt) Frost He d. Beaver Dams, Schuyler Co, N. Y, Mar. 9, 1855. She d there May 26, 1862

David Frost and family lived at Pleasant Valley, Dutchess County, N Y He was a private, 7th Regt Dutchess Co Militia, in the Revolution. David was a "bound out boy" when young. His parents came from England, the father dying on the voyage or soon after reaching America The mother m (2) a Mr. Thorn and lived on Long Island Joseph Cole settled at Beaver Dams about 1833 He served in the War of 1812, and was granted a warrant of 40 acres of government land for his services, but he never took up this land, probably sold his right to it Beaver Dams so named because of the fact that there were two dams, one at and one near by First called Beaver Dams in 1843, formerly West Catlin. First store there in 1832 Dates of births, marriages and deaths taken from Joseph's family record, now in possession of his great-grandson, Mortimer Cole Children·

    172 George Frost, b Dec 23, 1797, m May 5, 1822, Elizabeth Merrick He d Dec 4, 1826, aged 28 years, 11 months, 11 days, and is buried on Cole's farm near Long Pond, in the town of Carmel. Children·

        173 Infant daughter "buried Oct. 5, 1822."
        174 Harry, b 1824. Started to visit his grandmother, Phebe, at Beaver Dams, was taken sick, returned home and died

+175 Chas. Green, b Aug. 14, 1800
+176 Ira, b Mar. 15, 1804.
 177 Harlem, b Feb 4, 1810, d u m, Oct. 20, 1838
+178 Asahel, b June 5, 1814
 179 Minerva Ruth, b Aug. 30, 1817, m Beaver Dams, Oct. 17, 1843, Uriah R, b. Hornby, N Y, 1825. son of George and Phebe (Rockwell) Patchen. He d 1894. She d. New York City, Mar 21, 1904

33

SAMUEL (Joseph, Elisha); m. Prudence Barrett who was b. Jan. 2, 1779 They moved from Carmel to Western New York and in 1835 to Livingston Co, Michigan, being among the first settlers in that part of the State His descendents are mostly farmers He d. Mar. 26, 1851, at Oceola, Mich She d Aug 4, 1847 Children born Tompkins County, N. Y

 180 Elizabeth, b July 10, 1798; m Benjamin Jefferson. She d in N Y State, Aug 24, 1841
+181 Joseph, b Nov. 22, 1799
 182 Anna, b Mar. 9, 1801; m Abram Hendrickson He d and she m (2) at Dearfield,, Mich, William Sherborne She d at Byron, Mich He d at Detroit, Mich
+183 Enos, b Aug 30, 1802
 184 Zillah, b June 5, 1804, m George Lawrence. She d. at Mason, Mich.
 185 Catharine, b. May 6, 1806, m Dec 14, 1828, John Allen, b in New Jersey, Aug. 4, 1808, son of William and Anna (Allen) Van Camp. He d at Hartland, Mich, Jan 12, 1892 She d at Parshallville, Mich, Sept 14, 1890
 186 Samuel, b Aug 24, 1808; m Melinda Kellogg. Lived Otsego Co., N Y. They had a son named Marcus
 187 Marcus, b Mar. 14, 1810; m Hannah White, lived Huron Co, Ohio
 188 Minor, b Mar 15, 1812, d May 13, 1812

NATHAN COLE
SON OF JOSEPH COLE
No. 34

The Descendants of Elisha Cole

  189 Dr Ebenezer, b May 24, 1813, d Apr. 20, 1864, m Martha Downer, and had one son

      190 Milo, b Feb. 2, 1837 Unmarried and living in Texas in 1880.

+191 Rev. Nathan, b Jan. 30, 1815

  192 Louisa M, b June 8, 1817, m John, son of Edmund and Betsey (Edwards) Beach.

  193 Ada Jane, b June 4, 1819; m Riley, son of William Earl. Both died at Oceola, Mich.

+194 Isaac Thompson, b June 21, 1821.

34

NATHAN (Joseph, Elisha), m Apr 26, 1800, Anna Rowland. She was b Sept 6, 1782 At the time of his marriage he lived in Kent, Dutchess Co On Oct 14, 1809, "Brother Nathan Cole received letter of recommendation from Carmel Baptist church as he was about to move to another part of the vineyard' He soon afterwards settled in Covert, N. Y. He was a farmer He d there Feb. 10, 1877. She d there Jan 26, 1849.

He was a man of exemplary habits and an earnest Christian Held office of deacon for half a century His face was always illuminated with a smile and he was loved by all Children:

+195 Watson, b. May 9, 1801.

  196 Cynthia b Nov 28, 1802; m. Nov. 11, 1821, Walker Bennett She d May 9, 1834 He m a second time and died at Danby, N Y

  197 Ursula, b Oct 26, 1804; m Feb 26, 1826, Benjamin Arrowsmith. He was b. in New Jersey, Apr 17, 1795 She d Covert, Aug 13, 1836, and he m (2) Hannah M Durrand He d Covert, May, 1867.

  198 Sarah Anna. b Oct 10, 1807, m Feb 22, 1824, Sylvester, b. Mar. 14, 1800, at Covert, son of Asaph and Deborah (Ferris) King. He d Covert, June 11, 1889 She d there Nov 16, 1885

+199 Eli, b Jan 17, 1809

+200 Edwin Wildman, b May 18, 1814.
201 Myron Rowland, b Jan. 27, 1816, m Covert, 1840, Eliza, b. July, 1820, dau of Isaac and Elizabeth (Auble) Emmons He d Kidder's Ferry, N. Y, Aug. 6, 1894 She d there Feb 26, 1907 No issue.
+202 Milo Van Duzen, b Sept. 26, 1819

36

ASAHEL (Joseph, Elisha); m Jan 13, 1808, at Carmel, Elizabeth, b Nov. 13, 1790, daughter of Jedediah and Abigail (Ganung) Wood. He d Oct. 23, 1875 She d May 20, 1857

He was a farmer by occupation, and lived for many years In the very south-east corner of the town of Kent. He possessed a very strong mind, and when once convinced that a course was right, followed it without regard to consequences He outlived his wife by many years and died at the residence of his son Milan in Carmel Village at the age of 89 years Children born at Kent:

203 Hannah, b Dec 5, 1808, m Jan 2, 1834, Ezra, b Kent, Dec 15, 1811, son of Thomas and Charlotte (Kelley) Colwell He was a farmer; d Apr. 20, 1882, aged 70 years She d May 10, 1882, aged 73 years
204 Azmon Wood, b. Nov 17, 1817; d u m Oct 20, 1857.
205 Milan Jedediah, b Dec 16, 1819, m Nov 15, 1870, Susan, b May 8, 1837, daughter of Ebenezer and Huldah (Foster) Kelley, and wid of Jerome B Hazen. He d Aug 10, 1899, aged 79 years, 7 months, 25 days She d Nov 30, 1905, aged 68 years, 6 months, 23 days. No issue

Asahel's is the first Cole line to become extinct

Ebenezer Kelly, 1797-1877
Huldah (Foster) Kelley, 1800-1851
Jerome B. Hazen, d. Sept., 1866

38

LEVI HALL COLE (Joseph, Elisha), m Dec. 3, 1814, by Elder Ebenezer Cole to Hannah, b Jan. 16, 1798, dau of Daniel and Susan (Ogden) Cole. She was his own cousin. In his early married life he lived in what was called "Cole's Street," the highway leading from Cole's Mill to Mahopac, but later purchased a farm in the south-west part of the town of Carmel on which he lived until his death For many years he was a deacon of the Baptist church at Red Mills. He was a good neighbor, a true friend, a respected citizen and a zealous Christian He d Oct 17, 1860, aged 69 years She d Dec. 16, 1876, aged 78 years 11 months Children:

- 206 Mary Jane, b July 31, 1815, m. at Red Mills, Nov. 14, 1837, Dr. Isaac, b July 16, 1808, at Red Mills, son of Marcus and Mary (Barrett) Barrett They lived at Red Mills and two of their children married Coles. He d. Feb 29, 1880, aged 71 years, 7 months, 13 days. She d. Aug 20, 1895, aged 79 years, 11 months, 10 days

    He studied the Thomsonian practice of medicine He never claimed to be a physician, yet was very skillful in compounding extracts and syrups from native herbs that were efficacious in purifying and giving tone to the system He was a disciple of the healing art, but never accepted any pay for his services
- +207 Ramah, b. Oct. 1, 1818.
- +208 John Berry, b. Apr 10, 1821.
- 209 Caroline, m Sidney Brooks, b June 22, 1830, in Courtlandtown, Dutchess County, son of Elias Querereau and Eliza (Griffin) Tompkins He d Nyack, N. Y, about 1900 She d Brooklyn, N Y, 1861-62
- 210 Amanda, b Oct. 4, 1826, m. Jan 14, 1854, Theron, son of Eleazer and Betsey (Cole) Cole.
- +211 Alonzo Ojida, b. Oct. 8, 1827
- 212 Cynthia, b Nov 6, 1829; m. Nov. 14, 1855, Amos Lane, b. June 10, 1827, son of Silas and Elizabeth

(Tompkins) Austin They lived at Red Mills He d. Apr. 21, 1897. She d. Aug 12, 1906.
213 Adaline Minerva, b. Feb 6, 1832, m. Feb 18, 1857, Ira Travis, b at Red Mills, Feb 4, 1833, son of Elijah and Betsey Ann (Travis) Horton He is still living She d Oct 29, 1877.
+214 Joseph Watson, b. May 20, 1834.
215 Antoinette, b Feb. 18, 1837, m. Jasper, son of Laban and Ann (Sheldon) Cole.
216 Daniel Webster, b. 1840, d u. m at New Orleans, La, July 20, 1863 "Died a soldier while in the service of his Country."

39

RAMAH (Joseph, Elisha), m. Esther Mills He m. (2) Cynthia Martin, m (3) Lucy Winans. He d near Byron, Mich May 31, 1865, aged 70 years, 3 months, 4 days. She d. about 1852.

Ramah settled at Ovid, N. Y. He removed from there about 1824 and took up east half of section 24 in Troy, Oakland Co, Mich. He afterwards went to Shiawassee Co His wife Esther, who died at Troy in 1826, was the first grown person to be buried in the Crook's Cemetery During the winter of 1825-26, he taught in a log schoolhouse He was a tender-hearted man, and although his discipline was lax, his pupils loved him dearly The benches in the school house were made from basswood logs split through the center, flat side up and raised from floor by legs inserted in under side, no cushions and no backs The school was warmed by wood in a Dutch fireplace where half a dozen boys and girls would be standing in turn trying to warm themselves. Later he kept a hotel and helped many a new settler with gratuitous meals and lodging Cynthia Martin died six months after the birth of her son, William M Cole Lucy Winans died three weeks after Mary Jane Cole. Children by (1) marriage·

217 Freeborn (the mother and child died soon after its birth);

(2) marriage:

    218 Mary Jane, b. at Troy, Mich.; d. u m., aged 22 years.
+219 Adoniram Judson, b. Apr. 18, 1831.
+220 William Martin, b ———.

By (3) marriage, no issue.

40

JOHN (Daniel, Elisha), m. Mary (Polly), b Apr 1, 1780, dau. of Philip Smith   He d Jan 14, 1867, aged 91 years, 4 months, 15 days   She d July 16, 1862, aged 82 years, 3 months, 16 days.

In Carmel church records he is mentioned as "for many years a zealous consistent christian," and same records under date of July 16, 1862, mention death of Polly and "that her eyes had long been shut upon things of earth "   Also, "died July 29, 1862, Eliza, daughter of John and Polly—thus mother and daughter separated for a few days, have commenced a companionship never to be broken "   Children b at Carmel:

+221 Levi, b ———.
 222 Lovisa, b 1798, m for his (1) wife, Zachariah Smalley   She d May 9, 1840 in her 43d year. No issue.
 223 Ivah, m. Lauren Newton   Had Louisa, who m (1) Henry Woodin, m (2) Frederick Abbott.
+224 Horace, b. July 8, 1806
+225 Hiram, b June 25, 1811.
 226 Viola, b Dec 27, 1813, m there Nov., 1883, Marcus, b ———, son of Samuel and ——— (Williamson) Barrett   He d Tyrone, N Y, Aug 27, 1880   She d there Dec. 19, 1894
 227 Eliza, b Oct 2, 1816, d unm, July 29, 1862, aged 45 years, 10 months, 27 days

45

JESSE (Daniel, Elisha); m Apr 19, 1807, Mary, b Nov. 15, 1788, dau of Cornelius and Rachel (Barrett) Organ.   They lived at

Kent and he was an invalid for many years He d. Feb 26, 1861, aged 76 years, 5 months, 10 days. She d. Sept. 23, 1857, aged 69 years, 8 days

Cornelius Organ enlisted at the age of 16 years in the 2nd Regt Westchester Co Militia and served 7 years during the Revolution He was born in Virginia and d. at Carmel, Oct 5, 1818, aged 57 years His wife, Rachel, d Sept. 18, 1836, aged 73 years, 3 months Children, born in Kent·

+228 Allen, b Jan. 27, 1808.
229 Jesse, b Nov 29, 1809, d May 29, 1812, aged 2 years, 7 months.
230 Rachel, b. Jan 31, 1813; m. May 13, 1832, to her cousin, Eleazer H. Cole.
+231 Reuben, b Jan 6, 1816.
232 Norman, b March 21, 1821, m Phebe J., dau. of Morris and ―――― (Brown) Russell He d Peekskill, April 19, 1898, aged 77 years, 23 days She d South East, April, 1904 They had·
Elon G , who d y.

46

DANIEL H (Daniel, Elisha), m Sarah, b Nov 9, 1791, dau of Josephus and Ruth (Owen) Tillott They lived at Coles Mills He d. Nov. 2, 1856, aged 70 years, 2 months, 9 days She d May 21, 1860, aged 68 years, 6 months, 12 days Children born Kent:

+233 Ogden, b March 14, 1810
+234 Tillott, b Dec 29, 1811.
235 Julia, b. Feb 28, 1817; m. Harmon, son of Eleazer and Sarah (Hitchcock) Cole No issue
236 Emily, b. March 6, 1818, m Chauncey, son of Lewis and Adah (Cole) Nichols He was a brother of Zillah Nichols, the wife of Tillott Cole She d. Carmel, Dec 20, 1864, aged 46 years, 9 months, 14 days He left Carmel and was never heard from They had a son Edward, who died unmarried.

PRE REVOLUTIONARY CHURCH
HILLSIDE CEMETERY, PEEKSKILL, N. Y.

49

ELISHA J (Daniel, Elisha), m. (1) Rachel, b. 1793, dau of Josephus and Ruth (Owen) Tillott She d Jan. 1, 1815, in her 22nd year, and he m (2) 1815, Lydia, b 1799, dau of ——— Frost He d Kent, June 4, 1879, in 87th year She d there Oct 14, 1873, in 74th year Children—1st marriage

- +237 Thomas Owen, b Dec. 22, 1814
- +238 George Harrison
- 239 Zillah, d. Nov 10, 1821, aged 2 years
- +240 Charles Norton, b Jan 1, 1820
- 241 Antoinette, d July 23, 1837, aged 12 years, 9 months, 7 days

56

NATHANIEL (Ebenezer, Elisha), m Ann Elizabeth, b 1785, in New York City, dau of Anthony and Katharine (Brown) Woolheizer She was the only one of her family born in America Other children of her family were Jacob, Frederick, John, and Katharine, who m Wm Steele

Nathaniel was a farmer and lived in what is now Putnam Valley, which was taken from the town of Carmel in 1861. He was Supervisor, 1839-43-45; Sheriff, 1832 It is claimed that he served in the War of 1812 She d April 28, 1863 He d. May 4, 1868 Both buried in Hillside Cemetery, Peekskill, N Y Children, born Putnam Valley

- +242 Nathaniel, b 1807
- +243 Ebenezer, b 1809
- 244 Mary Margaret, b April 3, 1812, m. Oct 25, 1834, Alanson, b Oct 29, 1802, son of John and Charlotte (Dingee) Adams He d Nov. 7, 1839, in North Fenton, N. Y., and she m. (2) April 21, 1841, at Greene, N Y, Ephriam, b Nov 23, 1817, at Walton, N Y, son of Thaddeus and Hannah (Seymour) Hoyt He d at Port Jervis, N Y, April 15, 1868 She d there April 14, 1868.
- +245 Henry, b ———, 1813.

58 THE DESCENDANTS OF ELISHA COLE

+246 Anthony William, b March 16, 1818
247 Katharine Ann, b April 16, 1820; m Washington Wiloby Mead, who was b Putnam County, Oct 14, 1818 He d Sun Prairie, Wis, Sept 29, 1877, aged 59 years. She d there Oct 25, 1873
248 James Ogden, b. March 30, 1823 He d. unmarried at Carmel, May 15, 1888, aged 65 years, 1 month, 15 days Supervisor, 1877. Sheriff of Putnam County, 1873-79, and at the time of his death.
249 Maria Elizabeth, b Feb. 22, 1826; d Aug. 22, 1829

57

WILLIAM (Ebenezer, Elisha); m ———, Sally, b. July 20, 1786, dau. of John and Susanna Odell He was a farmer and miller and lived near Craft's Corners. He was a soldier in War 1812. He d. ———. She m. (2) Absalom Likely Children:

+250 John Benjamin, b May 28, 1811
251 Mary, b ———; m Nathaniel Tompkins
252 Vashti Susan, b March 16, 1817; m March 1, 1835, to George Washington, b Sept. 9, 1813, son of George Washington and Deborah (Jacobs) Depew She d. Oct. 21, 1849, aged 32 years, 7 months and 5 days He m. (2) Elmira Cole. He d. at Baltimore in 1872 She d. there ———
253 Elmira, b. ———; m her brother-in-law, Geo W Depew.

58

EBENEZER (Ebenezer, Elisha); m. ———, Elizabeth, b July 18, 1792, dau. of Jeremiah and Lurana (Ferris) Chapman. He was a farmer and d at Putnam Valley, June 2, 1855, aged 69 years She d. there May 26, 1876, aged 84 years. Children

254 Child, d. y.
+255 James, b Dec. 22, 1807
+256 Charles

+257 William, b. Dec. 5, 1814.
258 Lucretia, b June 3, 1819, m. Jan 28, 1837, Charles, b Nov. 7, 1814, son of Silas and Azubah (Cole) Selleck He d. March 23, 1903 She d. June 28, 1894.
258½ Mary, b May 5, 1823, m Feb. 4, 1849, Abijah, b Sept. 5 1820, son of William N. and ——— (Morris) Platt. Lived at Peekskill He d April 20, 1900 She d. April 25, 1894. Their children were: William C, b June 20, 1857, and Ebenezer, b April 2, 1859
259 Jeremiah, b Jan 26, 1826, d. unm. Jan. 21, 1871
260 Lurana, b June 1, 1828; m William, b. Dec. 27, 1828, son of John Richards He d. April 16, 1904 She d. April 24, 1891.

59

JOSEPH (Ebenezer, Elisha), m Elizabeth Redfield They lived at Caramel He d Jan 28, 1843, aged 53 years, 11 months, 3 days. She d May 5, 1871, aged 75 years He was Sheriff of Putnam County in 1829 (Jos G Cole's record gives wife's name as above, while another record calls her Betsy Odell) Child

261 Mary, d Feb 7, 1848, aged 16 years, 9 months, 12 days

64

JAMES (Ebenezer, Elisha), m at Kent, Sept. 15, 1825, Adah, b there Feb 3, 1805, dau of Thomas and Charlotte (Kelley) Colwell He d May 22, 1872, aged 69 years, 3 months, 18 days She d Oct. 26, 1878, aged 73 years, 8 months, 23 days

James was born, lived and died in the town of Kent. He was a farmer, stone mason, and Justice of the Peace for sixteen years. In his father's will he is mentioned as the youngest son Children·

+262 Thomas, b March 21, 1822
+263 Edwin, b Sept 18, 1824.

+264 William, b July 4, 1825
+265 Alvah, b April 26, 1827
 266 Catharine, b ———, 1829
 267 Susan, twin of the above
    Catharine d Dec 2, 1842, aged 13 years, 10 months, 20 days; Susan d y
 268 Mary, b Oct 21, 1832, m. Nov 23, 1875, at Martindale, Columbia County, N. Y., Howard Tompkins She was his second wife and they lived at Kent He d Mar 3, 1899 She living No issue.
+269 Ebenezer, b. Jan. 14, 1834
+270 Charles, b Aug. 14, 1836
 271 Charlotte, b Dec 21, 1838, m May 12, 1881, Edward, b April 12, 1849, son of John and Mary (Heacock) Metcalf He living at Danbury, Conn She d Jan 27, 1899 No issue
 272 Amanda, d Jan 27, 1843, aged 1 year, 8 months, 29 days.
+273 James Wood, b ———

65

LEWIS (John, Elisha), m Feb 4, 1805, Hannah Rogers She d ———, and he m. (2) Aug. 1, 1819, Fanny, dau of Moses and Mary (Caldwell) Hazen. Lived at Hector, Tompkins County, N Y. He d. April 15, 1854 Children, born at Hector, N. Y

+274 Amos Rogers, b June 23, 1806
 275 Cyrus, b Sept 5, 1809
+276 Darius, twin of above.
    Cyrus, m ——— Potter and moved to Wisconsin about 1842 Had a son.
+277 Elvin Clinton, b Dec. 4, 1812
+278 Elmer C , twin of above
 279 Adaline, b May 1, 1820, d unm Feb 10, 1854
 280 Moses Hazen, b Dec 8, 1824, d. unm Jan. 1, 1863
 281 Dewitt Clinton, b Jan 14, 1828, d Jan. 14, 1868

70

HARVEY (John, Elisha), m Aug. 1, 1819, Anna, b Feb. 17, 1801, dau of Moses and Mary (Caldwell) Hazen He d. June 20, 1892 Children.

    282 Mary Washburn, b Dec 31, 1820.
    283 Eliza, b Oct 12, 1823
    284 Fanny Hazen, b April 15, 1826.
    285 Marvin, b. June 15, 1828
    286 Adelia Tidd, b Dec. 31, 1830.
    287 Washburn Ogden, b Feb 1, 1834
    288 Ann Elizabeth, b July 18, 1836.

72

OGDEN (John, Elisha), m. June 15, 1839, Clarinda Smith. Children

    289 John Elkanah, b Sept. 7, 1840
    290 Romaine Harvey, b Aug 2, 1848.

74

HEMAN (Reuben, Elisha, Elisha), m. November, 1806, Chloe, b Feb 12, 1785, dau of Joseph and Elizabeth (Townsend) Hopkins. Lived at South East, Dutchess County, N Y Farmer. He d. Jan. 19, 1832, aged 46 years, 4 months, 12 days She d Jan. 30, 1865, aged 79 years, 11 months, 18 days Children·

    291 Ira, b Dec 18, 1807, d unm Nov. 18, 1859, aged 52 years, 1 month, 22 days.
    292 Adilla, d y
    293 Zillah, b April 7, 1815; m Sept. 23, 1834, in South East, Jeremiah, b Woodbridge, Conn, Jan. 20, 1795, son of Charles and Anna (Baldwin) Hine. He graduated at Yale in 1815 Was Surrogate of Putnam County, 1822-23 Elected District Attorney in 1829 and served until his death, Aug 24, 1838, aged 43 years, 6 months, 28 days She m (2) May 31, 1842, William Edgar, b

Apr. 30, 1824, son of Nathan Alva and Clara (Crosby) Howes. He d Oct. 12, 1849, aged 25 years, 5 months, 12 days. She d. April 16, 1876

 294 Edwin, b. Feb. 21, 1822
+295 Edmund, twin of the above.
Edwin disappeared
+296 Heman Hopkins, b ———, 1823

75

CHARLES (Reuben, Elisha, Elisha)　He m ———. Went West. Alive in 1840　Children:

   297 Le Grand, b ———.
   298 Eliza, b. ———

78

EBENEZER (Reuben, Elisha, Elisha), m Betsey Ellis Lived at Carmel He d. Feb 6, 1870, aged 76 years, 5 months, 16 days. She d June 30, 1873, aged 76 years, 10 days Children:

   299 Ellen, b Jan 1, 1819, d unm. April 16, 1867, aged 45 years, 3 months, 15 days
   300 Mary Ann, b Sept 22, 1819, m. at Carmel Aug. 20, 1840, Benjamin, b Sep 1, 1806, son of Major and Martha (Watts) Fowler. He d. Sep. 8, 1858, aged 52 years, 2 months, 7 days, and she m. (2) for his third wife, on Nov 5, 1867, at Brewster, N. Y, George Doughty, b May, 1814, at Beekman, N Y He d. at Carmel, March 16, 1889, and she d at Brewster Jan 17, 1890.
+301 John, b. ———, 1822.
   302 Nelson, b. Aug. 15, 1826; d unm Nov 14, 1890

83

ELI (David, Elisha, Elisha); m at Cazenovia, N Y, May 29, 1825, Malina, b there March 2, 1803, dau of Abner Sweetland Farmer He d Geneva, O, Aug 14, 1881 She d Saybrook, O, Dec 4, 1873 Children born at Cuba, N Y.

 303 Amarilla, b and d Jan 7, 1826.
+304 Abner Sweetland, b. Dec 22, 1826
+305 David Orlando, b Oct 13, 1828.
 306 Clarissa Malissa, b July 18, 1830, m Oct 14, 1851, Caleb M Rude She d. at Cuba, N Y., July, 1833.
 307 Mary Elizabeth, b July 27, 1832, m Aug 17, 1854, Daniel L Hart. She d. at Geneva, O, June 16, 1884
 308 Hannah Maria, b Sept 12, 1834, d unm. at Cuba March 10, 1863
 309 Caroline DeForest, b. May 27, 1837; m Sept. 6, 1866, Effingham Bower
+310 Lyman Mason, b Aug 7, 1840
 311 Harriet Albing, b Oct 3, 1842, d. at Cuba, N. Y, Sept 24, 1848
 312 Susan Adelia, b and d May, 1846

85

ABNER BANGS (David, Elisha, Elisha), m July 10, 1827, Lucy, b July 21, 1809, dau of Chester and Abigail (Hackett) Scott She d in Wisconsin, 1847 He d at Friendship, N. Y., June, 1876 Soon after his wife's death, he, with his two sons, returned to Friendship, his former home In 1851 he m a Mrs McCall, who d the following year No issue by second marriage Children (b Friendship, N Y) ·

 313 Clemina, b Aug. 6, 1829; d. 1847 in Wisconsin
+314 William Wallace, b May 24, 1831
+315 Chester Scott, b July 1, 1836

87

NATHAN (David, Elisha, Elisha), m in N Y State Dec 5, 1831, Louisa, dau of James and Lavina (Hodge) Henderson. She d at Lyons, Mich, 1851. He m (2), 1854, Susan C

Bailey. Farmer. He d at Lyons, Mich., 1878 Children (b at Charlotte, Chautauqua County, N Y.):

+316 Horace, b. March 19, 1833.
+317 James, b July 22, 1835.
+318 Leander, b. May 24, 1837.
+319 Dwight H., b. Oct. 9, 1842.
  320 Florence, b 1855; d. 1860.

88

DAVID (David, Elisha, Elisha); m at New Berlin, N Y, Sept 7, 1837, Almira, b at Manilius, N. Y, Jan. 10, 1811, dau of Perese and Mary (Nickerson) Bradford Farmer, lived at South Edmeston, N. Y He d Aug 12, 1888 She d March 24, 1887 Children:

321 Juliette, b Dec. 12, 1841, m Oct 15, 1863, Henry L, b West Laurens, N Y, Feb 6, 1838, son of Benj. J and Ruth (Smith) Haight She d July 25, 1906. He living.
322 Lewis, b Oct 29, 1843, d 1847.
323 Augusta, b Feb 22, 1845, m Feb 20, 1868, Herbert Walker, b at New Berlin Aug. 11, 1841, son of Albert W and Roxie B (Babcock) Hills Both living at New Berlin, N. Y.
324 Eugene, b April 17, 1846; d. 1848
325 Alice E, b June 5, 1849; d. 1853
326 Charlotte Eva, b. Nov 1, 1852; m. April 8, 1878, William, b. New York City Feb 22, 1830, son of Joseph and Nancy (Sigerson) Ward He d. in Michigan April 14, 1907. She living in Oregon.
327 Adelia, b Feb 8, 1855, m. August, 1883, John, b. Feb 12, 1852, son of John and Elspeth (Oliver) Rutherford.

89

ELISHA (David, Elisha, Elisha); m Nov. 27, 1836, Delia, dau of Rev. Henry Chapman He d Jan 9, 1844 Children

+328   Charles Henry, b Dec 2, 1837
 329   Merrick L , b June 3, 1843.

90

JOHN (David, Elisha, Elisha), m Jan 25, 1833, Eliza E , dau. of Chester and Abigail (Hackett) Scott She d 1846, and he m (2), 1847, Mary, dau of Lyman and Fanny (Mason) Scott Abigail's father, Josiah Hackett, was a Captain in the Revolution Chester s father, Nathaniel Scott, was also a Captain in the Revolution Children

    330   Henrietta, b. ———, m 1851, George Scott.
    331   Warren, b ———, m ———, May Marsh
    332   John Tyler, b ———; m. 1882, Franc Stratton
    333   Lester, b 1844 , d. 1853
    334   Arabella, b 1850, d 1853
    335   Nellie Belle, b 1856, d 1877

91

CHESTER S (David, Elisha, Elisha), m May 6, 1835, at Sinclairville, N. Y , Virtue Elvira, b there Feb 3, 1815, dau of Maj Samuel Sinclair and his second wife, Mrs Fanny Edson. He was a hatter and lived at Hillsdale, Mich He d. there Feb 2, 1885 She living in 1896.

Chester lived at Edmeston, N Y, at the time of his marriage and lived at Mayville, N Y, before going to Michigan (Maj Samuel Sinclair served in the 1st N. H Regt , Col John Stark, in the Revolution He enlisted in Capt Amos Morrell's company on June 20, 1777, for 3 years At the time of his enlistment he was in his 16th year Was at Fort Ticonderoga, Bemis Heights and Valley Forge. at which place his brother, Bradley Sinclair, died from exposure He was discharged at West Point April 6, 1780) Children

    336   Chester Sinclair, b March 8, 1836, d Jan 28, 1839
    337   Frances Eliza, b Oct 26, 1839; m July 5, 1860, Nathaniel L Randall Lived at Hillsdale, Mich Their children were Frankie, Emma and Nathan

+338 Henry Clay, b Aug 4, 1841
339 Walter Sinclair, b June 21, 1851; m Sept 30, 1874, Julia Randall. Live at Hinsdale, Mich. No issue

94

ALONZO (David, Elisha, Elisha); m Louisa Lewis. They had
340 One child

95

HIRAM (Eleazer, Elisha, Elisha); m Rachel Organ. She is said to have been a dau of Cornelius and Rachel (Barrett) Organ and an aunt to wife of Hiram's brother, Eleazer H Cole. Children

341 Green, b ———; m ——— Haight
342 Barnum, b. ———.
343 Hiram, b ———.
344 Laura J, b ———.

98

ELEAZER H. (Eleazer, Elisha, Elisha), m May 13, 1832, Rachel, b. Carmel Jan 31, 1813, dau of Jessie and Mary (Organ) Cole. He d. April 13, 1834, aged 29 years, 10 months. She d May 1, 1883, aged 70 years, 3 months, 1 day. Child.

345 Louisa Jane, b March 7, 1833, living unm at Peekskill

100

HARRISON (Eleazer, Elisha, Elisha); m. Oct 26, 1828, Anna Eliza Philips, b. Nov. 22, 1808. Lived in Ohio. Children.

+346 Edward Eleazer, b. Nov 19, 1829
347 Mary Ann, b ———, m Dec 30, 1851, Thos H Brown
348 Almeda, b ———; d y
349 Walter Todd. Member Company G, 49th Ohio. Killed in battle, Chicamaugua, Sept 20, 1863

350 Althea, b ———; m 1861, James Boyd Had Nellie

351 Ann Amanda, b ———, m Feb 22, 1866, Henry A Saliers.

352 Harriet Eliza, b ———, m Feb. 22, 1874, Ira Geo Labounty

104

THERON (Eleazer, Elisha, Elisha), m Jan 14, 1854, Amanda, b Oct 4, 1826, dau of Levi H and Hannah (Cole) Cole. She d Oct 6, 1860 He m. (2) Jan 13, 1862, Amanda Longwell, wid. of Andrew Houch She d Sept 9, 1877 He m. (3) at Peekskill, N. Y, Oct 16, 1884, Antha Jane, b Mahopac Falls, Aug. 21, 1840, dau. of Isaac and Mary Ann (Cole) Barrett She was a niece of his first wife. He d Campbell, N Y, Dec 16, 1906 She still living Child.

353 Spencer Houghton, b Brooklyn, N. Y, Oct. 20, 1855, m. Jan 1, 1884, Minnie, b Nov. 30, 1863, dau of Elah B. and Eliza Ann (Ballard) Hopkins He living at Savona, N Y. Their children were

Leon Edwin, b Jan 6, 1885
Theron Hopkins, b Feb. 28, 1888.

110

ALFRED (Obed, Elisha, Elisha), m at Carmel, June 19, 1836, Calista Jane, b May 1, 1819, dau. of Jeremiah and Fanny (Ballard) Wilson. Farmer and lived and d at Black River Falls, Wis He d March 24, 1874 She d May 11, 1903.

(Fanny Ballard was a dau of Tracy and Mercy (Cole) Ballard She m (1) Jesse Wilson, a brother of her second husband, Jeremiah Wilson) Children (b. at Carmel):

+354 Henry B, b July 6, 1838
355 Hortense, b Aug 10, 1840; d. May 10, 1845.
356 Jerome, b Oct 15, 1842; unmarried
357 Francis Wayland, b. Aug. 8, 1846

114

LABAN (Elisha, Elisha, Elisha), m Oct 29, 1827, Esther, dau of William Fowler She d Sept 10, 1833, aged 33 years, 5 months, 16 days, and he m (2) Aug. 30, 1835, Ann, b Dover, Dutchess County, April 12, 1800, dau. of Ebenezer and Hannah (———) Sheldon Lived at Red Mills He d May 2, 1848, aged 49 years, 7 months, 5 days She d. Aug 20, 1887, aged 86 years, 8 months Child

    358 Jasper, b. 1828, m Antoinette, dau of Levi and Hannah (Cole) Cole Lived in New York City She d Dec 22, 1878, aged 41 years, 10 months, 4 days No issue

        A few years before his wife's death he left his home one evening and was never seen or heard from afterwards He had quite a sum of money with him and it was thought he was robbed and murdered

117

JACOB (Elisha, Elisha, Elisha), m June 5, 1834, Jane, b Aug. 4, 1805, dau of John and Rachel (Sunderlin) Kelley She d Dec 7, 1849, aged 44 years, 4 months, 7 days, and he m (2) March 14, 1851 Mrs Julia Augusta, b in Franklin County, dau of Gates Hoyt and wid of Dr George W Paddock He lived at South East, having gone there from Carmel April, 1833 Farmer He d Sept 23, 1883, aged 78 years, 3 months, 23 days She d at Salt Lake City, 1890

(John Kelley was a son of John Kelley who came from Cape Cod Rachel (Sunderlin) Kelley m (2) Epenitus Yeomans and d March 4, 1850, aged 72 years.) Children

    359 Antoinette Kelley, b May 16, 1836, m Feb 17, 1858, Theodore F, b South East, Jan 10, 1832, youngest son of Jesse and Eleanor (Foster) Kelley He d May 7, 1897 She living at Carmel
        (Three of the children of Jesse and Eleanor Kelley married Coles. Susan m Jonathan; Isaac m Antoinette (dau of Elisha Cole 3d), and

The Descendants of Elisha Cole

Theodore m as above Antoinette, by her marriage to Theodore, became the aunt of her own cousins)

360 Harriet Newell, b June 4, 1838 Still living at Carmel She furnished many records and a great deal of information concerning the Cole family, and greatly aided in the compilation of this work

361 Minerva, b. Feb 6, 1841; m April 7, 1870, Irvin, b Lagrange, N Y, Aug. 12, 1843, son of Anson Lawrence and Hannah Simmons (McOmber) Thomas He living at Cuba, N Y She d. Franklinville, N Y, June 18, 1891

+362 Elisha Kelley, b Lodi, O, May 26, 1843

363 Emma Jane, b Aug 7, 1845, m. Nov 1, 1878, George, b June 29, 1847, at Bolton, Canada, son of Henry and Maria (Bolton) Nunn He living at Hamilton, Canada She d Aug 19, 1887.

365 Susan, b. Sept 18, 1847 Living at Carmel, unm

118

DAVID (Elisha, Elisha, Elisha), m. May 14, 1836, Emily Preston, b Sept 25, 1812, dau of William Sheldon She d at Greenfield, O, May 19, 1839, aged 26 years, and is buried there He m (2) Aug 31, 1840, Amanda, b Carmel June 2, 1810, dau of Andrew and "Anor" (Kniffen) Ferris He d July 9, 1844, at Steuben, O, aged 36 years She d. at Cleveland, O, Dec 28, 1898

David was a pioneer farmer in Greenfield, now Steuben, Huron County, Ohio, locating there about 1835

Andrew Ferris, b June 15, 1769; d. June 15, 1837

"Anor" Ferris, d at Carmel Feb. 8, 1837

Children (first marriage, b at Greenfield):

+366 Norman Sheldon, b. Sept 3, 1837
367 Emily, b ———.

Children (second marriage)

368 Emily, b May, 1842, d. Nov 14, 1843, aged 1 year, 6 months
+369 David Elliott, b April 16, 1844

120

JONATHAN (Elisha, Elisha, Elisha); m June 19, 1836, Susan, b. South East Nov 17, 1820, dau of Jesse and Eleanor (Foster) Kelley.

He was an undertaker and farmer and was ordained a minister by the Carmel Baptist Church April 10 1844 He d. May 2, 1884, aged 73 years She d. Jan 3, 1899, aged 78 years, 1 month, 17 days Children (b at Carmel):

370 Eli Kelley, b Jan. 14, 1837, d unm at Donaldsonville, La, Oct 5, 1865, aged 23 years, 3 months, 21 days He was a surgeon, 8th N. Y Cavalry Buried at Carmel

371 Mary Elizabeth, b June 23, 1838, m Feb 17, 1858, James Alonzo, b 1831, son of Henry and Julia (Dean) Knapp He d. March 22, 1865, aged 33 years. 7 months, 6 days She d Nov. 19, 1858, aged 20 years, 4 months, 6 days No issue

+372 Onken Willard, b Aug 27, 1846.

124

RUFUS (Elisha, Elisha, Elisha), m in Siskayon County, Cal, May 19, 1869, Ellen. b West Jefferson, Me, Dec 4, 1842, dau of John and Nancy (Boynton) Clary He settled on a ranch in the northwestern part of California The S P R. R was built through his land and a station built and named "Coles" His wife went West as a teacher He d Nov 24, 1889 She still living Children (b at Coles, Cal) ·

373 Irma Estelle, b. Oct 11, 1871. d. unm April 10, 1889

374 Rufus Jay, b Jan 5, 1873. Unmarried and lives at Hilts, Cal He is a farmer and stock raiser

125

BYRON (Elisha, Elisha, Elisha), m. at Norwalk, Conn., May 3, 1860, Chloe Ann, b at Carmel Sept 9, 1838, dau of Edmond and Hannah (Henion) Knox Lived in Oregon. He d Jan 18, 1894. She living at Martinez, Cal

In 1850 he went to California by the way of Panama and settled in Oregon A mineral spring was found on his farm He started a sanitarium and called it "Colestin" Children (b at Colestin)

375 Ella Ann b May 4, 1861; m. at Sisson, Cal, Oct 2, 1881, Charles Frank, b Hawkinsville, Cal, May 16, 1857, son of William and Mary (Parker) Sullaway Both living at Sisson He is a lumberman

376 Jules Francis, b May 28, 1863, m Isabel Williams, have children, Edith and Aileen

377 Emma Jane, b. June 5, 1866, m Oct 25, 1890, Joseph, b Portland, Me, Dec 1, 1864, son of Fred Allen and Annie Maria (Mowe) Poor Both living at Ashland, Ore Their children are:

    Herbert Knox, b April 8, 1894
    Alice Mowe, b Aug 19, 1899

378 Willard Leonard, b Jan 6, 1868; m Shasta, Cal, June 29, 1903, Alice, b Melville, Cal., Feb 18, 1879, dau of Thaddeus Fairbanks and Alice Jane (Wilkinson) Harvey Both living at Martinez, Cal Children, b in San Francisco, Cal

    Alice, b June 27, 1905.
    Willard, Harvey, b. Aug. 8, 1906

379 Hugh Franklin, b Dec 14, 1868, m Yreka, Cal, Nov 14, 1894, Lillie, b Woodville, Oregon, May 5, 1872, dau of Stephen and Elizabeth (Evans) Beers Both living at Hilts, Cal Have an adopted son, Howard Loud

380 Grace Elizabeth, b. Apr 8, 1871; m at Yreka Cal Sept 8, 1892 Frank Lane, b May 11, 1867,

Thornton, Ind, son of Alexander and Mary (Williams) Park Both living at Camino, Cal Their children are

>   Jessie Cecil, b. Apr 10, 1895
>   Percy Cole, b Oct 29, 1896
>   Lloyd Clayton, b June 23, 1899
>   Gertrude Celia, b. Aug 25, 1905.

381 Byron Hopkins, b Dec 28, 1873.

382 Jessie Edith, b. Jan. 16, 1875; m Dec 25, 1897, Isaac Chase, b. June 25, 1868, Toledo, Ohio, son of Isaac Weaver and Mary (Ruland) Zent Both living at Merced, Cal Their children are:

>   Grace Zerelda, b Apr 28, 1899
>   Willard Clinton, b Jan 15, 1901
>   Claude Raymond, b Oct 26, 1902

383 Herbert Bailey, b July 5, 1877; m Yreka, Cal, Sept 20, 1905, Mary A, b Hamburg Bar, Cal, June 7, 1887, dau of John and Mary (Murphy) O'Neill Child:

>   Gladys Colestin, b. Ashland, Ore., May 26, 1907.

384 Henry Clay, b. June 8, 1880; m Talent, Ore, Nov 30, 1904, Frances Ellen, b there Feb 23, 1880, dau of Welborn and Mary Catharine (Brophy) Besson. Both living at Talent He is a railroad engineer Child:

>   Kenneth Besson, b Ashland, Ore, Feb 24, 1907

129

EZRA (Daniel, Elisha, Elisha), m Feb 2, 1828, Angeline Porter, b Oct 6, 1810 Ezra went West while a young man and settled near Adrian, Mich He d Weston, Mich, Mar 12, 1895, aged 86 years, 11 months, 12 days She died there Dec. 26, 1886 Children

385 Orville Porter, b. Nov 10, 1828, d unm Nov 12, 1851.
386 Samantha, b. Jan 5, 1831, m May 8, 1849, Cornelius Quick She d. Jan 4, 1870.
387 Lydia, b Sept. 28, 1832; m Apr 28, 1852, George Holden She d July 21, 1903.
388 Lois S , b Jan. 10, 1834; m Dec 25, 1854, George Price. He d and she m. (2) Mar. 22, 1877, George Acker She d May 3, 1902
389 Harriet Pixley, b June 23, 1836, m Oct 4, 1859, David Holden. She d Oct 10, 1899.
390 Sarah H., b Jan. 19, 1838 Living at Weston, unm
391 Daniel Harrison, b. June 24, 1840, d unm Nov. 29, 1900.
392 Jane Thursey, b Feb 4, 1842, m. Dec. 19, 1867, to William Tenbrook.
393 Miner, b Jan 4, 1845, d. Apr. 24, 1846.
394 Matilda Louisa, b Mar 30, 1847; m. Apr. 13, 1868, William Henry, b Sept. 19, 1840, son of Eli and Harriet R. (Horton) Cole
395 John Hall, b Dec 21, 1848, m Nov. 30, 1876, Minnie Rappleye.
396 Asaph E , b Oct 26, 1850, d Sept 26, 1851
397 Adelbert, b. Dec. 4, 1853; d Feb 4, 1854.

131

AARON HAZEN (Daniel, Elisha, Elisha); m. at Covert, N. Y., March 21, 1835, Lydia Bloomer, b there Feb. 18, 1817, dau of William and Barbara (Swick) Rappleye They moved from Covert to Spencer, O , in June, 1835 He took up 240 acres of heavy timber land He invented a buckle known as "Cole's Wedge Trace Buckle." He was licensed to preach by the Baptist Church. He d Adrian, Mich , Oct 27, 1867. She d Dallas, Tex , Oct 8, 1889 Children (b at Spencer):

398 Harriet Calista, b. Dec 20, 1835, m West Barre, O , June 30, 1861, Rev. Howard Bailey, b. Aug.

74   THE DESCENDANTS OF ELISHA COLE

8, 1830, Baldwinsville, N Y., son of Dea Amos and Sarah (Bailey) Taft. She d Salem, Mich, March 4, 1868, and he m (2) Nov 26, 1868, Emma F Brigham. He entered Kalamazoo College in 1855 and graduated in 1859 In 1861 he graduated from the Theology Seminary and was ordained pastor of the Baptist church at Perrysburg, O, the same year. He living at Weston, Mich.

+399 William Rappleye, b. Sept 25, 1837.
+400 Miner Thomas, b July 3, 1839
 401 Adoniram Judson, b Oct 11, 1843; d West Barre, O, Jan 4, 1861
+402 Frank Marion, b Dec. 25, 1851, Maumee City, O
+403 Ralph Tunis, b. Dec 25, 1853
+404 George Ide, b April 24, 1857, Grand Blanc, Mich.

133

IRA HAZEN (Daniel, Elisha, Elisha), m at Covert, N. Y, Jan 3, 1849, to Mary Caroline, b there Oct 11, 1822, dau. of Beckwith and Mary (Hurd) Denison She d Sept 26, 1892.

Ira H Cole was b on his father's farm in the town of Covert, Seneca County, N Y, in the house where he now lives, a hale and hearty man for one well into the last decade of a century's span of life.

All his lines of ancestry run back to the earliest New England families

Through his father he is descended from the Daniel Cole who came to Plymouth from England in 1632, and through his mother, from Elder William Brewster and Stephen Hopkins, of the *Mayflower*

His grandfather and great-grandfather, both named Elisha Cole, and his grandfather Joseph Hopkins, were revolutionary soldiers, all serving in the 7th Dutchess County Regt.

He is the last of a family of eleven children, four boys and seven girls, all of whom reached maturity, seven living to advanced old age, one being 96 and five over 85 years of age at death

IRA H. COLE
No. 133

Mr Cole has spent his whole life without interruption on the farm of his nativity He m. Jan 3, 1849, Mary Caroline Denison, dau of Beckwith Denison, a neighbor Through her father she was a descendant of Capt. George Denison, of Stonington, Conn, and John Howland, of the *Mayflower*. And through her mother she traced her lineage to William Leete, the first Governor of Connecticut Her great-grandfather, Christopher Denison, died in the military service under Wolfe at Quebec To this woman's Christian character and strength and refinement of mind this branch of the Cole family is much indebted.

Ira H Cole has always been a respected and influential member of the community in which he has lived for nearly ninety-two years Always possessing the full confidence of friends and neighbors, and looked up to by them as a strong man, both mentally and physically, he never sought political preferment, choosing rather to pursue the even tenor of a quiet life He has, however, creditably filled political offices of minor importance, and has always held a keen and intelligent interest in politics His first vote was cast in 1838, his first in a Presidential election in 1840, for William Henry Harrison He was a strong supporter of Henry Clay in 1844, but went with the Free Soilers under Van Buren in 1848, voting again with the Whigs in 1852 His training, cast of mind, and predilections lead him to espouse the cause and principles of the Republican party, which he joined upon its organization, voting for Fremont in 1856, for Lincoln in 1860, and for every Republican candidate for the Presidency since

While possessing, primarily, but a common school education, years of reading and study on broad and liberal lines, has made him a very well-informed man Bringing a strong and naturally free mind to the study of questions political, social and religious, he has, notwithstanding the narrowness of his environment and field of activity, developed into a man of rare, broad, independent judgment on almost every question of the day His life and growth well illustrate the truth that while the city develops best the objective, the country best develops the subjective man

His is a character of great native strength and nobility. We assert with confidence that none have ever honestly assailed or had reason to assail the absoluteness of his integrity To him it is as natural and necessary to be honest, open and direct, both in act and word, as to breathe Hardly willing to tolerate the ordinary social conventions, hypocrisy and all forms of pretence are entirely foreign to his nature Deceit and trickery are with him simply impossible, and in others unpardonable Whatever the quality or appearance, he loves and wants to know naught but the genuine. No less strong is his sense of justice and his uncompromising adherence to it regardless of results. If slow to forgive the wounds of malice, he has always been quick and unhesitating in the recognition and just estimate of others' virtues.

In religion he has been, and is still, a conscientious, sincere and logical investigator, loathe to accept any conclusion that does not appeal to reason and rationality, regardless of tradition or creed But convictions once formed he never would, or could, deny until sound reason moved them Reared amid religious teachings severely orthodox and strongly sectarian, yet by his native strength and original and independent mode of thought, he long ago reached an attitude upon this subject, forcing the conviction that true religion is the religion of universal law, perhaps the same attitude to which the world, through the stress and storm of centuries of religious controversy has been steadily tending, and will, eventually, attain While not a communicant in the church, he would as soon deny the sunshine of a cloudless summer day as to deny his God Reason, conscience and rationality working on the broad plane of nature and the universal, with simple right and justice as standards, rather than the comparatively narrow man-made doctrines and dogmas of orthodoxy, are and have always been his guides

Mr. Cole, we believe, is the oldest living resident of his county The playmates of his boyhood, friends and associates of his young manhood, and most of his acquaintances of middle life have passed on He stands, as it were, an aged oak, alone in the midst of a clearing, bearing rugged evidence of strength that is waning, full of suggestions of departed fellows and a long gone past, but still bravely shooting its leaves to the sun. A true child of nature he is passing on as naturally and normally as he came and has lived. Patient and confident, courageous but resigned, he is ready at any time for the end.

To us of the younger generations, it is interesting, almost incomprehensible, to note some of the conditions existing, and some of the great changes which have been wrought in the world, all within the lifetime of this man with whom we may talk face to face.

George III. was still on the throne of England when he was born. Napoleon Bonaparte had met his Waterloo almost within the year, and was then living in banishment at St Helena. The associates and co-laborers of Washington were the statesmen of our country. Madison, just retired from the Presidency, was still in the vigor of his statesmanship. Monroe was but five months in his first term as President. John Adams, Thomas Jefferson and John Jay all lived several years after. Louis XVIII ruled France. The preaching of John Wesley still rung in the ears of living men and women. The associates of Voltaire and the courtiers of Frederick the Great were still in the prime of life. Lafayette made his last visit to this country seven years after. The tragedy of Hamilton was still being told by its witnesses. Goethe and Warren Hastings had just passed maturity. Keats and Charles Lamb were young men. Bismark and Bronte were babies. Lincoln, Gladstone, Darwin, Tennyson and Poe were all lads of eight, Dickens and Thackeray of five and six, Longfellow of ten, and Emerson, Hugo and Dumas of fourteen. Webster, Clay and Calhoun had but commenced their political careers. The charm and power of the eloquence of Chatham, Burke and Fox were being extolled by their colleagues. Queen Victoria, Victor Emanuel, Tyndall, Huxley, George Eliot, Grant, Sherman, Sheridan, Blaine, Garfield and McKinley have all since come upon the scene, stamped their lives upon the world and passed beyond.

The religious world was still narrow, dogmatic and intolerant—almost fanatical. New England puritanism was still predominant Science was in its infancy Metapsychics as a science was unthought of

The difference between the world then and of to-day as regarding all the arts of civilization is beyond wildest imaginings. Most all the uses of steam and electricity were undreamed of. Every method of lighting except by the wax and tallow candle, and of heat except by the woods of the forest, and of locomotion except by man and beast were practically unknown. Coal was just discovered. Twenty-eight years were to elapse before the discovery of petroleum It was the day of the household spinning wheel and loom. No means of travel except by foot or sail The use of steamboats had barely begun. Then it was a question of weeks and stage-coaches Now the traversing of a continent is but a question of hours. Then to encircle the globe was an adventure of years. Now it is a holiday excursion of forty days. Then the sending of a message of a few hundred miles was a matter of weeks and slow mails, while now the subject of this sketch can sit by his fireside and flash his word to the world's capital or actually converse at any moment with most any city on the continent Then when the slow-going ocean-crossing vessel was lost to sight below the horizon it was for months beyond the ken of man Now we communicate in a moment with the mariner anywhere on the broad seas The railroad, telegraph, telephone, phonograph, locomotive, automobile, photograph, artesian well, sewing machine, matches, in fact most of the principal mechanical inventions, were things of the future

The then higher grades of education were beyond the reach of the masses. Now it is almost thrust upon them

In that year the Erie Canal was but started. But seven States had been added to the original thirteen The great body of our country's territory was yet a howling wilderness Our population was but eight million, while now it is eighty million souls.

From one of the smallest and poorest, we have grown to be the greatest, richest and most powerful nation on earth

And this is due in no small degree to the thousands of strong and simple men our country produced in the first half of the nineteenth century, of the stamp of Ira H Cole.

Children:
- 405 George Herbert, b Jan. 3, 1850, unm ; living at Seattle, Wash
- 406 Adelaide, b. July 25, 1851; m March 6, 1878, at Farmer Village, N Y, to Dr Mathew L, b Geneva, N Y, Oct 20, 1845, son of Henry A and Mary Ann (King) Bennett He living at Watkins, N Y. She d May 11, 1889.
- 407 William Denison, b. March 30, 1853; d. unm. at Seattle, Wash., Sept 18, 1906.
- 408 Sarah Louisa, b April 14, 1855, m Nov. 26, 1879, at Covert to Charles Samuel, b. April 6, 1856, at Varick, N. Y, son of Harry and Electa (Blaine) Sniffen Both living at Interlaken, N. Y Their child
  Edna Caroline, b July 24, 1884.
- +409 Fremont, b Sept 18, 1856
- +410 Irving W, b. Sept 21, 1859
- +411 Hervey Denison, b Aug 25, 1861
- 412 Wirt, b. June 3, 1863, d Feb. 7, 1865
- 413 Elbert, b Sept 19, 1865, d unm April 29, 1896

143

HYMAN (John, Elisha, Elisha), m Mary, b Jan 7, 1814, dau. of James and Abigail (Roberts) Hughson She d April 14, 1838, aged 24 years, 4 months, 7 days, and he m (2) April 25, 1839, Hannah, b Nov. 14, 1809 (Jos. Cole records Nov 8, 1808), dau of David and Mary (Fowler) Merrick. He d at Mahopac March 9, 1881. Was a farmer She d at Carmel March 12, 1895, aged 85 years, 3 months, 26 days Children:
- +414 John Roberts, b Nov. 4, 1832
- +415 Addison, b Jan 24, 1840.
- +416 Amanda L, b May 12, 1842; d unm April 16, 1901

149

JARVIS WASHBURN (John, Elisha, Elisha), m Carmel Jan 1, 1845, Phebe Jane, b Jan 24, 1826, at Philipstown, dau of

Levi and Mary (Colwell) Kelley. He was a farmer and enlisted Sept 13, 1862, for three years in Company A, 4th Regt, N Y, Hart's Volunteers Dischaiged May 22, 1865 His health was affected by exposure during service and his death resulted therefrom He d at Carmel April 9, 1868, aged 48 years, 11 months, 10 days She d at Stamford, Conn, May 23, 1894 Children

   417 Albert, b Carmel Dec 15, 1846; d unm at Williamsport, Pa, May 30, 1891.
   418 Mary Jane, b. Nov 20, 1848, m May 11, 1889, at Stamford, Conn, to John V Laethum He is dead She d. in New York City May 27, 1907
   419 Emma Frances, b Mahopac Feb 4, 1852 Living unm
+420 James Kelley, b Mahopac Oct 22, 1853
   421 Thaddeus, b Apr. 7, 1855 Living at Sheridan, Wyo, unm.
   422 Florence Nightingale, b Aug 26, 1868, unm

151

ABNER BANGS (Nathan, Nathan, Elisha), m at Chester, Ill, Nov 22, 1837, Nancy R Cochrane, b Dec 17, 1816 She d at Chester, and he m. (2) Jan 13, 1853, Jeannette, b. Roxburyshire, Scotland, Sept 25, 1816, dau of James and Jeannette (Lo) Douglas He d. at Turner, Ore, June 3, 1890 She d at Portland, Ore, Feb 23, 1899 Children (b at Chester).

+423 John Peck, b. Nov. 7, 1838.
   424 Abner Bangs, b May 24, 1840, d May 8, 1846
   425 Mary, b Aug 8, 1842, m. Oct. 16, 1866, Morris Cocks, b New Cannan, Conn, May 11, 1837, son of Frederick and Mary (Cocks) Crissey. Both living at Chester
   426 William Van Zant, b April 21, 1845 Living in Alaska; unm
+427 Oliver Garrison, b March 23, 1849
   428 Circassia Jenette, b April 12, 1858; unm

HERMAN CAMP COLE
No. 153

THE DESCENDANTS OF ELISHA COLE   81

429   Agnes Olympia, b Nov 3, 1861; m at Turner, Ore, June 14, 1888, Jarvis Varnel, b Millport, Mo, Jan 31, 1854, son of Harney H and Eleanor Isabella (Henry) Beach   Both living in Portland, Ore   Their children.

   Varnel Douglas, b Nov. 9, 1889
   Jarvis Douglas, b April 15, 1891, d July 23, 1895

153

HERMON CAMP (Nathan, Nathan, Elisha), m in New York City June 26, 1844, Emily Cocks; b April 16, 1821, d Chester, Ill, Oct 14, 1859   He m (2) at Carrollton, Ill, Feb 13, 1862, Mrs Sarah Jane, b at Winfield, N Y, March 24, 1832, dau of Rev Isaac D and Sarah (Green) Newell and wid of Joseph Sheppard Flanagin   He d at Upper Alton, Ill, Oct 20, 1874, and she m Nov 24, 1879, John C Clark   (For account of his life see his father's record)

Children

+430   Charles Briggs, b. May 6, 1845
+431   Zachary Taylor, b July 4, 1847.
 432   Alice Emily, b Feb 21, 1850, m at Alton, Ill, Sept 24, 1873, William Elliot, b St Louis Dec 31, 1844, son of William Henry and (his second wife) Ellen (Smith) Smith   Their children·
   Eunice, b ———
   Ellen, b ———
+433   Henry Clay, b May 13, 1852
 434   Eunice Elizabeth, b Sept 16, 1854, m George J Kendall. They had three children·
   Alice, b ———.
   Eugene, b ———
   Henry C, b ———
+435   Edward Everett, b March 6, 1857
 436   Cora Verna, b Sept 3, 1863, d Feb 19, 1892
 437   Grace, b. Dec. 9, 1865; living; unm

+438 Hermon C, b July 15, 1868.
 439 Nathan, b May 27, 1874.
 440 Newell, twin of above

> Nathan m at Boston, Mass., Aug. 31, 1907, Estelle, b Logan County, Ill., June 18, 1884, dau of Charles Steinberger and Eliza (Westfall) Lawrence. He an investment broker living at Springfield, Ill
>
> Newell d unm Jan 24, 1896.

156

JAMES MADISON (Nathan, Nathan, Elisha), m at Chester, Ill., Jan 5, 1843, Eleanor Clement, b Westerlo, N. Y., Oct 11, 1824. He d. Chester April 22, 1855. She d there July 18, 1904. In September, 1850, he and his brother Abner went overland to California. He returned the following spring. Was a farmer and stock raiser. Children:

 441 Sarah Louisa, b Dec 10, 1843, d May 12, 1846.
 442 Clementina, b March 12, 1846; living
 443 Anna Maria, b. Sept. 11, 1848, d Feb 26, 1854.
 444 Agnes Eleanor, b Nov 20, 1850, m at Chester Oct 24, 1877, Albert Stephen, b Greenville, Ill., July 17, 1848, son of Kendall Parker and Elizabeth Brown (Holden) Morse. Both living. Their child:

> Edwin, b Jan 10, 1879

 445 Edwina Jeanette, b April 17, 1853, d March 9, 1854
 446 Jennie Medora, b March 30, 1855, d Dec. 26, 1857.

157

NATHAN (Nathan, Nathan, Elisha), m at St Louis Jan 30, 1851, Rebecca Lane, b at Richmond, O., June 29, 1832, dau of Aaron W. and Sarah (Bradbury) Fagin. He d at St Louis March 4, 1904. She living

He was born in a house that stood at what is now Eighth Street and Lucas Avenue, St. Louis. He was first employed in the wholesale grocery firm of Wm. L. Ewing & Co Later founded the Cole Brothers grain business and the Nathan Cole Investment Company, of which he was president until his death In 1868 he was elected Mayor of St Louis and was a member of Congress, 1876-1878 He was president of the Merchants' Exchange and a director of the Bank of Commerce for forty-three years, and most of this time was vice-president of the institution. He was prominent in church and charitable work and a life-long member of the Second Baptist Church Children:

  447 Sarah Fagan, b. Dec 30, 1851, d. Dec. 9, 1854
  448 Burtena Scott, b Aug. 13, 1853, d Dec. 21, 1854
+449 Amedee Berthold, b Sept 21, 1855
  450 Henry Ernest, b Dec. 9, 1857, unm.
+451 Nathan, b March 16, 1860.
  452 Rebecca Genevieve, b. July 2, 1863, d May 17, 1868
  453 Hallie Rachel, b May 17, 1864, m March 20, 1888, Joseph Louis Hebert. He d in California Dec 18, 1896.
  454 Richard Hood, b Nov. 13, 1866; unm
  455 Rebecca Lane, b Dec 1, 1868; m May 27, 1897, Harry Wilson, b March 6, 1875, at Savannah, Mo, son of Lewis Cunningham and Catharine (Ford) Stiles Living at Ann Arbor, Mich Their children:
     Nallie C., b 1898
     Susan Jane, b 1900
  456 Hermon Camp, b May 24, 1871; m at Galena, Kans, Mae, b there Sept 23, 1872, dau. of John and Elizabeth (Lyons) Rawson No issue.
  457 Percival Victor, b May 25, 1874, d unm at Denver, Col, June 26, 1901

164

ORMOND HAYES (Berry, Joseph, Elisha); m at Carmel Dec. 30, 1830, Mary, b there Feb. 1, 1813, dau of Alexander and

Elizabeth (Dean) Ganong He d March 3, 1875. She d April 29, 1879

He was born in the town of Carmel on the farm since owned by Jeremiah L Green, and spent his youth there When about eighteen he started traveling with a circus and menagerie owned by his father, his brother-in-law, Selah Ballard and Jared Crane, and during the following seven years visited every State in the Union and the principal cities of the United States and Canada. About 1835 he purchased a part of his father's farm and resided there until his death At one time he was in the blacksmithing business and ironed in his shop the first spring wagon made in that part of the country Children

+458 Joseph Ganong, b June 30, 1832
 459 Amanda Jane, b. July 12, 1834, d Sept 3, 1834
 460 Mary Fayette, b Aug 20, 1837; m. Dec 28, 1886, Alonzo O. Cole No issue.

175

CHARLES GREEN (Joseph, Joseph, Elisha), m Jan 14, 1824, Susan Wood She d Feb. 9, 1827, aged 21 years, 4 months, 1 day, and he m (2) Feb 6, 1830, Mary, b Dec 12, 1808, in Brewster, N Y, dau of Samuel and Hannah (Wright) Bailey He d at Beaver Dams April 7, 1846 She d June 17, 1897

Charles G and his brother Ira settled near Beaver Dams, Schuyler County, N Y., in 1830, their father and brother Asahel followed a few years later They came from Carmel via the Erie Canal to Geneva, up Seneca Lake to Watkins and from there to Beaver Dams The journey took one week. Their mother's brother, Underhill Frost, had previously settled there. The two brothers bought a farm of 64 acres and worked it together and lived in a log house with their families for three years Then Charles G built another log house in the same yard and they lived in this way until the death of Charles. Each family had seven children Children:

461 William F, d. July 21, 1827, aged 11 months, 21 days; buried in family plot on farm near Long Pond

462   John Wood, d. in 24th year.
+463 Joseph Bailey, b. Sept 2, 1832, at Catlin, N Y
+464 Harvey Townsend, b Oct 31, 1834, at Catlin, N Y
465   Jane Ann, b Feb 28, 1837; m at Beaver Dams Jan 24, 1860, Otto Marshall, b. at Wheeler, N Y, Nov 3, 1839, son of James, Jr, and Elizabeth Maria (Fritcher) Paris She d at Jerseyville, Ill, Feb 11, 1872, and he m (2) Oct 2, 1889, to Rebecca Gay. He living in California He descended from Col Isaac Paris, who came from Strasbourg and settled near Stone Arabia in the Mohawk Valley He and his son Peter, who was not yet eighteen years of age, were both killed in the battle of Oriskany Aug 6, 1777 At this time Isaac was somewhat over sixty, yet had children at home scarcely out of the cradle He was a member of the State Senate and one of the Committee of Safety
466   Aurelia, b Feb 12, 1839, m there Oct 16, 1860, Francis L, b in Wyoming County, Pa, July 6, 1837, son of Jacob and Christiana (Lockhart) Koons They living at Vinton, Ia
467   Caroline, b April 13, 1841, m Feb 6, 1867, to Leroy Deven, b at Reading N Y, July 6, 1842, son of Peter and Maria (Cross) Obert He d at Bancroft, Mich, Oct 19, 1906 She living at Corning, N Y.
+468 Jarvis Asahel, b Nov 6, 1843
469   Martha, b Sept 30, 1846, m Beaver Dams, Mar 2, 1869, to Charles Nehemiah, b Hornby, N Y Aug 27, 1847, son of Silas Mathias and Jane Ann (Ferro) Masters They living at Decorah, Ia

176

IRA (Joseph, Joseph, Elisha), m Brewster, N Y, Mar 10-18. 1826, Nancy, b there Apr 7, 1807, dau of Samuel and Hannah (Wright) Bailey He d Beaver Dams, Mar 3 1877

She d there Nov 16, 1868. He was a farmer Children b. Catlin, N. Y.

    470 George, d. June 12, 1827, aged 2 months Buried in family plot near Long Pond.
    471 Phebe Ann, b. Mar 26, 1828, m. Catlin, N Y. July 4, 1844, William, b July 24, 1824, at Candor, N. Y., son of Harrison and Nancy (Petty) Loomis He enlisted in 1862 in Co F, N Y. State Engineers, and d in hospital in Virginia, Sept. 2, 1864 She d Post Creek, N. Y, Nov. 5, 1856
+472 George Frost, b Apr 2, 1829
    473 Minerva, b Dec 9, 1832
    474 Marinda, twin of the above.

        Minerva m. Beaver Dams, Aug 6, 1850, to Thomas K, b Hornby, N. Y, July 10, 1828, son of William and Mary (Mapes) Hurley He living Paris, Mich She d Beaver Dams, May 30, 1858

        Marinda m. July 3, 1851, to James Lion, b. Mar 9, 1829, at Wayne, N Y., son of John Lion and Mrs. Sarah (Hodge) Schuyler Gardner He d Luther, Mich., Feb. 25, 1901 She living at Clarkstown, Mich.

    475 Susan, b. Feb 8, 1838; m. Horseheads, N. Y, Oct 3, 1855, Lovett, b. Reading, N Y, Sept. 8, 1828, son of Minard and Margaret (Obert) La Fever. He d. Beaver Dams, Aug 13, 1894. She living at Corning, N Y
+476 Charles Lewis, m. Mar 21, 1842.
+477 Samuel Bailey, b Jan. 24, 1847.

178

ASAHEL (Joseph, Joseph, Elisha), m June 23, 1835, Mary Ann Ball, b Marcellus, N Y, June 3, 1817, dau. of Ira and Lavina (Richardson) Savory. He a farmer. The Savorys came to Beaver Dams from Hartford, Conn, and Ira's father was b in England He d Havana, N Y, Sept 25, 1884 She d Moreland, N Y, Mar 21, 1889 Children·

> 478 Melissa, b June 23, 1836, m June 22, 1869, to Charles, b. Montour Falls, N. Y., June 11, 1826, son of Col Green and Cynthia (McClure) Bennett Both living at Watkins, N. Y.

+479 Harlem, b Nov. 7, 1837.
+480 Ira Savory, b Mar 28, 1839

181

JOSEPH (Samuel, Joseph, Elisha), m Elizabeth Wicks She b. Aug 30, 1806 They went to Oceola, Mich, about 1833 He d Parshallville, Mich, May 11, 1878 He a farmer She d. at Parshallville, Apr 17, 1898

(Parshallville was first settled by Isaac Parshall He built a grist mill and named the place after himself He was b Chemung, N Y, Feb 5, 1798, and was the oldest of 17 children. Israel Parshall, his brother, after clearing up a farm moved to Parshallville, a distance of two miles, bought the grist mill and opened a general store in connection with it He drew his flour 50 miles to Detroit by team and brought goods for his store on the return trip He moved to Havana in 1855, and built a grist mill He was a great hunter and was killed by his own gun while standing on a log watching for dogs to drive deer in the river His gun slipped down and discharged The bullet entered his chin and came out of his temple, killing him instantly Warren R Cole was hunting with him at the time) Children·

> 481 Minerva, b Dec 8, 1823, m May 19, 1839, Israel, b Chemung, N Y, May 4, 1815, one of 17 children and son of Asa and Susannah (Kinney) Parshall He d at Chesaning, Mich, Aug 25, 1865, and she m (2) Dec 31, 1871, Guy, b Chemung, N Y, Nov 25, 1835, son of John and Sarah (Baldwin) Van Gorder She d at Havana, Mich, Feb 15, 1899 He d May 22, 1907

482 Warren Ramah, b June 17, 1827; m 1850 Catharine, b in New York State, dau of John N. and Sarah (Sutphen) Huff She d and he m (2) Mary Horton, dau of Matthew and Esther Marie (Mudge) Palmer He d Aug. 21, 1907 Farmer at Gaines, Mich She still living at Parshallville. Children by first marriage
Fremont, b ———, d. y
Jay, b ———, d y

483 Prudence b Jan 28, 1830, m Feb 20, 1850, Jesse, b Chemung, N Y, son of Asa and Susannah (Kinney) Parshall He d Parshallville, Mich, July 22, 1893 She d Fenton, Mich., Oct. 29, 1900

484 Elizabeth, b Aug. 23, 1832, at Harrison, Pa , m Feb 8, 1850, Aaron, b Ovid, N Y , Mar 6, 1821, son of John N and Sarah (Sutphen) Huff

+485 Yates Thompson, b Apr 24, 1836

486 Maria, b ———, d at the age of 12 years

+487 Joseph W , b Apr 16, 1842

+488 Charles C , b Jan 17, 1852

183

ENOS (Samuel, Joseph, Elisha), m Dec 16, 1830, Laura, dau of Hiram and Lena (Jefferson) Mason. He d Oct. 24, 1865 She d Feb 8, 1856. Children

489 Fidelia Elizabeth, b Jan 31, 1832, m Jan 1, 1852, Robert Wesley, b Maryland, Feb 5, 1832, son of Henson and Matilda (Arnold) Walker Both living at Howell, Mich

+490 Delevan Samuel, b Apr 21, 1833

491 Sarah A , b July 3, 1835, m July 8, 1856, Aaron B , b July 21, 1833, son of Borden and Mary A (Haslet) Durfee He d Oct 8, 1879 She living at Fowlersville, Mich

492 Ada Olive, b Aug 5, 1837, m at Corunna, Mich , Feb 25, 1862, Edgar Lucius, b Hannibal, N. Y ,

Jan. 9, 1837, son of James W. and Eunice (Wiltse) Rathbun Both living at Fowlersville, Mich

+493 Hiram Mason, b June 12, 1839.
+494 Webster Knapp, b Jan. 19, 1841.
+495 Arthur Enos, b Oct 3, 1853

191

NATHAN (Samuel, Joseph, Elisha), m Green Oak, Mich, Feb 10, 1836, Esther M, b. in Connecticut Sept 15, 1811, dau. of Edmund and Betsey (Edwards) Beach. She d Osceola, Mich, Nov 3, 1853, and he m. (2) April 2, 1854, Mrs Adaline, wid of Giles Barbour He was a Baptist minister and came to Michigan in 1835. He d. West Bloomfield, Mich, July 21, 1865 She d in Michigan 1877-8 Children, b Osceola

496 Betsey, b Mar 5, 1838, m Oct 11, 1859, at Troy, Mich, David, b Orange County, N Y, Nov 22, 1820, son of Frederick Roat. He d at Pontiac She d. West Bloomfield, Mich, Jan 25, 1880 No issue.

497 Adah, b June 29, 1841, m Dec 26, 1866, Frederick, b Orange Co, N Y, Oct 18, 1844, son of David Roat Both living at McMillan, Mich.

498 Zuba, b. Mar 24, 1843, m Osceola, Mich, Apr 3, 1859, Giles, son of Giles and Adeline (Richmond) Barbour He d Osceola and she m. (2) Charles Benjamin She d Conway, Mich, Aug 27, 1866 Children, (1) marriage:

    Chas. N, b ———, m Emma Young; (2) m, no issue.

499 Hannah b Nov. 18, 1845; m at Commerce, Mich, Feb 8, 1865, Robert, b. Dec 16, 1837, son of Edward and Jane (Mourtland) Clendening He d Ventura, Cal, Feb 24, 1878 She living at Pontiac.

500 Maria, b Aug 1, 1847, m. Pontiac, Oct 20, 1880, Geo W, b Elba, Lapeer Co, Mich, Mar 20,

1845, son of Abel and Clarissa (Davenport) Hubbard Both living at White Lake, Mich. No issue

+501 Adelbert, b. Jan 14, 1851.

194

ISAAC THOMPSON (Samuel, Joseph, Elisha); m Livingston Co., Mich, May 2, 1847, Harriet B, b. Sodus, N Y, Mar. 20, 1829, dau of Jacob and Sarah (Mudge) Debar He a farmer He d Livingston Co, Mich, June 28, 1897 She d there May 18, 1894 Children:

    502 Alfred, b Jan 8, 1848, d. Jan 11, 1848.
    503 Guy A, b Dec 30, 1848, m Livingston Co July 3, 1883, Alma R, b. in Michigan Jan. 8, 1863, dau. of Alonzo and Mary C. (Hawley) Doolittle. No issue He a carpenter and hay dealer Both living at Owosso, Mich
    504 Harriet, b Apr 30, 1851, d. May 24, 1853
    505 Laura J, b. Nov. 30, 1852, m Apr. 6, 1875, Edward, b. Penn Yan, N. Y., son of ——— and Lydia (Bristol) Townsend He d Michigan, Dec 30, 1903. She living at Howell
    506 Ira T., b May 28, 1855; m. Malcourt Co., Mich, Jan. 25, 1884, Mary Von Deleer No issue.
    507 Frank J, b Jan 22, 1863, d Jan 11, 1872

195

WATSON (Nathan, Joseph, Elisha); m Feb 10, 1825, Nancy, b. May 31, 1802, at Hopewell, Orange Co, N. Y., dau. of Alexander and Mary (Shaw) Thompson They lived at Moreland, N Y, where he was a farmer Their children were born there and the dates regarding births, deaths and marriages were taken from their Bible He d. Corning, N Y, Oct. 12, 1889 She d. there Nov. 4, 1887 Children:

    508 Mary Ann, b. Feb 5, 1826, d Oct 29, 1843
+509 Alexander Hamilton, b Feb 8, 1827.

510 Nathan Thompson, b Aug. 4, 1830; m Dec 20, 1870, Mrs Nancy, b Montour Falls, N. Y, Nov 13, 1842, dau. of Peter and Loraine (Bryant) Fero, and wid of Pulaski Miller. He d. at Corning, N. Y, June 17, 1892. She living No issue.

511 Edwin, b Apr. 3, 1835; m Frances Delaney

199

ELI (Nathan, Joseph, Elisha), m Covert, N Y, Nov 17, 1831, Harriet Rebecca, b Aug. 6, 1810, in Connecticut, dau of Jesse and Lydia (Darrow) Horton He was a farmer and moved to Michigan about 1878 He d Cedar Springs, Mich, Mar 21, 1895 She d. there Feb 13, 1893. Children

512 Mary Louisa, b May 29, 1834, m. Covert, N Y, Dec 25, 1855, Thomas Judson, b there Sept 29, 1832, son of Thomas Anson and Eliza (De Groot) Hopkins He d Jan 28, 1905 She living in Michigan.

513 Harriet Ursula, b. June 23, 1836, d Feb 19, 1837

514 Oscar T., b. Jan 21, 1837, d July 2, 1842

+515 William Henry, b Sept 19, 1840

+516 George Washington, b Feb 3, 1843.

517 Emma Louisa, b. Sept 6, 1845, m Dec 12, 1866, William R Murphy He living She d Sept. 14, 1869. Children.
Fred. b. ———
Lena, May, b ———

518 Julia Fenn, b July 27, 1848, m Covert, N Y, Dec 6, 1876, Charles Samuel, b Covert, June 28, 1847, son of Thomas Anson and Anna Eliza (De Groot) Hopkins Both living in Michigan

519 Ada Frances, b July 14, 1851, m Mar. 19, 1873, Edmund C, b Covert, Nov 3, 1849, son of Nestor and Phebe (King) Woodworth Both living in Michigan

+520 Edgar Thomas, b July 26, 1855

521 Anna Sarah, b Apr 23, 1858, m Sept. 16, 1886, Arthur Bates She living at Craik, Canada

200

EDWIN WILDMAN (Nathan, Joseph, Elisha), m Sept. 10, 1835, Emma, b. Covert, N. Y., July 7, 1814, dau. of Lewis and Samantha (King) Porter. She d Nov 27, 1848, and he m (2) Mary Ann, b. Apr 7, 1825, dau of Peter and Mary (Everitt) Quick He was a farmer. In 1851 a merchant in Adrian, Mich He d Adrian, Mich , Jan 6, 1861. She living Children, b Fairfield, Mich.

(1) marriage:
- 522 Wilbur Milton, b Sept 3, 1836, d. Mar 7, 1839
- +523 Hascall Myron, b. Oct 7, 1838
- +524 Nathan W , b Feb 11, 1841.
- 525 Harriet Porter, b Oct 4, 1842, d Mar 27, 1845
- 526 Ursula, b Jan 31, 1845, m June 18, 1873, at Covert, Herbert, b there Oct 23, 1845, son of Truman and Aurilla C (Whitney) Boardman He d Rochester, N Y , July 4, 1875 She living Toledo, O.
- 527 Lewis Porter, b Weston, Mich M,ar 3, 1847, m. Beloit, Wis , June 12, 1889, Mary Ann, b. Troy, Wis , Nov. 26, 1844, dau of Augustus and Almira (Stiles) Smith He d. Beloit, Mich , May 28, 1901 She living there He was cashier Mil & S P R R No issue

(2) marriage:
- 528 Rachel Emily, b Nov 27, 1849, m Aug 12, 1869, William H , b Brockport, N Y., Oct 19, 1837, son of John and Jane (Graham) Parker.
- 529 Maria, b Aug. 25, 1851; m. June 30, 1867, Henry Clay Clements
- 530 Edwin, b June 29, 1853, d y

202

MILO VAN DUZEN (Nathan, Joseph, Elisha), m at Elysses, N. Y , Nov 23, 1843, Druzilla, b there Feb 17, 1819, dau of Edmund and Mary L (Estrange) Hopkins He d Covert, Oct 24, 1902 She d there Apr 23, 1895. He a farmer. Children:

531 Carrie Frances, b Nov 17, 1844, m Covert Oct 6, 1869, Ira Cole, b there Oct 9, 1846, son of John Chapman and Adelia (Cole) Hall. He d. Interlaken, N. Y, Apr 27, 1908 She living. The following is from the Interlaken (formerly Farmer Village) Review of May 1, 1908

IRA COLE HALL

Ira C. Hall, a life-long resident of the town of Covert, and one of the best known and honored citizens of Seneca County, died at his home in Interlaken, Monday evening, Apr 27, 1908

Mr Hall was a man of wide acquaintance, of broad sympathies, of pure and noble character. His father was a member of Assembly from Seneca County, and for several terms a member of the Board of Supervisors

Ira C Hall was graduated at the Trumansburg Academy in 1864 and at Yale College in 1868 He was a member of the Alpha Delta Phi fraternity, of the senior "Scroll and Key," and one of the nine "Wooden Spoon Men" in the junior class He was a member of the surveying corps of the Geneva and Ithaca Railroad, and was the first station agent at what was then, Farmer Village.

In company with his father, he conducted for many years a coal, hay and grain business For four years he served as Supervisor for the town of Covert, and for two years was chairman of the board Although not a member of the Baptist church, he was deeply interested in its wellfare, and for many years was a member of its board of trustees

Funeral services held at the home yesterday afternoon were conducted by Mr Hall's former pastor and life-long friend, Rev Lewis Halsey, D D, of Clyde, assisted by Rev Dr T. A Hughes and C W McNish Many friends were in attendance, including the members of the Board of Supervisors of Seneca County, and delegations from the Masonic lodges of Ovid, Lodi and Trumansburg The burial service was conducted by the Masonic fraternity, under direction of Past Master Rev. E B. Van Arsdale

The Board of Supervisors were the honorary pall bearers, the active bearers being members of Farmersville Lodge, Messrs E. C Grant, W E Peterson, E F Chase, J B Moore, T P. Hause and C W Bogart.

Many loving friends will say, "Farwell my brother!" and will remember Ira C. Hall as a man true to his friends, loyal to his convictions, faithful in the discharge of every duty.

+532 Arvah Hopkins, b. Oct. 17, 1847
533 Ella Louise, b Dec. 27, 1849, unm.
534 Anna Mary, b June 19, 1852; m. at Covert, N. Y., Sept. 29, 1877, John George, b at Schney, Germany, Nov 12, 1848, son of John George and Elizabeth (Schramm) Mohr (Moore) Living at Minneapolis, Minn. Child William C
535 Sue Alida, b Nov 20, 1854, d July 10, 1855
536 Evalina Hall, b Apr 19, 1862, m at Covert Dec. 5, 1889, to Frank Loren, b Enfield, Conn , Apr. 30, 1858, son of Loren and Maria (Loomer) Griswold. Living at Hazardville, Conn

207

RAMAH (Levi H , Joseph, Elisha); m Charlotte, b Carmel, Dec 27, 1821, dau of James and Sarah (Townsend) Carver He d at Brooklyn, May 8, 1892. She d there Nov. 30, 1888. Children:

+537 Wallace Henry, b. Dec 16, 1844, at Mahopac, N. Y.
538 Abiather Ballard, b. July 30, 1847, d Feb. 11, 1851.
+539 Frank Josiah, b Brooklyn, N Y., Dec 7, 1858.

208

JOHN BERRY (Levi H , Joseph, Elisha); m. Apr 28, 1853, Maria, b Mar. 20, 1826, dau. of James and Tamar (Sloat) Hart She d Sept 16, 1881, at Brooklyn, and he m. (2) Aug 8, 1889, Margaretta Crocker, b New York City July 30, 1850, adopted dau of John and Catharine (Brazin) Gold He d. June 27, 1893 She living Children, b Brooklyn

RED MILLS—NOW MAHOPAC FALLS
PULLED DOWN 1881

540 Hester Amelia, b Dec. 8, 1853, m Brooklyn Dec. 8, 1879, Henry Morgan, b. Elba, N Y, June 24, 1847, son of George Hall and Elizabeth (Morgan) White Living at Lee, Mass

541 Ella Euphemia, b. New York City, Sept. 28, 1860; m. at Brooklyn June 4, 1889, Harry Whitehouse, b Brooklyn July 30, 1864, son of Andrew Jackson and Sarah Emma (Cross) Doremus. Both living at Staten Island, N. Y.

542 Alice, b. May 8, 1864, d. May 2, 1868

+543 Herbert Milton, b Apr 10, 1871.

211

ALONZO OJIDA (Levi H, Joseph, Elisha), m Emily Augusta, dau of L Augustus and Jane (Jessup) Reed She was b. Apr 8, 1834, d Sept 14, 1856. He m (2) Emma Matilda, dau of Jacob and Sarah (Russell) Browner She was b Dec 27, 1834, d Nov 20, 1873 He m (3) Mrs Sarah C., b. Dec. 7, 1832, dau of Frederick and Mary E (Kohler) Hederick, and wid of Abiather R Ballard, who d Feb 28, 1875. She d. Nov 4, 1885 He m. (4) Dec 28, 1886, at Carmel, Mary Fayette, b. Aug 20, 1837, dau. of Ormond Hayes and Mary (Ganong) Cole. He was in the trucking business He d Brooklyn Mar 12, 1899 All buried at Mahopac Falls. Fourth wife living No issue 3rd and 4th marriages Children by 1st marriage

544 Jennie Augusta, b. New York City Oct 8, 1854; m. at Brooklyn, Jan 21, 1885, Millard Fillmore, b Mahopac Falls, Jan 10, 1858, son of Elisha Cole and Agnes Ann (Horton) Agor She d. at Mahopac Falls, July 14, 1901, and he m. (2) Jan 19, 1903. Mrs Sarah Amanda, b Oct. 2, 1863, dau. of Peter B and Sarah K (Smith) Curry, and wid. of Kelsie Agor.

(Elisha Cole Agor, mentioned above, was a grandson of Elizabeth (Cole) Agor, dau. of Elisha Cole Millard F Agor is a merchant and postmaster at Mahopac Falls.)

By 2nd marriage:

545 Carrie Adina, d. Apr. 6, 1862, aged 5 years, 9 months.
546 Sarah Browner, b 1860, d Apr. 8, 1862.
547 Edwin D, b. Aug 3, 1863, d Aug. 23, 1864
548 Annie Louise, b. June 6, 1865, m Brooklyn, Apr. 20, 1886, Dr William Fenton, b. Buffalo, May 28, 1855, son of Edwin H and Rebecca (Holledge) Millington He graduated from New York University Medical College and was house physician and surgeon at Seamen's Retreat, S I, N. Y., 1878-80 Both living in Brooklyn.
549 Hattie Isabel, b Oct 10, 1868, d. unm, Mar 11, 1892
550 Fanny Estelle, b. Sept. 13, 1870; m. Brooklyn, Feb 21, 1894, William Ross, b. Nova Scotia, July 4, 1858, son of Ebenezer and Jane (Ross) Kinsman.

214

JOSEPH WATSON (Levi H, Joseph, Elisha), m New York, Oct 29, 1859, Mary Elizabeth, b New York, Sept. 4, 1837, dau. of James and Rachel (Dargavel) Pope She d. Feb 15, 1872, and he m. (2) New York, Jan 20, 1875, Mrs Ann W., b. 1832, dau. of William T. and Caroline L (Wood) Ryer, and wid of Chas A. Hilliker She d June 15, 1891 He living in Brooklyn. Children·

551 Nellie Louise, b Sept. 9, 1860, unm.
552 Carrie Augusta, b. Apr 8, 1864; m Apr 8, 1885, David Campbell Austin. She d Mar 18, 1893.
553 Jessie Lena, b Oct 12, 1866, m May 30, 1888, to Chas Irving, b New York, Feb 17, 1860, son of John H. and Hannah M. (Onderdunk) Smith
554 William Sylvester, b Sept 17, 1870; m Roslyn, N. Y., June 30, 1905, Ruth Payne, b there July 8, 1876, dau of John Weeks and Hannah Maria (Axtell) Wood

219

ADANIRAM JUDSON (Ramah, Joseph, Elisha), m Linden, Mich, May 2, 1861, Augusta Malvina, b Sacket Harbor, N Y, Dec 10, 1840, dau, of Samuel Reed and Mary Kendall (Stone) Campbell. He was a farmer and was killed by a bull while driving it out of his corn-field. He d. Byron, Mich, Sept. 22, 1882 She living at Shepard, Mich   Children, b. Byron.

- 555 Belle Frances, b Jan 20, 1862, m Nov 30, 1882, Rev Sidney Cornish, b Wiggaton, England, Oct. 24, 1858, son of William and Elizabeth (Daw) Davis   He is a Baptist minister and both living at La Junta, Col
- +556 Edward Judson, b June 13, 1864.
- 557 Loella Augusta, b Aug 29, 1872, m Cheyenne, Wyo, May 24, 1899, to William Henry, b England, Sept 16, 1866, son of William Davis and a nephew of Rev Sidney Davis Both living Children

    William Howard, b May 1, 1900
    Philip Judson, b. Sept 12, 1901.

- 558 Grace Emma, b Dec 17, 1879; m. Nov 1, 1897, Rev George Washington, b Lindon, Mich, 1873, son of Verge and Annie (Green) Bedell Children:

    Clara, Frank, Paul, Lula Bell.

220

WILLIAM MARTIN (Ramah, Joseph, Elisha), m Byron, Mich., Sept 2, 1858, Alice, b Poughkeepsie, N. Y, Apr. 25, 1841, dau. of John and Maria (Doughty) Williams He was a farmer and d Fitzgerald, Ga, Mar 19, 1904 She d Mar 17, 1907 Children:

- +559 Charles, b Byron, Mich, Jan. 20, 1860
- 560 Claude, b Lansing Mich, Mar. 18, 1867, m Cadillac, Sept 27, 1893, Zora Belle, b Olivet, Mich, Apr 5, 1871, dau of James M and Maria L.

(Day) Flagg Both living at Kalkasha No issue:
+561 Clyde, b Dewitt, Feb 19, 1869

221

LEVI (John, Daniel, Elisha), m Abigail Smalley Lived in Michigan Children:

    562 Zillah, m John English, m (2) ———— Larzalese.
    563 Cyrus, b ————
    564 James W, b ————, d unm
    565 Zachariah, b ————, d unm
    566 Mary, b ————, m Augustus Schigler.

224

HORACE (John, Daniel, Elisha); m Carmel, Oct. 5, 1833, Goolda Ruth, b there May 8, 1812, dau of Enos and Cynthia (Cole) Hopkins He was a farmer at Bradford, N Y He d July 29, 1894 She d Dec. 17, 1903 Children

  +567 Chester Enos, b Carmel, June 6, 1835.
    568 Mary Cynthia, b Bradford, Jan 18, 1841, m. there Nov 13, 1861, Hosea, b May 8, 1841, son of Hosea and Harriet (Brundage) Longwell. He d. Oct 6, 1905 She living
    569 Ansel L, b Mar 18, 1852, d Aug 31, 1864

225

HIRAM (John, Daniel, Elisha); m Fanny, b. Carmel, Nov 2, 1821, dau of John and Sarah (Drew) Barrett He was a farmer and lived at Carmel He d June 5, 1888 She d Sept 4, 1888 Children·

    570 Annie Augusta, b Nov 1840, m. Oct 26, 1859, Byron E, b. Aug 14, 1835, son of Ansel and Eliza A (Hopkins) Hazen She d June 6, 1862, and he m (2) June 11, 1868, Zillah, dau of Samuel Addison and Hannah (Colwell)

Townsend He d Mt. Vernon, N Y, May 12, 1906 She living

+571 Charles William, b June 15, 1845

228

ALLEN (Jesse, Daniel, Elisha), m Jan 29, 1840, Susan, b Mar. 22, 1813, dau of John and Betsey (Washburn) Cole He was a farmer and lived at Carmel He d Dec. 28, 1880 She d July 16, 1887 Child.

+572 Henry Clay, b May 12, 1841.

231

REUBEN (Jesse, Daniel, Elisha), m Dec. 19, 1859, at Roxbury, Conn, Harriet L, b there May 9, 1829, dau of Sherman and Jerusha Esther (Morton) Minor He d. Dec 28, 1891, aged 75 years, 11 months, 22 days She d May 13, 1897.

He was born at Kent and his early life was spent on a farm. Later he taught school He was one of the early settlers of St Paul, Minn, and made considerable money in real estate in that city He also owned property in North and South Dakota, California and Washington He d at Rock Elm, Wis, and is buried at Sleepy Hollow, Tarrytown, N Y. Child

573 Cornelia Minor, b Roxbury, Conn, Nov 2, 1860, m in New York City, Dec 9, 1889, Clinton Sears, b. New York City, Aug 16, 1858, son of James and Mary (Bourbon) Arnold Both living at Scarboro, N. Y.

233

OGDEN (Daniel H, Daniel, Elisha), m Sarah, dau of Harry White. He d Dec 29, 1849, aged 39 years, 9 months, 15 days. She d about 1855 at the home of her sister, Mrs Solomon Barrett, and is buried at Farmers Mills Children:

+574 Theodore Frelinghuysen, b at Cole's Mills, 1844

575 Charles E , b Jan 7, 1847, d unm at Atlanta, Ga , July 30, 1864, from a wound in the head He enlisted in the 6th N Y Heavy Artillery in 1862, and was later a private in Co E , 5th Regt. Conn Vols.

234

TILLOTT (Daniel H , Daniel, Elisha) , m Zillah, b. Kent, Mar. 23, 1823, dau of Lewis and Adah (Cole) Nichols They lived at Cole's Mills. He d. June 4, 1890, aged 78 years, 5 months, 9 days. She d. May 11, 1905, aged 82 years, 1 month, 18 days. Children :

+576 George Richardson, b. Oct. 28, 1845.
+577 Lewis Edgar, b Oct 13, 1850

237

THOMAS OWEN (Elisha J , Daniel, Elisha) ; m. Jan. 8, 1837, Antha Jane, b Apr 17, 1814, dau of Enos and Cynthia (Cole) Hopkins She d. Sept. 13, 1840, and he m (2) Sept. 1, 1847, Marie Antoinette, b June 24, 1824, dau. of Ira and Phebe (Merritt) Terry He d July 1, 1871 She d. Feb. 17, 1907 Children ·

578 Newman, b July 20, 1840, d Jan 29, 1842, aged 1 year, 6 months, 2 days
579 Emma Eliza, b Jan 9, 1856; m Oct 16, 1878, at Bethel, Conn , Coleman Robinson, b Kent, Jan. 20, 1843, son of Steven R and Emily (Townsend) Barrett Both living at Carmel No issue
580 Jessie Fremont, b Mar , 1857, m Nov. 7, 1878, John Francis, son of Joseph and Loretta (Northrup) Nichols He d Jan , 1904 She living No issue

238

GEORGE HARRISON (Elisha J , Daniel, Elisha) , m. at Croton Falls, Charlotte, dau of Cyrus and Zillah (Colwell) Chase

THE DESCENDANTS OF ELISHA COLE

He was a wholesale liquor dealer He d at Chicago, May 20, 1903 She d there June 24, 1898 Children·

581 Cyrus E , m Clara W Beardsley He d. Chicago, in the '80's She still living They had two sons, Walter and George
582 Gertrude O , b ———, d unm at Chicago, Mar 29, 1903
583 (Daughter), d aged 3 years.

240

CHARLES NORTON (Elisha J , Daniel, Elisha), m. Jane Ann, b Nov 23, 1826, dau of James and ——— (Sowber) Budd. He was a school teacher and farmer He d Sept 4, 1891. She d at Poughkeepsie, July 28, 1908 Children, b Pleasant Valley, N Y

584 Edward, b ———, d y.
+585 Mortimer Belding, b Dec 13, 1854.

242

NATHANIEL (Nathaniel, Ebenezer, Elisha), m. Jane Galloway. He d. at Sun Prairie, Wis , June 30, 1882 She d there Sept 13, 1889, aged 76 years, 10 months Children, b Chenango Co , N. Y.

586 Sarah, b Apr , 1833 , m ——— Jenkins She died Oct. 29, 1859, aged 26 years, 6 months.
587 Anthony William, b ———, 1838; m. Annie Hammersley Lives at Zanesville, Wis.
588 Malvina. b Oct , 1840, d unm Dec 26, 1860
589 Mary Ellen, b Dec , 1842, d unm. July 7, 1857
590 Adoniram Judson, b ———, 1845.
591 Charles Ogden, b ———
592 Maria Elizabeth, b ———
593 Jennie, b. ———.
594 George Henry, b ———, 1854 , m Harriet E Miles, b. Jan 6, 1860 Have two children, Frank Nathaniel and Alice Jane.

243

EBENEZER (Nathaniel, Ebenezer, Elisha), m Eliza Horton He d at Sun Prairie, Wis, Mar 4, 1884 Children:

    595 Margaret Ann, b ———.
    596 William H., b ——— Lives Mineral Point, Wis.
    597 Emeline, b ———, m (1) ——— Raymond; m. (2) ——— Shaw.
    598 John Emory, b. ———. Lives in Iowa
    599 Mary Elizabeth, b. ———; m. ——— Jenkins.

245

HENRY (Nathaniel, Ebenezer, Elisha), m Betsey A. Purdy. She d Mar 16, 1849 He m (2) ——— Lives in California. Children:

(1st) marriage only:

    600 Esther Ann, b ———, 1840
    601 George, b ———, 1842, d in Civil War
    602 Ogden, b. ———, 1843, d in Civil War
    603 Angevine, b ———, 1845, m Jennie Norton He d Argentine. Kans. They had Charles, Edith
    604 Francelia, b ———, 1846, m Charles Pease
    605 Joseph, b Apr 3, 1848, d Nov 14, 1849.

246

ANTHONY WILLIAM (Nathaniel, Ebenezer, Elisha), m about 1843, Mary, dau of Cyrus Horton She d at North Fenton, N Y He m (2) in the spring of 1845, Frances, b 1819, dau. of Capt James and Ann (Curry) Sherwood She d at North Fenton, Dec 5, 1861, and he m (3) in 1863, Letitia, b North Highland, N. Y, Mar 9, 1819, dau of James Cargill He d Putnam Valley, Dec 9, 1891 He was a farmer. She d Feb ———, 1894 Children

    606 Child—died at birth with mother
    607 Two children, b at North Fenton, d y.
+608 Horton Sherwood, b Jan 28, 1850.

609 Mary Frances, b May 16, 1853, m Reuben Burr Gilbert
610 Herbert, b Oct 14, 1856, d Apr 1, 1871, aged 14 years, 5 months, 15 days
611 Emma Louise, b Sept 21, 1861, m Shrub Oak, N. Y, Mar 27, 1889, to Chas Barmore, b. Putnam Valley, May 29, 1865, son of James Henry and Lucy (Lickley) Travis Both living at Peekskill.

250

JOHN (Benjamin, Ebenezer, Elisha), m ———, Mary Jane, b ———, dau of Thomas and ——— (Pratt) Gillett She d 1835, at Adams Corners, and he m (2) Mrs. Sarah, b ———, 1804, dau of ———, and wid of James Sherwood She d Aug. 27, 1876, and he m (3) Apr 17, 1877, Mrs Margaret Hawkins He d Virginia, Jan. 22, 1896 She d Aug 8, 1886 He was a carpenter Child

+612 William John, b Putnam Valley, Oct 28, 1832

255

JAMES (Ebenezer, Ebenezer, Elisha), m 1847, Sarah, b Jan 18, 1826, dau of Peter and Elizabeth (Haight) Mekeel He was a farmer and lived at Putnam Valley He d Jan 26, 1869 She d Mar 3, 1891

The Mekeels were French and the name originally was Mekeer There were three brothers, one settled in Westchester County, one in Putnam County, and the third disappeared Children.

613 Ann Elizabeth, b Sept 11, 1841, drowned Aug 4, 1862.
+614 Charles Ogden, b July 2, 1852
+615 Peter James, b Feb 9, 1854

256

CHARLES (Ebenezer, Ebenezer, Elisha), m Melissa Kimbel She d and he m (2) Priscilla Moore He d Apr. ———, 1894. Children.

616 Mary, b ———; m Tremaine Finch.
617 William R , b ——— Lived at Susquehanna, Pa.
618 Elmer, b ———.
619 Lurana, b ———, m ——— Jacobs.

257

WILLIAM (Ebenezer, Ebenezer, Elisha), m. Apr 29, 1837, Hettie Maria, b. Mar 22, 1817, dau of Lemuel and Charity (Kirkham) Smith Farmer and lived at Putnam Valley He d Dec. 3, 1892 She d Dec. 25, 1901 Children·

620 Susan Jane, b. Apr. 9, 1838; m Apr 9, 1861, to the Rev Thomas Stockton, b Nov 23, 1839, at Phillipstown, N. Y., son of Benson Oakley and Julia Ann (Gilbert) Lent Both living Children:
Hettie A , b Aug. 4, 1863, d Aug 9, 1894
William Benson, b May 1, 1865

621 Elizabeth, b May 9, 1840, d y

622 Julia Frances, b. Oct 12, 1842, m Dec 19, 1860, to William Benjamin, b Dec 3, 1840, in Putnam County, son of Steven V and Phebe Ann (Terry) Weeks Both living at Peekskill Children:
Libbie, b Nov 23, 1861
Arthur, b Oct. 16, 1868.

623 Margaret, b Oct 12, 1843; m Oct. 22, 1862, to Selah b. Apr 15, 1840, son of Alexander and Sarah A. (Chapman) Armstrong Both living Children·
Harriet R , b ———.
Emma B , b. ——— .

624 Ebenezer, b Oct. 14, 1848; d at age of 6 years.

262

THOMAS (James, Ebenezer, Elisha), m at Kent, Nov 3, 1849, to Polly (Mary) b there Dec 20, 1827, dau of Morgan and

Hannah (Ketcham) Brownell He was a farmer and d at Danbury, Conn , Mar. 6, 1903 She d. at Kent, N Y , May 29, 1899 Child

+625 James Henry, b Kent, N Y , July 15, 1851.

263

EDWIN (James, Ebenezer, Elisha), m Catharine, b. Sept 29, 1829, dau of Freeman and Eunice (Russell) Sprague He was a farmer, and lived at Kent, N. Y. He d Apr 20, 1876 She d June 20, 1894. Children

+626 Theron, b. Dec. 1, 1852
627 Lavenia, b. Apr 16, 1853, m at Kent, Feb 17, 1875, to Abel Evans, b there Dec. 29, 1849, son of William and Elizabeth (Selleck) Ballard, both living at Paterson, N. Y
+628 Ebenezer, b. Feb 7, 1855
629 Estelle, b Nov 18, 1856, m Nov 12, 1879, to Chas. E (No. 635), son of Alvah Cole No issue.
630 Charlotte, b Sept. 16, 1858, m at Paterson, Dec 6, 1882, to Charles L., b. East Fishkill, Apr 16, 1857, son of Albert and Sarah (Davis) Turner Both living at Paterson Child

Georgiana, b Kent, Nov 18, 1890.

631 Eunice, b Apr 7, 1860, m Freeman Smalley
632 Gilbert, b. Sept 19, 1869, m. Louise, dau of Caleb and Louise (Russell) Smalley

264

WILLIAM (James, Ebenezer, Elisha), m Susan Elizabeth, b at Carmel, Mar. 22, 1827, dau of Robert and Nancy (Tompkins) Wixson. He d Sept 2, 1873, aged 48 years, 1 month, 29 days She d Nov. 16, 1892 (Tombstone gives her age 65 years, 7 months, 24 days Town records, as 64 years, 9 months, 24 days

(Robert Wixson was a son of Shubel Wixson, who came with his brother Pelig from Cape Cod and bought land in Kent in 1782) Children

633 Mary,
634 Martha, twins, b. Jan 17, 1855
Mary d Mar. 4, 1861. Martha m. in New York City, May 1, 1872, Freeman, b. Dec. 26, 1849, in Carmel, son of Edwin and Marion (Hopkins) Fisher Both living at Carmel Child Bertha, b May 15, 1873.

265

ALVAH (James, Ebenezer, Elisha), m at South East, Apr. 26, 1851, Louisa, b there Sept. 26, 1829, dau. of Charles and Elizabeth (Hoyt) Everett They moved from Kent to Northfield, Minn, in 1856 He d there Mar. 9, 1863. (She m (2) at South East, Mar. 15, 1864, Orson Beach, and had a son Leonard D. Beach) She d. Brainard, Minn, Mar 15, 1895 By first marriage:

635 Charles E, b Northfield, Minn, Mar 26, 1859; m. at Kent, Nov 12, 1879, his cousin Estelle, b. Nov. 18, 1856, dau of Edwin and Catharine (Sprague) Cole He is a machinist Both living at Brainard, Minn No issue

269

EBENEZER (James, Ebenezer, Elisha); m. at Ludingtonville, Putnam County, Oct 28, 1857, Rachel Jane, b at Kent, Feb 3, 1834, dau of Freeman and Eunice (Russell) Sprague. He was a farmer and lived at Kent. He d. Jan. 31, 1896. She living at Holmes, Dutchess County, N Y. Children.

+636 Eugene, b. June 3, 1861.
+637 Albert G., b Mar. 1, 1864
+638 Ferris E, b Oct 22, 1865.

270

CHARLES (James, Ebenezer, Elisha); m. at Carmel, Oct. 31, 1860, Sarah Jane, b there July 14, 1836, dau. of Reuben and

Minerva (Hughson) Hopkins   He d. New York City, June 16, 1895, she living at Peekskill   Children, b Carmel

639   Georgiana Irene, b Oct 3, 1861; m. Peekskill, Nov. 24, 1895, John Wildy, b in Illinois, Aug. 2, 1858, son of John Joseph Wildy and Mary Elizabeth (Baker) Place. Both living
640   Nellie Josephine, b New York City, Oct 13, 1871, unm

273

JAMES WOOD (James, Ebenezer, Elisha), m Elizabeth A, b. Paterson, N. Y., June 25, 1849, dau. of Alvin and Betsey (———) Eastwood   She d Danbury, Conn, Apr. 9, 1888, and he m. (2) Carrie L, b Norwalk, Conn, May 17, 1871, dau of Henry and Harriet (Vany) Rotherforth   He d ———. She d Danbury, June 6, 1902   Children

641   Oliver, b ———, d y
642   Ida, b ———, d. y.

274

AMOS ROGERS (Lewis, John, Elisha), m at Egypt, Monroe Co, N Y, May 14, 1829, Hannah Gannett, b there Oct. 11, 1806, dau of Gideon and Hannah (Smith) Randall   He d at Rochester, N Y, Jan. 29, 1882   She d. May 5, 1881, at Pittsford, N. Y.   He was a farmer.   Children

+643   Otis, b Egypt, N. Y, Sept. 14, 1834.
644   Lydia Hathaway, b Egypt, N. Y., Mar 28, 1841; m there Apr 6, 1861, Albert, b. May 14, 1839, son of Nathan and Margaret (Pierce) Case
Both living in Michigan

276

DARIUS (Lewis, John, Elisha), m New York State, Feb 4, 1841, Mary Ann, b. Sept ———,1818, dau of Spencer and Sophia (Kelley) Allen   They settled in Lenawee County, Mich. He d at Rollin, Mich., Sept 20, 1846, and she m Apr 5, 1848, his brother, Elvin C Cole He was a farmer Children by first marriage, born at Rollin

+645 Lewis W , b Sept 20, 1844.

646 Darius, b July 9, 1846, m. Jan 6, 1864, Chloe, dau. of Levi and Mary (Baker) Sherman. Farmer He d at Rollin, Nov 28, 1880 She dead (No issue)

277

ELVIN CLINTON (Lewis, John, Elisha); m Seneca County, N. Y , Mar 7, or 12, 1837, Lydia, b Jan. 21, 1821, dau. of Philip and Magdalena (Covert) Tunison She d at Covert, N. Y, Dec 17, 1843 He m (2) at Macedon, N Y., Apr. 5, 1848, Mrs Mary Ann (Allen) Cole, wid of his brother Darius, and dau of Spencer Allen She d at Rollin, Mich , Sept 17, 1849. He m (3) May 2, 1852, Elvira Laura, b Van Buren, Onondaga County, N Y , June 2, 1826, dau of Asa and Amanda (Matson) Dayton He was a farmer and d at Rollin, Jan 6, 1889. She d there May 4, 1891

(Magdalena Tunison was a daughter of Col Ryneai Covert Col War 1812). She d. Mar. 16, 1880, aged 84 years She was the lineal descendant of Anneke Jahns and possessor of the Anneke Jahns Bible brought from Holland with family records written in Dutch It was taken by Electa (or Letta) Fulkerson across Seneca Lake about 1860 for one Dominie Sharp to translate He took the Bible to New York City where the family records were removed and all trace of them lost Sharp resigned his ministerial charge and left the country with a competency for life. (This statement made by adult members of the Tunison family who had seen the Bible) Children·

+647 Amos Rogers Tunison, b May 19 1839
648 Allen, b Aug 14, 1849
649 Emma Celia, b July 21, 1853, at Rollin, Mich , m there June 15, 1873, to J C , b Hergershausen, Germany, son of Wilhelm and Catharine (Bachman) Schneider. Living at Toledo, Ohio
+650 Elvin Dayton, b Feb 28, 1861, at Rollin

278

ELMER C (Lewis, John, Elisha), m Oct 8, 1842, Lucretia Smith, b Dec 4, 1812, in Delaware Co He was a farmer and d at Rollin, Mich, Mar. 10, 1854 She d. at Adrian, Mich Children, b at Rollin

+651 Ogden, b Mar. 16, 1844
+652 John Rogers, b Jan 9, 1847

295

EDMUND (Heman, Reuben, Elisha, Elisha), m at Croton Falls, N Y, Dec 31, 1845, Elizabeth, b Somers, N Y, Jan 11, 1818, dau. of John and Anna (Bailey) Owen. He a farmer, and d. July 14, 1853, aged 31 years, 4 months, 23 days She died at Oswego, N Y., May 29, 1904 Child.

653 Isabella, b Oct 19, 1848, m in New York City, June 5, 1867, Franklin Burbank, b. Oswego, Sept 1, 1844, son of Samuel Burbank and Sarah Clarkson (Doyle) Johnson He d July 3, 1868, and she m at Oswego, Dec 11, 1879, her brother-in-law, Edgar Doyle Johnson, who was b Jan 5, 1847 Both living at Oswego

296

HEMAN HOPKINS (Heman, Reuben, Elisha, Elisha), m Hannah Jane, b ———, dau of Jacob Orson and Maria (Van Blarcom) Howes He was a farmer and lived at South East. He d Aug, 1864 She d Croton Falls, Dec 14, 1896, after being a wid for 32 years Children:

654 Orson, b. Sept 7, 1849, m Dec 5, 1871, to Ida Elizabeth, b. Aug 25, 1852, at Pound Ridge, dau of Linus and Catharine (Thatcher) Olmstead Lived at South East. He d Oct 9, 1891, aged 42 years, 1 month, 2 days She d. Feb 7, 1890, aged 37 years, 6 months, 13 days Children:

Jennie Louise, b Oct 21, 1874, d Oct 31, 1894.

655 Emma M, b ———, d Aug 14, 1855, aged 3 years, 2 months, 7 days
656 Ida, b June 10, 1854, m at South East, Sept 25, 1878, Charles Byington, b there June 18, 1849, son of George Washington and Elizabeth (Byington) Gregory. He a farmer, living at Croton Falls She d at Somers, Dec 8, 1896
657 William H, d unm.

301

JOHN (Ebenezer, Reuben, Elisha, Elisha); m Dingle Ridge, South East, Jan 12, 1853, Jane Ann, b at South East, dau of Ezra and Sarah (Ritchie) Rundle She d Sept 7, 1857, aged 29 years, 11 months, 11 days, and he m (2) 1861, Susan Elizabeth, b at Dykmans, July 19, 1839, daughter of John and Deborah Jane (Barnes) Wood He was a butcher, and d at Brewster, July 28, 1884 Aged 62 years, 11 months, 17 days She d there Feb 21, 1899 Children, born at Brewster:

658 Medora Jane, b June 11, 1856, m there May 28, 1890, Alonzo Augustus, b at Paterson, N Y, Jan. 15, 1857, son of Alonzo and Jemima (Stripling) Palmer, both living at Towners
659 Herbert R, d Oct 8, 1857, aged 1 month, 14 days.
660 Ida Belle, b. July 7, 1863, m Dec 18, 1890, Harry Clark, b. at Chenango Forks, N Y, June 27, 1867, son of Jean and Emily (Price) Hicks Both living at White Plains, N. Y.
661 Chester, b May 30, 1865, d Sept 21, 1873
662 Edwin, b June 4, 1867, unm
663 Wilbur, b July 5, 1868, m Bertha Owen

304

ABNER SWEETLAND (Eli, David, Elisha, Elisha), m Oct 10, 1848, Roena Herrick Children

664 Addie May, b Mar 30, 1854; m May 9, 1878, Lafayette Holden He Capt 136th N Y Infantry, Civil War.

665 William L , b May 10, 1857; m Apr , 1878, Lillie Fuller He d Sept. 29, 1880 Child

Louis, b Dec 23, 1878; d. Nov 22, 1881.

305

DAVID ORLANDO (Eli, David, Elisha, Elisha) , m Oct 28, 1852, Anadella C Rude She d and he m (2) Aug 16, 1855, Susan Jane Nash Lived Downer's Grove, Ill. Children·

666 Son, b and d Feb 22, 1854
667 Arthur B , b Jan 22, 1857, m Mar 22, 1882, Lulu Stanley Child

Alice, b Mar 5, 1885

668 Halbert, b Aug 3, 1860, d Mar 31, 1861
669 Adele M , b Victor, Ill , Feb 22, 1863, m Nov 14, 1883, C C Van Horn Children:

Roy C , b Sept 17, 1884

669a Clarence L , b Oct 9, 1865, d Apr 15, 1872.
669b Rollo M , b Sept 29, 1870
669c Alonzo E , b Jan 8, 1874
669d Allen M , b Dec 3, 1879

310

LYMAN MASON (Eli, David Elisha, Elisha) ; m Westfield, Ohio, Nov 4, 1869, Angeline Mary, b there 1852, dau of Duane and Mary Elizabeth (Reynolds) Rouse He an engineer Both living at Geneva, Ohio He was also a First Lieutenant, in Company B, 56th Illinois, during the Rebellion Children

670 Ivy Louise, b Westfield, O , July 6, 1871 ; m Geneva, O , May 23, 1906, John Newton, b. Richfield, O , May 15, 1863, son of William and Rebecca (Newton) Weld Living Cleveland, Ohio.
671 Arthur Lawrence, b Saybrook, O , Sept 27, 1874; m July 24, 1897, Flora Donk Child:

Charlotte Angeline, b Chicago, Feb. 21, 1899.

314

WILLIAM WALLACE (Abner Bangs, David, Elisha, Elisha), m at Cuba, N Y, Oct 28, 1852, Mary Jane, b there Feb. 12, 1836, dau of James Stewart and Lois (Shaffer) Graham. He d Denver, Col, June 4, 1900 She living in Chicago.

He enlisted at the first call for volunteers in April, 1861, for two years in Company B, 23d N. Y. Vols, made 2nd Lieut, and in Sept., 1862, upon resignation of Capt Loybon, he was promoted to fill the vacancy Served two years and was honorably discharged Children, born, Cuba, N. Y

- 672 Eugene, b Nov 7, 1853, d. Aug 3, 1862.
- 673 James Graham, b Sept 27, 1855, d Aug. 10, 1862.
- 674 Charles, b Mar 25, 1860, d Aug 9, 1862.
    (The above children died of diphtheria while their father was with the army.)
- 675 Minnie May, b May 26, 1863, m at Cuba, May 26, 1885, Robert Carson, b there June 9, 1861, son of Henry Axtel and Jane (Orton) Mead They had.

    Lucy Alice, b Sept. 6, 1887.
- 676 Ada Eleanor, b Jan 5, 1868; m at Denver, Col, Apr 2, 1896, Melville b at Washington, Ia, Mar 15, 1866, son of George and Louisa Jane (Melville) Black.
- 677 Alice Bertha, b Oct 6, 1870; m in Brooklyn, Dec 24, 1889, Charles Evans, b Jersey City, N J, Apr 22, 1868, son of William Schuyler and Katharine (Peck) Winters
- 678 Jessie Lois, b Apr 21, 1875, d. Feb 4, 1879

315

CHESTER SCOTT (Abner Bangs, David, Elisha, Elisha); m at Painted Post, N Y, Nov 2, 1858, Adeline Eleanor, dau of George Charles and Mary (Gibbs) Wheat. He d at Corning, N Y, June 21, 1906 She living

He moved from Friendship, N Y, to Corning in 1854 He was greatly interested in the political affairs of Corning and held many offices He was President of the town several times and in 1868 was appointed U S Assessor of Internal Revenue for that District He was a delegate to the Republican National Conventions of 1872, 1876, 1880, and was one of the 306 who voted for Grant at the Chicago Convention In 1879 he was appointed captain of the port of New York by Governor Cornell, which office he held until it was abolished in 1894, in 1884-5 he was chairman of the Republican State Committee He retired from active politics in 1886 Children, born at Corning·

+679 Chester Glenn, b Aug 10, 1859.
680 May Belle, b Mar. 21, 1861, m Jan 14, 1890, Dr. Geo. Thompson, b Homer, N Y, Oct 14, 1862, son of Chester Warner and Eliza (Thompson) Hawley He d at Corning, Sept 14, 1897 She living.

316

HORACE (Nathan, David, Elisha, Elisha), m at Lyons, Wis, Feb 8, 1866, Aurelia Celestine, b Palmyra, Mich, Mar 5, 1841, dau of Joseph Thomas and Mary Emeline (Wright) Pendleton He was Postmaster, and d at Lyons, Jan 27, 1894 She living Child:

681 Cecil Aurelia, b July 26, 1877, d unm July 27, 1896.

317

JAMES (Nathan, David, Elisha, Elisha); m at Lyons, Wis., Apr. 20, 1864, Eleanor, b there, Nov 30, 1845, dau. of Harvey and Martha (Twentymen) Hand He d Dec 25, 1888, at Westbranch, Wash, and she m (2) Nov 1, 1899, Hiram Cordill. He was a farmer She living. Children

+682 Arthur, b Feb 20, 1871
683 Harvey, b Mar 25, 1873, unm.
684 Maude, b Jan 11, 1876, m at Moscow, Idaho, Oct 12, 1895, William, b Missouri Dec 4, 1864, son of John Alexander Both living at Westbranch
685 Willie, b Jan 25, 1879, unm

318

LEANDER (Nathan, David, Elisha, Elisha), m at Lawrence, Kans, Feb 27, 1860, Melinda, b Michigan Nov. 14, 1842, dau. of Sardinia and Theodosia (Raredon) Richards Farmer and carpenter Both living at McLoud, Okla Children

    Four children, all d y
686 Bertha, b Jan 6, 1867; m June 10, 1884, N Lemuel, b in Iowa, 1861, son of Noah and Melvina (Powell) Myer She d July 3, 1896

319

DWIGHT H (Nathan, David, Elisha, Elisha), m. June 1, 1869, Emma L Gillett He is dead She Postmistress at Lyons, Wis Child

687 Florence Viola, b April 14, 1870

328

CHARLES HENRY (Elisha, David, Elisha, Elisha), m Feb 2, 1865, Mary Luella Henshaw She b Jan 22, 1847 They lived at Jackson, Mich Children

688 Edward Carlton, b Feb. 2, 1866; d July 23, 1867.
689 Frank Elsworth, b July 23, 1869
690 Hugh Clifford, b June 30, 1872
691 Mary Gertrude, b Sept 7, 1877, d March 6, 1879
692 Charles Alland, b April 17, 1883

338

HENRY CLAY (Chester S, David, Elisha, Elisha), m Sept 13, 1875, Olive Beebe He, a farmer, living at Luddington, Mich Children·

693 Chester David, b Aug 18, 1876.
694 Millie, b March 2, 1878
695 Hannah, b April 11, 1880, d January, 1881
696 Annie Orlinda, b July 10, 1882
697 Walter Henry, b Oct 25, 1884.

346

EDWARD ELEAZER (Harrison, Eleazer, Elisha, Elisha), m March 2, 1855, Mary Wall Children

    698 Van Rensselaer, b ———, m ———, Ella Victoria Newkirk They had
        Daniel, b ———.
        Calvin, b ———.
        Grover, b ———.

    699 Harrison, b ———, m ———, Mary Jane Bellyet.
    700 William Walker

354

DR HENRY B. (Alfred, Obed, Elisha, Elisha), m. at Black River Falls, Wis., July 15, 1866, Clara L., b Annsville, Oneida County, N Y., May 5, 1848 dau of John B G and Lenora (Calkins) Baxter He was Asst Surgeon 128th N Y. Vols, 1862-1865 Both living Children

    701 Cepha Hortense, b Dec 6, 1869, d unm at St Paul, Minn, May 5, 1901
    702 Herbert B, b. Nov. 25, 1878, m at Granton, Wis, July 28, 1904, Tillie Grant Davis

357

FRANCIS WAYLAND (Alfred, Obed, Elisha, Elisha), m Black River Falls, Wis., Sept 13, 1877, Ella, b there Feb 16, 1856, dau of Samuel W and Sarah E (Hamilton) Bowman Both living at Black River Falls Children (born there) ·

    703 Rachel, b. Jan 3, 1881, m June 29, 1904, Frank L Cooper
    704 Katharine, b Nov 24, 1884
    705 Philip, b Sept 10, 1889.

362

ELISHA KELLEY (Jacob, Elisha, Elisha, Elisha), m Feb 29, 1869, Helen, b Aug 10, 1842, at Cuba, N Y, dau of Jesse and Lois

(Bennett) Newton He d May 24, 1890 Was a farmer She living in Michigan Children

    706 Henry Netwon, b March 27, 1870 m June 15, 1898, at Glenwood, Ia , Mary, b in Iowa, Oct. 3, 1872, dau of John Ellis and Sarah Jane (Wright) Scott Both living at Ann Arbor, Mich
    707 Francis A , b Nov 14, 1875; d June 6, 1876
    708 Maud Jane, b June 1, 1877, d Aug 29, 1877
    709 Leon Jacob, twin of above
    710 Raymond, b Feb 14, 1883, d May 16, 1883

366

NORMAN SHELDON (David, Elisha, Elisha, Elisha), m at Beekman, N Y , Oct 12, 1858, Melissa, b at Fishkill Dec 5, 1838, dau of Alfred and Mary (Gildersleeve) Schutt She d at Fishkill Aug 3 1898 He living at Fishkill Children

   +711 Clayton, b May 27. 1860
    712 Josephine Howes, b Jan. 26, 1864, unm

369

DAVID ELLIOTT (David, Elisha, Elisha, Elisha), m Hoosick, N Y , Aug 26, 1869. Mary b Harlem, N Y , Dec 26, 1847, dau of Thomas S and Margaret W (Ash) Rogers Both living at Painsville, O

In 1862 he went to California, via Cape Horn, on the steamer *Ariel*, of the Vanderbilt Line, which was captured by the *Alabama* The *Ariel* was released off the coast of Jamaica after being held two nights The officers of the *Alabama* intended to land passengers at Jamaica and burn the *Ariel*, but were informed of a yellow fever epidemic there On reaching San Francisco learned that the real reason for not landing at Jamaica was because a U S man-of-war was in the harbor Children (born at Cleveland, O)

    713 Mary Constance, b July 7, 1871 ; m July 7, 1895, Jay Nellis, b Painesville, O , March 19, 1872,

son of Robert Maynard and Alice (Gray) Murray She d at Cleveland May 5, 1904

714 Trenton Leland, b Jan 14, 1874, m at Collingswood, O , Oct 30, 1900, Helen, b Amboy, O , Oct 6, 1875 dau of Charles and Kate (Pomeroy) Buell, both living at Collingwood No issue.

372

ONKEN WILLARD (Jonathan, Elisha, Elisha, Elisha) , m at Hamilton, N Y , June 18, 1866, Cornelia A , b Otsego County, dau of Elihu F and Harriet N (Wood) Walker She d. at Carmel April 17, 1877, and he m (2) Annie C Little He lives at Brunswick, Ga Children (born at Carmel) ·

715 Eli Kelley, b. Sept 1, 1867, m at San Francisco May 10, 1893, Emily De Russy, dau of John William Cornish and Mary (Cunningham) Maxwell He is a Lieutenant Colonel of the U S. Marine They have

Maxwell, b Jan. 13, 1896

716 Nellie Walker, b Dec 8, 1875, m at Washington, D C , April 29, 1896, Herbert Augustus, b April 8, 1874, at Danbury, Conn , son of Thomas Gregory and Mary B (Kealer) Wildman Both living at Danbury, Conn Have.

Talbot Cole, b June 20, 1897
Frederick Starr, b Nov. 4, 1898

399

WILLIAM RAPPLEYE (Aaron Hazen Daniel, Elisha, Elisha) , m at Spencer, O , Oct 4, 1860, Eliza Corson, dau of William and Mary (Corson) Taylor She d at Ridgefield, O , June 13, 1874, and he m (2) Sept 4, 1875, Eva Jane, b Avon, O , Oct 27, 1852, dau of Robert and Jane (York) Baldwin He a farmer and nurseryman He went to Texas in 1875, and they are now living near Dallas, Tex Children:

717 Addie, b Richfield, O, June 1, 1870, m George Godsey.
718 Mary Lydia, b Dallas Sept 1, 1877, m J Htzenbuchler
719 William Ide, b Dec 18, 1878
720 Robert Frank, b Jan 23, 1880
721 Miner Thomas, b May 29, 1882.
722 Hattie C, b Sept 18, 1885, m Rawlins Douglass.
723 Clara Lucretia, b Sept. 18, 1887
724 Bertha Marguerite, b March 29, 1890
725 Frank M, b Jan 11, 1892.
726 Julia, b Aug 8, 1894.

400

MINER THOMAS (Aaron Hazen, Daniel, Elisha, Elisha) ·

Hon Miner T. Cole was b in Spencer Township, Lucas County, Ohio His father was Aaron H Cole, a native of Covert, Seneca County, N Y, where his birth took place Feb 20, 1813 Aaron Cole's father was Daniel Cole, a native of Putnam County, N. Y. The mother of Miner T Cole before her marriage was Lydia B Rappleye, dau of William Rappleye, of Covert, Seneca County, N Y Lydia B Rappleye was b. in Covert, Seneca County, N. Y, Feb 18, 1817. Aaron H Cole was m to Lydia B Rappleye at Covert March 21, 1835, and immediately moved to Michigan Territory and located on what afterwards became Spencer, Lucas County, Ohio They settled in a howling wilderness, infested with Indians, bears, wolves, deer, wild turkeys and quantities of small game. Seven children were born to them. Harriet Calista, b at Spencer, Dec 20, 1835 She d at Salem, Mich, March 4, 1868 William Rappleye Cole was b at Spencer, Ohio, Sept 25, 1837 Now resides at Dallas, Tex Miner T, b at Spencer July 3, 1839, now resides at Palmyra, Mich Adoniram Judson was b at Spencer Oct 11, 1843, d at West Barre, Ohio, Jan. 4, 1861 Frank Marion was b at Maumee City, Ohio, Dec 25, 1851. Now resides at Chester, Va Ralph Tunis was b at Maumee, Ohio, Dec 25, 1853 Now resides at Brighton, Col. George Ide Cole was b at Grand Blank,

MINER THOMAS COLE
No. 400

The Descendants of Elisha Cole 119

Genessee County, Mich, April 24, 1857 Now resides at Los Angeles, Cal

Miner T. Cole helped clear the farm from the tall timber, and attended the district school in the old log school house In the spring of 1851 his father moved to Maumee, Ohio, to give his children the privilege of attending a good school In 1856 they moved to Genessee County, Mich.

In the spring of 1858 Miner and his older brother, William R., and sister Harriet went back on the old farm at Spencer, Ohio On the 28th day of August, 1861, Miner enlisted in Company F, 14th Ohio Vol Infantry Soon after the regiment started for the South, where, during the War of the Rebellion, they served more than four years, participating in the battles of Mill Springs, Chattanooga, Mission Ridge, Jonesboro, and various other small battles Miner T was with the regiment at all the battles and skirmishes, also went with them under General Sherman from Atlanta to the Sea Upon his arrival at Golsdboro, N C, he accepted an appointment from the Secretary of War, Mr Stanton, as First Lieutenant in the 22nd U S Colored Troops He went with them to Brownsville, Tex, where, after seven months, he was mustered out as First Lieutenant On his return from the army he moved with his father to Adrian, Mich and engaged in the manufacture of the Cole wedge trace buckle, an invention of Aaron H Cole

On the 30th of May, 1867, Miner T Cole was m to Mary Jane Taylor, b Sept 14, 1842, at Spencer, Ohio Mary J was the dau of William and Mary M (Corson) Taylor, who was formerly of Lycoming County, Pa. For one year they resided in Adrian, Mich, and then moved to Palmyra, Mich, where they now reside Farming and dairying has been his occupation He was a member of the Michigan Legislature from Jan 1, 1887, to Jan 1, 1891 In January, 1901, he was appointed by Gov Bliss as Commissioner to the Pan-American Exposition, and had charge of the Agricultural, Horticultural and Dairy exhibits of Michigan There are 165 acres in the farm. All good land A large and commodious house, well furnished and surrounded by a large and well-kept lawn The barns are large and well built Some of the privileges are telephone in the house, rural mail delivery, electric road running by the side of the farm Children (born at Palmyra, Mich).

727 Harriet Calista, b Sept 29, 1868, m Nov 29, 1893, Herbert Ralph, b Palymra, June 14 1868, son of Ralph Jerome and Almira Ann (Corbitt) Clark Both living
728 Harley Lynn, b. March 20, 1874
729 Florence Marian, b Jan 25, 1876
730 Mary Taylor, b Aug 31, 1877; m Aug 31, 1898, Dr George Britton McClellan, b Rome, Mich, Aug 19, 1867, son of Eugene and Alice Amelia (Jenells) Seger Both living

He entered the Michigan College of Medicine at Detroit in the fall of 1889 and received his degree March 24, 1893 Practised for a time at Rome, Mich., and then removed to Adrian. He was Mayor of Adrian in 1902-3 He is also President of the Adrian Steel Castings Co

402

FRANK MARION (Aaron Hazen, Daniel, Elisha, Elisha), m Mobeetie, Tex, Oct 1st, 1892, Caroline C, b Philadelphia, Pa, April 4, 1859, dau of Gustav Henry and Caroline (Ebelmesser) Nesper. He is a farmer at Chester, Va Children (born at Mobeetie):

731 Frances Louise, b Sept 9, 1894
732 Hazel Dorothy, b July 20, 1896
733 Harold Marion, b Sage, Okla, Sept 10, 1898.

403

RALPH TUNIS (Aaron Hazen, Daniel, Elisha, Elisha), m at Adrian, Mich, Sept 4, 1875, Harriet, b Feb 3, 1858, dau of John Milton Moore and Cynthia Lovicia (Strong) Cavender. Both living at Brighton, Colo Child

734 Charles Cavender, b Aug 25, 1877.

404

GEORGE I. (Aaron Hazen, Daniel, Elisha, Elisha), m at Adrian, Oct 6, 1882, Ada Theresa, b Canandaigua, Mich, 1861, dau of John Milton Moore and Cynthia Loovisa (Strong) Cavender Both living at Los Angeles, Cal Children

    735 Ralph Dana, b April 15, 1885
    736 Ada Louise, b Sept 3, 1888
    737 Georgia Imogene, b Aug 23, 1896

409

FREMONT (Ira, Hazen, Daniel, Elisha, Elisha), m at Watkins, N Y, Sept 20, 1888, Charlotte Caroline, b Reading, N Y, Sept 22, 1863, dau of Cyrus and Frances (Shepherd) Roberts Both living in New York City. Child

    738 Faith Adelaide, b at Watkins, N Y, April 10, 1890

Fremont Cole, fifth child and one of the seven sons of Ira Hazen Cole and Mary Caroline (Denison) Cole, was born on the Cole farm at Covert, N Y He was educated in the Hall's Corners District and Farmer Village Union Schools and began the study of law with Surrogate of Schuyler Co, at Watkins, N Y, April 16, 1877 In January, 1878, he was appointed Clerk of the Schuyler Co Surrogate's Court, a position he held about three years, being succeeded by his brother, Irving W Cole He began the practice of his profession in March, 1881, at Watkins, in partnership with W L Norton, at that time District Attorney of Schuyler County Subsequently, in 1883, he was joined by his brother Irving, and the law firm of Cole Brothers continued to be a leading one in that section until the Spring of 1890, when Fremont removed to Seattle, Wash, and began the practice of law in that city He was elected to the New York State Assembly from his adopted county in 1884, and re-elected for five successive terms, being Speaker of that body during the sessions of 1888 and 1889 He was nominated for State Senator by the Republicans of the Seattle, Wash, Senatorial District in 1894, but after an exciting contest was defeated by 92 votes While at Seattle he was attorney for the

Cornell University, at that time having large investments in the State of Washington, and represented a number of other large eastern interests In the fall of 1895 he received an offer which induced him to return to New York, since which time he has had an office, and continued the practice of law, at No. 1 Madison Ave, New York City.

410

IRVING WASHINGTON (Ira Hazen, Daniel, Elisha, Elisha), m at Elmira, N. Y, June 27, 1893, Nelle Emeline, b Roseville, Pa, April 10, 1863, dau of Elmer Ross and Emeline Catharine (Watkins) Backer Both living at Buffalo, N Y Child:

739 Elmer Hopkins, b May 7, 1900

Irving W, son of Ira Hazen, and Mary Caroline (Denison) Cole was born on the Cole Homestead in the Town of Covert, Seneca Co, N Y He acquired his early education in the neighboring district schools, the Farmer Village Union School and Cook Academy, Havana (now Montour Falls), N. Y.

He commenced the study of law at Watkins, N. Y, in the Spring of 1880, was Clerk of the Surrogate s Court of Schuyler Co for two and a half years during his studentship, entered the Albany Law School, Union University, in the fall of 1882, and graduated therefrom in May, 1883, with the degree of LL B., having been admitted to the bar at Albany in January of that year The following fall he commenced the practice of law with his brother, Hon Fremont Cole, at Watkins, under the firm name of Cole Brothers In January, 1889, E O Boylen, District Attorney, was taken into the firm, which continued under the name of Cole, Cole & Boylen until the spring of 1890, when Fremont withdrew In January, 1892, Mr Boylen withdrew from the firm and Elbert Cole, a younger brother, was made partner, and the firm again, under the name of Cole Brothers, continued until the fall of 1893, when the subject of this sketch removed to Buffalo, N Y, where he has since continued the practice of his profession

Always a Republican, he has never sought political preferment, and never held office, except the clerkship above referred

IRVING W. COLE
No. 410

to, although active in politics while residing in Schuyler County, being Chairman of the Republican County Committee when he left that County to take up his residence in Buffalo Since then he has devoted himself exclusively to his profession, principally at litigated work, in which he has been successful in many important cases of which involved the judicial settlement by the highest court of important points in the law substantive, notably the cases of

> Wallingford vs Kaiser, 191 N Y, 392, 15 L R A (new series) 1126, 84 N E. 295
> Grand vs Livingston, 2 App Div, 589, aff 158 N Y 688, 53 N E 1125
> Waldron vs Fargo, 170 N Y, 130, 63 N E 1077
> Shephard vs Fulton, 171 N Y, 184, 63 N E 966

411

HERVEY DENISON (Ira Hazen, Daniel, Elisha, Elisha), m at Lodi, N Y, June 13, 1895, Mary, b there June 27, 1868, dau of J F and Lefferetta A (Phillips) Tinker She d at Lodi, May 8, 1906 He is a farmer and lives at Interlaken, N Y Children (born at Covert, N Y) ·

> 740 Ira Joseph, b Aug 16, 1896
> 741 Emily Charlotte, b Nov 29, 1898, d y.
> 742 Maude Evelyn, b Nov 29, 1900
> 743 Marion, b Jan 18, 1904

414

JOHN ROBERTS (Hyman, John Elisha, Elisha), m New York City, July 3, 1861, Helen Gertrude, b there Oct 15, 1840, dau of William Hiram and Jane Adeline (Tompkins) Burnett He d Brooklyn, N Y, Nov 23, 1903 She d there May 3, 1887. He went to New York City in 1850 In 1870 engaged in the trucking business with his son, Arthur, in which he continued until his death Children (born at Hoboken, N J):

> 744 Charles, b ———, d y

745 Elva Isabel, b Sept 1, 1865, m Carmel, N Y, Sept 14, 1904. Andrew James, b New York City, Sept 29, 1869, son of Andrew and Margaret (Alderdice) McClintock Both living in New York City

+746 Arthur, b Sept. 3, 1867
+747 George Edwin, b March 21, 1870
748 Emma Estelle, b New York City, April 4, 1872, m there April 23, 1896, Andrew James McClintock She d May 10, 1899, and he m (2) her sister Elva.

415

ADDISON (Hyman, John, Elisha, Elisha), m at Mahopac, N Y, Nov 8, 1865, Emily Augusta, b there Aug 11, 1845, dau of David Augustus and Julia A (Bailey) Ferris Both living near Mahopac In early life he travelled with Seth Howe's Circus. He enlisted in the Union Army at Chicago and was sworn in at St Louis under Gen Thomas He was discharged Sept 16, 1864 In 1873 he bought a farm of 100 acres near Lake Mahopac Child·

+749 Walter Bailey, b Sept 23, 1868.

420

JAMES KELLEY (Jarvis W, John, Elisha, Elisha), m New York City, Jan 22, 1893, Eleanor Florence, b. there Nov 1, 1873, dau of David Lyman and Celia (Simpson) Mersereau Both living in New York City Children

750 James Kelley, b June 28, 1894
751 Thaddeus Lincoln, b Feb 12, 1902

423

JOHN PECK (Abner B, Nathan, Nathan, Elisha), m Jan 5, 1865, Mrs Mary A (Reasoner) Condit He is a farmer at Aurora, Ore Children (born there)·

+752 Abner Bangs, b Nov 16, 1865
+753 John Reasoner, b. July 28, 1867.

CHARLES B. COLE
No. 430

+754 Nathan Edward, b. Oct 22, 1869.
755 Emma Agnes, b Feb 8, 1873, m June 30, 1898, at Aurora, to Claude H Nosler They had
   Lynde Claude R, b April 23, 1899
+756 Christopher Oliver, b Feb 16, 1878
757 Rebecca Augustine, b Aug 16, 1880, m June 5, 1906, Edward G Miller

427

OLIVER GARRISON (Abner B, Nathan, Nathan, Elisha), m Oct 9, 1878, Salem, Ore, Alice Jane, b at Fairfield, Ore, Dec 16, 1856, dau of John Cannon and Elizabeth Jane (Mart) Peebles He, a farmer, living at Turner, Ore

(John C Peebles was b at Westmoreland Co, Pa, Jan 22, 1826, d Feb 11, 1895 Elizabeth J Mart was b Harlin Co, Ky, June 5, 1837. They were m Nov 27, 1851

Children

758 Zella Alice, b Salem, Ore, June 23, 1880, m. Oct 27, 1906, Rowland Giddings
759 Oliver Kenneth, b Canby, Ore, Oct. 29, 1886

430

CHARLES BRIGGS (Hermon C, Nathan, Nathan, Elisha); m at Walshville, Ill., May 12, 1869, Laura Amelia Layman, b in Tennessee, June 21, 1847, d Chester, Ill, July 11, 1878 He m (2) at Hampton, N H, Jan 3, 1882, Mary Ellen, b there March 30, 1857, dau. of Josiah C and Miriam (Moulton) Palmer They live at Chester, Ill

Children

760 Burt, b June 25, 1870, m at Webster Park, Mo, Jan. 25, 1908, Catharine, b St Louis, Mo, Oct 25, 1882, dau of Justin Smith and Ida (Harsha) Kendrick He is a Mining Engineer and lives at Chester, Ill
761 Alice, b Jan 6, 1872

126   THE DESCENDANTS OF ELISHA COLE

   762 Una, b. April 16, 1874; m Dec 29, 1898, at Chester, Ill, to Perry Carter, b Feb 3, 1869, at Adrian, Mich, son of Alford and Hannah (Carter) Withers They live at Mount Vernon, Ill. They had

      Hannah, b. Aug. 11, 1900
      Laura, twin of above.

   763 Edna, b March 22, 1877
   764 Marion, b Dec 17, 1882

431

ZACHARY TAYLOR (Hermon C., Nathan, Nathan, Elisha), m Brooklyn, N. Y, May 2, 1870, Martha, dau of Alexander S and Elizabeth A. (Bennett) Kennedy. She d at Philadelphia, Pa, 1896. In 1882 he removed to Chicago and took active charge of the Star and Crescent Mill. He continued in this position until 1890, when his health failed and he located at Los Angeles, Cal, where he still resides Child (born Chester, Ill):

+765 Austin, b. Jan 27, 1876

433

HENRY CLAY (Hermon C, Nathan, Nathan, Elisha); m Alton. Ill, April 24, 1878, Blanche Owens, b Alton, June 5, 1851, dau of Shadrack Rodney and Hannah Elizabeth (Pettingill) Dolbee Both living at Chester, Ill He is President of the H. C. Cole Milling Co Children (Born at Chester)

   766 Jewett, b June 13, 1879
   767 Saxon, b Sept 3, 1884
   768 Dorothea, b Oct 5, 1886
   769 Blanche, b Dec 8, 1888
   770 Harriet, b July 31, 1891

435

EDWARD EVERETT (Hermon C, Nathan, Nathan, Elisha); m at Chester, Ill, April 27, 1878, Minnie, b there Dec 1857, dau.

HENRY C. COLE
No. 433

of Savimen and Virginia (Guthrie) St Vrain She d at Fargo, N D, Feb 20, 1884, and he m (2) at Fargo, April 26, 1886, Lelia Floyd, b near Natchez, Miss, April 25, 1867, dau of Thomas Winn and Jeannette (January) Hunt They live at Fargo Children

771 Rudy, b at Chester, March 11, 1879
772 Irma, b Chester, June 23, 1880
773 Edward Hanford, b Hot Springs, Ark, Dec 29, 1890
774 Dunbar, b Fargo, Sept 5, 1891

438

HERMON C (Hermon C, Nathan, Nathan, Elisha), m May 22, 1889, Ella Lillian, b Nov 14, 1868, dau of Daniel Brown and Virginia Narcissa (Harrison) Gillhan Both living at Upper Alton, Ill Children.

775 Cora Lillian, b July 8, 1890
776 Herman, b Feb 6, 1893

449

AMEDEE BERTHOLD (Nathan, Nathan, Nathan, Elisha), m at St Louis, June 18, 1879, Anna Mary, b there, Dec 19, 1860, dau of John and Jane (Rogers) Jackson Both living at St Louis

He was educated at Washington University and Shurtleff College, Upper Alton, Ill At one time he was President of the Cole Brothers Commission Co After serving for two years as a Director of the Merchants' Exchange he was, in 1896, elected Vice-President, and also member of Public Library Board In 1897 he became President of the John Jackson Investment Co, which office he still holds, and is a Director in the Nathan Cole Investment Co He was a Director and Vice-President of the St Louis Public Museum in 1904, 1905 and 1906 Mr Cole is a 32nd Degree Mason Children (Born St. Louis)

777 Annie Jackson, b April 10, 1881
+778 John Jackson, b March 18, 1883
779 Ernest Jackson, b March 4, 1887
780 Rebecca, b Aug 23, 1889.
781 Marjorie Jackson, b Dec 22, 1891

451

NATHAN (Nathan, Nathan, Nathan, Elisha), m at Woodland, Cal, Aug. 28, 1881, Mary Ellen, b Stockton, Cal, Jan 17, 1862, dau of William Zachary and Hannah (Gadbury) Corbet Both living at Los Angeles Children (born Los Angeles)·

    782 Rebecca Fagan, b Aug 19, 1882, m March 30, 1904, Roscoe Lorenzo, b Wilmington, Cal, Feb 28, 1873, son of John and Anna Matilda (Eames) McCrea
    783 Mary Gladys, b Nov. 26, 1888
    784 Nathalie Rachel, b Aug 8, 1892

458

JOSEPH GANUNG (Ormond H, Berry, Joseph, Elisha), m June 14, 1854 Zellah Celeno, b Carmel, Sept 7, 1833, dau of Ansel and Eliza A (Hopkins) Hazen She d Feb 17, 1859, and he m (2) Oct 3, 1869, Lucena Catharine, b Sept 4, 1843, dau. of Lewis H. and Martha A (Cummings) Gregory He d. April 13, 1893, aged 60 years, 9 months, 13 days

He graduated from the State Normal School, Albany, N Y, 1852 Taught school for several years He was proprietor of the Carpenter House and Cole House at Lake Mahopac He was also Justice of the Peace He was Coroner, 1874-77-80 About 35 years ago he commenced the collection of records of his family, which the author of this work has had access to through the kindness of his son, Otis H Cole At the time Mr Cole collected his records there were a number of aged people residing in Carmel and vicinity who were acquainted with the children of Elisha Cole, the settler, and their testimony has been used in compiling this work Among them being

Mrs John Barrett, who, when Mr Cole saw her in Feb, 1886, was 98 years old, having been born Jan 17, 1788 At this time she was in good health and possessed a remarkable memory She remembered Elisha and his wife and was more or less acquainted with all but two of their children, John and Priscilla Children

785 Anne Amelia, b May 9, 1866, m at Mahopac, Feb. 22, 1883, Frederick Randall, b Brooklyn, Jan. 4, 1859, son of John and Abigail (Kraft) Tripler Both living.
786 Otis Hazen, b Jan 1, 1858.
786½ Twin Sons, b July 17, 1872, d y
787 Lewis Gregory, b May 21, 1874, m April 3, 1901, Marion E, b Aug 12, 1876, dau. of William H and Mary (Morton) Herring He is a physician and surgeon and both live in New York City. They have.
   William Gregory Cole, b Feb 1, 1902
788 Daughter, b and d Aug 30, 1878.
789 Joseph Ganong, b Dec 12, 1882, m April 25, 1906, Clara C, daughter of Joseph L and Lillian F. (Robbins) Naylor He, a mining engineer, living at Newburgh, N Y.
790 Marion Lucena, b Jan 30, 1886.

463

JOSEPH BAILEY (Chas G, Joseph, Joseph, Elisha), m at North Greenbush, N Y, Dec 24, 1866, Lucy Harriet, b Troy, N Y, Sept 20, 1836, daughter of David and Ann Eliza (Stephenson) Goewey She died at Barrington, Yates Co, N Y, Sept 23, 1878 He m (2) at Dundee, N Y, Feb 23. 1884, Mary, b Orange, N Y, Sept 19, 1849, dau of Norman and Caroline (Reuiff) Putnam He is a farmer Both living. Children.

791 Grover C., b Barrington, N Y, Jan 10, 1885
792 Louise Laura, b Starkey, N Y, March 15, 1889

464

HARVEY TOWNSEND (Charles G, Joseph, Joseph, Elisha), m, Hornby, N Y, March 20, 1861, Elizabeth, b. there July 14, 1840, dau of James Burton and Ann (Wands) Humphrey He a carpenter and living at Corning, N Y Children (born at Catlin, N Y)

    793 Victor Leroy, b Feb 25, 1863, unm
    794 Charles Erastus, b Nov. 5, 1866, d Sept 28, 1869
    795 Flora Linda, b May 22, 1868, m at Corning, Jan 10, 1889, Walter Joseph, b Covington, Pa Sept 14, 1866, son of John and Catharine (———) Blair. He d Corning, March 3, 1899, she d April, 1903
    796 Luella Jane, b Corning, Jan 26, 1870, d Sept 25, 1888
+797 James Stanley, b May 20, 1872
+798 Harvey Townsend, b April 12, 1874
+799 Otto Paris, b Sept 10, 1876.
    800 Mary Elizabeth, b March 17, 1879, unm
+801 Nathan Thompson, b Aug 3, 1881

468

JARVIS ASAHEL (Charles G, Joseph, Joseph, Elisha), m at Beaver Dams, N Y., Nov. 25. 1868 Adeline, b Orange, N Y, May 5, 1840, dau of Jacob and Temperance (Owens) Frost. He was a farmer and died at Beaver Dams, Nov 30, 1881 She living Children

    802 Grace, b Jan 15, 1870, unm
    803 Charles, b May 3, 1871; d unm Oct. 20, 1897.
    804 Lucy, b. Nov 17, 1874; m Monterey, N Y., Sept 3, 1893, Walter Franklin, b Sugar Hill, N Y, Jan 20, 1868, son of David and Jane (Caldwell) Wasson Both living at Schenectady, N Y
    805 Edna, b Dec 25, 1877, m at Montour Falls, N Y, Oct 23, 1895, William Stevenson, b New York City, Sept 15, 1875, son of Andrew and Rachel

(Atherton) Harwood Both living near Watkins, N Y

472

GEORGE FROST (Ira, Joseph, Joseph, Elisha), m Post Creek, Chemung Co, N. Y, Dec 24, 1850, Mary Almira, b Ulysses, Tompkins Co, N Y, May 8, 1825, dau of Henry and Hepsibah (Van Loom) Stewart He was a farmer, d at Beaver Dams, Sept 8, 1884 She living at Corning, N Y Children (born at Beaver Dams) ·

- 806 "Jack," b July 24, 1851, d 1861
- 807 Fannie Fern, b. Sept 10, 1853, m. at Beaver Dams, Nov 19, 1874, Lyman, b Post Creek, June 23, 1849, son of John and Lany (Traver) Smith. She d Sept 17, 1906, he living
- 808 Orville Seymour, b Jan 10, 1855, m May 21, 1890, Delephine, b May 28, 1855, dau of Samuel and Mary (Harvey) Van Loom He a carpenter. Both living No issue.
- +809 Albert George, b March 28, 1857
- 810 Ida May, b May 1st, 1860; m. at Corning, Aug 19, 1877, John Wilson, b Geneva, N Y, Dec 23, 1855, son of William and Jane (Wilson) Bryan He d Geneva, Aug 21, 1898, and she m (2) March 22, 1899, Jay, born Seneca Castle, Jan 16, 1856, son of Prosser and Catharine (Fitch) Jones, he d at Geneva, May 8. 1906 She living
- 811 Edward Earle. b Oct 28, 1862, m at Beaver Dams, Sept 19, 1894, Addie J, b Orange, N Y, Dec 2, 1869 dau of John and Charity (Chambers) Vosburgh Both living at Corning, N Y
- 812 Burr Marion, b April 15, 1868, unm

476

CHARLES LEWIS (Ira, Joseph, Joseph, Elisha), m Horseheads, N Y, Dec 13, 1865, Sarah Almira, b Oak Hill, N Y, April 22, 1842, dau of Charles Hyde and Betsey (Hunting) Walkin Both living at Watkins, N Y

132   The Descendants of Elisha Cole

He enlisted at Elmira, N Y, July, 1862, in 107th N Y Inf and arrived in Washington Aug 15 He was in the battles of Antietam, Chancellorsville, and Gettysburg In Sept, 1863, the regiment was sent West and made a part of the 20th Army Corps, under Gen Joe Hooker The regiment was in the battle at Resaca and Gainesville, Ga, in May, 1864 Mr. Cole also took part in engagements at New Hope Church, May 25, 1864, Pine Knob, Ga, June 15, Cuff's Farm, June 22; Kemmison, June 27, Peachtree Creek, July 20, and was at the siege of Atlanta, July 23 to Aug 24, and was in the March to the Sea, Nov 15 to Dec 10, 1864 At Rockingham, N C, March 8, 1865, he was shot through the right breast, taken prisoner, and left to die in an old log house at Browning Creek, about twelve miles from Rockingham His shoes and clothing were taken from him and he was unconscious for over thirty-six hours, during which time he was nursed and cared for by two women who lived in the hut During this time he was unattended by a physician He remained there until the latter part of May, then walked with the help of a negro to Wilmington, then to Newburn, Washington and Elmira He was discharged in June, 1865 Children (born at Watkins, N Y):

+813 Frank, b Nov 16, 1866
 814 Florence Elizabeth, b Oct 22, 1871, m Elmira, N Y, Oct 1, 1888, Walter, b Burdett, N Y, son of Silas C and Mary E (North) Colgrove She m (2) at Watkins, N Y, Jan 13, 1906, Edward Clarence, b Elizabeth, Pa, Sept 19, 1874, son of William and Mary (Martin) Cooper Both living at Watkins, N Y
+815 Ira Woodruff, b June 22, 1873

477

Samuel Bailey (Ira, Joseph, Joseph, Elisha), m Townsend, N Y, July 27, 1869 Ersula, b Six Nations, Schuyler County, N Y, April 10, 1849, dau of Jervis and Mary (Miller) Dean He is a dealer in general merchandise Both living at Townsend, N Y Children (born at Catlin, N Y)

THE DESCENDANTS OF ELISHA COLE 133

    816 Dean Jervis, b Oct 16, 1870
    817 Don Samuel, b April 16, 1873
    818 Lloyd Albert, b Sept 26, 1875, d Oct 13, 1884
    819 William Jay, b June 24, 1879

479

HARLEM (Asahel, Joseph, Joseph, Elisha); m June 13, 1860, Helen, b. Havana, N Y, Aug 27, 1840, dau of Seth Gregory and Esther (Crawford) Leonard. He was a farmer and d. March 6, 1902 She living at Detroit, Mich Children

  +820 Mortimer, b Havana, N Y, June 17, 1861
    821 Edith Leonard, b Watkins, N Y, June 28, 1863, m there Jan 10 1883, George White, b there Aug 19, 1859, son of Artemus Bodman and Lydia Caroline (White) Hurd Both living at Detroit

480

IRA SAVORY (Asahel, Joseph, Joseph, Elisha), m Burdett, N Y, July 4, 1867, Mary, b there in 1848, dau. of Jacob and Phebe (Everts) Hendricks He a farmer Both living at Montour Falls, N. Y. Children:

    822 Clarence, b June 26, 1869, d April 14, 1873
    823 George, b Aug 28, 1871, d April 28, 1874
    824 Donnie, b May 31, 1877, d Feb 28, 1880
    825 Claude Burton, b Sept. 21, 1882

485

YATES THOMPSON (Joseph, Samuel, Joseph, Elisha), m at Parshallville, Mich, April 24, 1856, Seraphina, b Clay County, Mo, Dec. 17, 1874, dau. of Elipheanet and Lovica (Allen) Luther He was a farmer and d at Parshallville, now Oak Grove, July 6, 1901 She living Children (born at Parshallville)

    826 Cynthia L, b April 21, 1857; m March 25, 1875, Morris Gilbert, b. Baptist Hill, N Y, Jan 10,

1852, son of Benjamin and Lucinda (Francis) Andrews He d Nov 13, 1901, and she m (2) Dec 24, 1904, David Henry, b at Pinckney, Mich, Jan 1, 1868, son of Elijah and Julia (Gainey) Stoddard Both living at Oak Grove, Mich.

+827 Jay C, b Dec. 21, 1859.

828 Millie M, b. Jan 8 1877, m June 27, 1906, Adelbert Marcellus, b Michigan, May 15, 1870, son of John and Harriet (Dexter) Farnham They live at Fenton, Mich No issue

487

JOSEPH W (Joseph, Samuel, Joseph, Elisha), m Oak Grove, Mich., Jan 2, 1867, Rachel Adelia, b. Osceola, Mich, April 21, 1845, dau of John and Eliza (Miller) Hetchler. He was a farmer and d at Fenton Aug 14, 1902. She living Children (born at Osceola).

829 Son, b and d Aug 14, 1868

830 Effie Elizabeth, b Oct 19, 1875; m. at Parshallville, Mich, May 29, 1901, Fred C, b. South Lyon, Mich, Dec 25, 1875, son of William and Anna (Brundell) Reed He d at Saranac, Mich, Sept 10, 1901 She living No issue.

831 Minnie Rachel, b July 16, 1878, m at Lansing June 23, 1906, Charles Erna, b Fleming, Mich, July 19, 1877, son of Isaac and Hortense (Bushnell) White Both living.

832 Edith Pearl, b Parshallville Dec 16, 1880, d Dec. 30, 1889.

488

CHARLES C. (Joseph, Samuel, Joseph, Elisha), m at Parshallville, Mich, May 27, 1875, Carrie Amelia, b Bristol, Ontario County, N Y., May 23, 1857, dau of Benjamin F. and Lucinda H. (Francis) Andrews. Both living at Flint, Mich. Children

833 Maude, b Osceola April 5, 1880, unm
834 Luke Salathiel, b Owosso July 8, 1886; unm

490

DELEVAN SAMUEL (Enos, Samuel, Joseph, Elisha), m Jan 12, 1856, Laura, b Hannibal, N Y, June 16, 1836, dau of Jason Haven and Sarah (Wiltsie) Scott He d at Hastings, Neb., Aug 1, 1892, she d. there Aug 1, 1894

He was a farmer and fancy stock breeder He came to Hastings from Michigan in 1867 and settled upon what is known as the Cole Farm Coming after the Union Pacific R R had received its grant he could not homestead more than 80 acres This he did, and shortly after purchased 160 acres railroad land for $8 an acre. He bought this land on time and by strict economy succeeded in paying for it Fourteen years later, from an outlay of $1,280, this property, including Cole's Park, is worth $72,000 Children (born in Saginaw County, Mich)

   835 Elwin Samuel, b Oct 30, 1858, m at Hastings, Mich, March 20 1877, Ida, b June 6, 1860, dau of H J and Margaret E (Munsell) Higgins He is a farmer Both living at Hastings. No issue
+836 Elmer Ellsworth, b April 26, 1860
+837 Eugene Enos, b May 24, 1865
+838 Jason Haven, b. Nov 1, 1865
+839 Robert Walker, b Hastings July 9, 1868
   840 Ada Elvira, b at Atlanta, Neb, July 2, 1870, m George Emmons, b Davenport, Delaware County, N Y, Jan 11, 1867, son of Thaddeus Delos and Mary Jane (Mills) Michael He d. in Colorado May 4, 1900, and she m (2) Aug 28, 1907, Alexander Semple, b Lanarkshire, Scotland, March 15, 1865, son of William and Jane (Semple) Murray Both living at Atlanta, Neb She had (first marriage, b at Hastings)

     Laura Mary, b Dec 7, 1889.

136   THE DESCENDANTS OF ELISHA COLE

> Ada Isadore, b Aug 9, 1893
> Eunice Lucy, b Jan 20, 1895

841 Arthur Bliss, b at Hastings Jan 17, 1877, m in 1894 Hattie Robbins   They have.
> Bessie, b ———.

493

HIRAM MASON (Enos, Samuel, Joseph, Elisha), m at Fenton, Mich, May 1, 1864, Rachel, b Edinburgh, Scotland, dau of Thomas and Eliza (McAllister) Minto   He a farmer living at Freeland, Mich   She d March 28, 1907   Children:

843 Addie Belle, b Jan 1, 1868, m. Richland, Mich., June 24, 1891, William Thomas, b Ingersoll, Mich., son of Thomas and Marguerite (Glover), McCulloch   Both living   They have·
> Mason William, b. June 22, 1904.

844 Della Mason, b Feb. 22, 1877, m March 8, 1898, William Dewey, b Osseo, Wis, August, 1877, son of Guss and ——— (Peterson) Johnson

494

WEBSTER KNAPP (Enos, Samuel, Joseph, Elisha), m. Oct 31, 1863, Annie Day, she d and he m (2) Samantha L Coburn. He living at Nashville, Mich

He enlisted Aug 10, 1862, at Osceola, Mich, in Company E, 26th Mich Vol Inf   He was at Alexandria, Va, from December until April, 1863, and from there he went to Suffolk and Yorktown   They were ordered to New York City in July to quell the riots   His regiment was then ordered to the Army of the Potomac   Mr Cole participated with his regiment in engagements at Morton's Ford Feb 6 and 7 1864, and also in the Battle of the Wilderness, and on the 12th of May was in the memorable charge when the Rebel works were carried with the bayonet   The regiment loss was 27 killed, 98 wounded, and 14 missing   The regiment also distinguished itself at Spotsylvania and Gaines Hill   He participated in 33 engagements and was on the skirmish line when Gen Robert E Lee surrendered He was wounded twice slightly and was honorably discharged June 4, 1865. Children (first marriage only):

845 Hortense R., b. ———, d. y.
846 George Samuel, b ———
847 Clarence Webster, b ———, d y
848 Jane Elizabeth, b ———

495

ARTHUR ENOS (Enos, Samuel, Joseph, Elisha), m Howell, Mich., Dec 30, 1872, Ruth Esther, b Oct 26, 1850, in Conway, Mich, dau of Thomas and Esther (———) Stanfield He a lawyer Both living Children

+849 Orville Webster, b July 24, 1874
850 Inez Elvira, b March 28, 1877
851 Ada Esther, b Jan 1, 1880, m May 19, 1904, Roy Truman, b Fowlerville, Mich, June 11, 1877, son of Truman and Lucinda (Ackley) Sprague

501

ADELBERT (Nathan, Samuel, Joseph, Elisha), m at Farmington, Mich, March 6, 1872, Cynthia M, b Berlin, Mich, Aug 27, 1850, dau. of Nathan S and Dency E (Button) Nichols He a farmer. Both living in Michigan Child

852 Ada Blanche, b Vernon, Mich, July 8, 1875, m Jan 17, 1900, Ward L Scranton They have: Winona Cole, b Feb 23, 1901

509

ALEXANDER HAMILTON (Watson, Nathan, Joseph, Elisha), m at Moreland, N Y, May 29, 1878, Frances, b there Dec 29, 1846, dau of John and Mary (Catlin) Crawford He d June 12, 1881 She living at Corning, N Y.

He went to California in 1850 and returned to Moreland in 1875 While in California he was a farmer and interested in mining Child

853 Norma, b May 8 1881, m. at Corning Dec 5, 1900, Henry, b Welsbach, Germany, May 12, 1878, son of John and Elizabeth (Christ) Herr.

515

WILLIAM HENRY (Eli, Nathan, Joseph, Elisha); m. at Fairfield, Mich, April 13, 1868, Matilda Louisa, b. there March 30, 1847, dau of Ezra and Angeline (Porter) Cole. He d. at Nashville, Tenn, Oct 23, 1907 She living

He enlisted in Company C, 126th N Y State Vols., Aug 5, 1862, was wounded in the right thigh at Gettysburg, in the right leg at the Battle of Mine Run; in the right hand at the Battle of the Wilderness. Because of these injuries he was discharged Feb 6, 1864. Child:

854 Alta Belle, b Covert, N. Y., Jan 25, 1873; m. May 25, 1892, Edward Ernest, b. Morenci, Mich, Oct. 13, 1869, son of William and Elizabeth (Schoonover) French Both living They have.
Eleanor Louise, b March 27, 1904

516

GEORGE WASHINGTON (Eli, Nathan, Joseph, Elisha); m. at Clinton, Ia, Dec 17, 1873, Frances Augusta, b Comanche, Ia, Jan 26, 1857, dau of Oliver Herman and Mary Cornelia (Stetson) Jackson. He a carpenter Both living at Chicago Child:

855 Charles Herbert, b Clinton, Ia, Dec 1, 1879, m. Chicago June 6, 1905, Cecilia Almira, b. there Oct 14, 1883, dau. of John James and Wilhelmina Ann (Rector) Patterson No issue

520

EDGAR THOMAS (Eli, Nathan, Joseph, Elisha), m. at West Troy, N Y, Oct 31, 1877, Nellie, b. New York City Sept 16, 1855,

THE DESCENDANTS OF ELISHA COLE 139

dau of Thomas Firth and Hannah Lavinia (Stevens) Green He a farmer Both living in Michigan Children (born at Fairfield, Mich)

 856 James Garfield b Feb 17, 1880
 857 Roy Edgar, b Aug 17, 1881
 858 Bessie, b Feb 10, 1885
 859 Florence, b Oct 14, 1886
 860 Harly, b June 22, 1890.
 861 Oscar Gregory, b Aug 8, 1893
 862 Milo Van Dusen, b Sept 21, 1899.

523

HASCALL MYRON (Edwin W, Nathan, Joseph, Elisha); m at Adrian, Mich, May 30, 1867, Alaida, b Albany, N. Y, Nov. 22, 1846, dau of Peter, Jr, and Almeda Maria (Brayton) Van Loon Both living at Adrian, Mich

He enlisted in the 18th Regt, Mich Vol Inf, and was mustered in Aug 26, 1862, was Sergeant-Major of the regiment for several months previous to Sept 24, 1864, on which date he was captured with 250 other men of the regiment by Gen. N B Forrest and was held prisoner until April 29, 1865 He was commissioned Second Lieutenant March 22, 1865, although absent, a prisoner He was never wounded but received a bullet through coat sleeve Children (born at Adrian) ·

 863 Walter Hascall, b Sept. 14, 1869, m at Denver, Colo, Oct. 8, 1904, Mary Lillian, b Feb 11, 1871, in Wayland, Mich., dau of Edward Payson and Harriet (Morton) Hersey Both living in Denver. No issue
+864 Harry Putnam, b. Oct 25, 1871
 865 Van Loon Brayton, b Jan. 9, 1876; d July 27, 1882.
+866 Arthur Vincent, b Dec 6, 1879
 867 Florence Adelaide, b Jan 6, 1886; d Dec 29, 1906

524

NATHAN W (Edwin W , Nathan, Joseph, Elisha) , m at Afton, Wis , Sept 20, 1866, Carrie Anna, b Palmyra, N Y , Sept 20, 1845, dau of Philip and Lucinda (Potter) Palmer. He d. Chicago March 18 1877 She living

He enlisted in 1862 in the 18th Regt , Mich. Vols , was appointed Corporal, and being a printer by trade, was detailed on special service, having charge of the Government Printing Office at Nashville, Tenn , until the close of the war Child.

 868 Carrie Louise, b Chicago Feb. 29, 1868 , m at Kansas City, Mo , Jan 15, 1890, John William, b Grand View, Ill , Jan 15, 1857 son of James and Elizabeth (McCollum) Paxton Both living in Kansas City

532

ARVAH HOPKINS (Milo Van Dusen, Nathan, Joseph, Elisha) ; m at Covert, N Y , Oct 11, 1871, Mary, b there Jan 6, 1849, dau of Miner T and Jane (Uhl) Coburn Both living at Covert Children:

 869 Milo Wilbur, b Nov 13, 1872, d Jan 12, 1873
 870 Miner Coburn, twin of above , m Sept 8, 1898, Cora M Tichenor They have:

  Ralph Tichenor, b Sept 13, 1903

 871 Agnes Maria, b July 6, 1875 , m Gilbert D Townsend They have·

  Arvah C , b June 24, 1897
  Carlton G , b. June 16, 1899

 872 Carrie Moore, b Sept 11, 1879
 873 Jane Bradley, twin of above

  Carrie Moore m March 7, 1906, Don A Hopkins

537

WALLACE HENRY (Ramah, Levi H , Joseph, Elisha) , m at Brooklyn, N Y , Nov 21, 1866, Emma Louisa, b. there May

8, 1847, dau. of Samuel Wyatt and Maria (Waring) Marston He was a salesman, and d June 24, 1908 She living Children (born in Brooklyn)

    874 Lillian M , b May 28, 1868, d Dec 1, 1869
    875 Hayward C , b March 30, 1871 , d Jan 30, 1872
    876 Ida, b Dec 10, 1873; m at Croton Falls Nov 31, 1900, Jesse Foster, b Newburgh, N Y , April 8, 1875, son of Robert and Anne Eliza (McCann) Carr. Both living in Newburgh
    877 Edith, b Dec 19, 1875 , m at Mahopac Oct. 20, 1905, Chauncey Brooks, b Newburgh July 21, 1876, son of Charles Oscar and Leora (Brooks) Edmonds
    878 Alice, b March 20, 1884

539

FRANK JOSIAH (Ramah, Levi H , Joseph, Elisha) ; m at Brooklyn June 6, 1881, Evangeline Virginie, b Chancellorsville, Va , Nov 5, 1850, dau of Dr. Samuel Smith and Eliza Ann (Wyckoff) Guy. She d at Plainfield, N J , Nov 7, 1883, and he m. (2) at Brooklyn Feb 10, 1885, Marie Louise, b Brooklyn May 6, 1858, a sister of his first wife. Both living at Orange, N J. Children:

    879 Margaret, b June 21, 1882; d. Aug 2, 1883.
    880 Evangeline, b Dec 23, 1885
    881 Charlotte Louise, b. Sept 3, 1887, m Jan 7, 1907, George Wesley, b Glen Cove, L. I., Feb 21, 1883, son of William and Eliza (Hambridge) Maidment
    882 Ramah Elliot, b May 8, 1889
    883 Grace Manchester, b Aug 25, 1890.
    884 Frederick Tripler, b Feb. 23, 1893

543

HERBERT MILTON (John B , Levi H , Joseph, Elisha) , m at Hyde Park, Mass , Oct 27, 1897, Dorothy Elizabeth, b.

Augusta, Me, Dec 1, 1870, dau. of George Henry and Sarah (Barton) Snow. Both living Children (born at Hyde Park):

    885 Richard Barton, b May 23, 1900
    886 Horace Wellington, b Jan 23, 1903

556

EDWARD JUDSON (Adaniram J, Ramah, Joseph, Elisha), m. at Quincy, Mich, Oct. 26, 1887, Cora Electa, b. there March 31, 1864, dau of Milan Marcellus and Jane Hannah (McNeal) Brown He a mechanic Both living at Quincy Children:

    887 Bessie Jane, b Quincy Aug 24, 1888
    888 Arnet Judson, b Durand Feb 21, 1892
    889 Rama Milan, b Durand Oct. 1, 1893.
    890 Ruth Violet, b Quincy April 25, 1897.

559

CHARLES (William M Ramah, Joseph, Elisha), m at Mancelona, Mich, May 15, 1897, Edith, b April 8, 1880, dau of William and Docia (Soper) Mason Both living at Kalkaska, Mich Children (born at Leetsville):

    891 Clyde, b July 29, 1899
    892 Claude, b Sept 4, 1902.

561

CLYDE (William M, Ramah, Joseph, Elisha); m at Cadillac, Mich., Sept 27, 1893, Nettie, b Parma, Mich, Aug 26, 1874, dau of George Washington and Harriet (Graham) Campbell. Both living at Kalkaska Children (born at Kalkaska)

    893 Bernice, b Oct 12, 1895
    894 Bertine, b Jan 4, 1898
    895 Clarence, b May 22, 1904

567

CHESTER ENOS (Horace, John, Daniel, Elisha); m at Urbana, N. Y, March 12, 1857, Sarah, b there April 15, 1838, dau of

Almeran and Zillah (Longwell) Retan She d Savona, N Y., March 16, 1891, and he m (2) at Watkins, N Y, Aug 9, 1893, Mrs Harriet Esther, b Dansville, N Y., June 13, 1839, dau of Dr Charles and Esther (Hulbert) Brown, and wid of Rev Sylvester J Lusk Both living at Savona He is in the coal, grain and feed business. Child

   896 Almeran Horace, b Savona Nov 16, 1859; m there Nov 18, 1880, Alina Ann, b Owego, N. Y, Dec 4, 1859, dau of George Hunber and Mary (Parker) Bennett Both living. No issue.

571

CHARLES WILLIAM (Hiram, John, Daniel, Elisha), m at Altay, N Y, Oct. 12, 1870, Emma Frances, b Wayne, N. Y., April 10, 1849, dau of Marcus and Havilah (Cole) Barrett He was a farmer, and d at Carmel April 15, 1888, aged 42 years, 10 months. She living near Penn Yan, N Y Children (born at Carmel) ·

   897 Homer, b Oct 23, 1871; d in 1873
   898 Grace Lorena, b Feb 14, 1875, d April 26, 1888.
   899 Cassie Belle, b Feb 4, 1881; m at Penn Yan Sept. 30, 1902, William Henry, b Milo, N Y., Feb 23, 1882, son of John and Lucy Ann (Shepard) Armstrong Both living at Penn Yan.

572

HENRY CLAY (Allen, Jesse, Daniel, Elisha), m at New York City Jan 3, 1867, Hannah Ann, b Feb 8, 1845, dau of Stephen W and Juliette (Ballard) Carver. He was a farmer and d at Carmel Sept 25, 1896, aged 55 years, 4 months, 13 days She d there Dec 23, 1903, aged 59 years, 10 months, 14 days Children (born at Carmel):

   900 Jesse Allen, b Jan 22, 1868, d June 16, 1870
   901 Henry Ballard, b Nov 24, 1869, unm ; lives at Mahopac

902 Marie Antoinette, b March 17, 1876, m New York City March 28, 1901, Howard Robert, b Phillipstown July 31, 1878, son of William Henry and Phebe Elizabeth (Tompkins) Stevens They live at Kent Cliffs
  903 Ward Wallace, b July 4, 1878, d. Oct. 15, 1881.
 +904 De Witt Clinton, b Aug 28, 1879
  905 Norvin Green, b Oct 18, 1882
  906 John Roberts, b. Dec 21, 1886

574

THEODORE FRELINGHUYSEN (Ogden, Daniel H, Daniel, Elisha), m May 21, 1865, Emma Safronia, b April 5, 1846, dau of Dr. Isaac and Mary Ann (Cole) Barrett She d. at Cole's Mills July 26, 1893, and he m (2) at Carmel March 29, 1898, Mrs Emma, b Sept 25, 1852, at Fishkill, dau of Samuel and Elizabeth (Sprague) Sprague, and wid of James J. Dakin He was a miller and lived at Cole's Mills until the reservoir was built, when he removed to Carmel He d Dec 6, 1906 She living at Carmel. Children (born at Cole's Mills):

 +907 Charles Philip, b Feb. 19, 1867
 +908 Daniel H, b. Aug 6, 1868
  909 Annie E, b March 5, 1870, m June 24, 1893, Ernest Howard, b at Carmel in 1872, son of Eli and Elizabeth (Shears) Townsend Both living
  910 Arthur T, b Oct 18, 1872, d Oct 29, 1883.

576

GEORGE RICHARDSON (Tillott, Daniel H, Daniel, Elisha), m at Carmel Oct 29, 1890, Mary Downes, b Dec 6, 1853, dau of Lewis and Catharine (Pierce) GaNunn He was a druggist and later was in the livery business Was killed by a railroad train near Tilly Foster Station Dec. 21, 1901 She living at Carmel. Child

  911 George Tillott, b Carmel June 17, 1895

577

LEWIS EDGAR (Tillott, Daniel H, Daniel, Elisha), m at Kent Dec 28 1879, Sarah, b there June 12, 1858, dau of John and Pamelia (Sprague) Bennett She d Oct 29, 1904 He living at Carmel He was one of the contractors who built the New York & Putnam Railroad At one time he was proprietor of the Smalley House at Carmel He was appointed Sheriff of Putnam County by Gov Hill in 1888 Children:

- 912 Edith Z, b Oct 18, 1881
- 913 May Belle, b April 8, 1892

585

MORTIMER BELDING (Charles N, Elisha J, Daniel, Elisha), m. at Stanford. N Y, Sept 11, 1880, Antoinette, b Stanford, Dutchess County, Jan 14, 1857, dau of Isaac G and Sarah Ann (Badgley) Sands Both living In 1887 he settled at Salt Point, Dutchess County, N Y, where he now lives He is a miller Children.

- 914 Stanley Sands, b Nov 11, 1881, at Stanford.
- 915 Jennie Antoinette, b Clinton May 27, 1883
- 916 Peninnah Owen, b Stanford Dec 29, 1886

608

HORTON SHERWOOD (Anthony W, Nathaniel, Ebenezer, Elisha); m at Belleville, Kans Jan. 28, 1879, Hannah Elizabeth, b Romney, Va, July 17, 1856, dau of David and Mary Jane (McNemor) Doran He is a farmer and lives at Republic, Kans. Children (born at Republic)

- 917 Bertha May, b Nov 2, 1879, m Feb 21, 1900, Oliver Huff They have
    Dorothy May, b June 2, 1901
    Oliver David, b. Oct 22, 1903
- 918 George Eugene, b May 7, 1884
- 919 Jacob Edwin, b Nov 26, 1886

612

WILLIAM JOHN (John D, William, Ebenezer, Elisha), m at New York City May 15, 1856, Elizabeth Ann, b March 12, 1837, dau of James and Elizabeth (Radcliff) Belshaw, of Edinburgh, Scotland She d. New York City July 23, 1872, and he m (2) New York City June, 1890, Emily Augusta Frost. They are living at Rutherford, N. J

He attended the Peekskill Academy until 18 years of age and then went to New York and learned the carpenter trade, after which he settled at Virogua, Wis., in 1856, where he manufactured carriages, etc Returning in a few years to New York he entered the real estate business. At the time of the riots, July, 1863, in saving a drafting-wheel from the mob, he received a fractured shoulder Children.

- 920 Mary Elizabeth, b June 18, 1857, Virogua, Wis.; m New York City June 2, 1879, James, b there Dec. 20, 1851, son of Robert and Jane (Belshaw) Hodge. Both live in New York City. No issue.
- 921 Ida Elmira, b New York City March 20, 1860; m. Walter George Nurse. They have:

    Walter,. b ———.
    Ethel, b ———
    Harriet, b ———

- 922 John B., b in 1862, d at age of three months
- 923 Clara, b. in 1868, d. y.
- 924 Genevieve, b Dec 1, 1870, m New York City June 8, 1898, Willard Goldthwaithe, b Salem, Mass., July 13, 1868, son of Henry Merrill and Eliza Shatswell (Symonds) Bixby She d. New City Nov 29, 1901. He living.
- 925 William J, b in 1872, d y

Second marriage:

- 926 May, b. ———
- 927 Irene, ———.
- 928 William, b ———.
- 929 Frank, b ———.
- 930 Elsie, b ———.

614

CHARLES OGDEN (James, Ebenezer, Ebenezer, Elisha), m July 22, 1871, Selenia, b. Feb 13, 1852, dau. of William J. and Mary (Haight) Hoffman. He a hatter Both living at Putnam Valley Children

931 Vincent Peter, b Aug 11, 1874, m June 18, 1900, Josie, dau of William Kent
932 William J, b. Dec 8, 1875, m June 3, 1903, Viola Austin
933 Jeremiah, b. Aug 3, 1878, m Nov. 4, 1906, Nellie B Lewis
934 Lurana Elizabeth, b Jan 8, 1884.

615

PETER JAMES (James Ebenezer, Ebenezer, Elisha), m Nov 11, 1874, Margaret Lavinia, b Putnam Valley Dec 31, 1859 dau. of Reuben and Eliza Jane (Miller) McKeel He a hatter. Both living at Peekskill Child.

+935 Edward James, b Feb 28, 1876

625

JAMES HENRY (Thomas, James, Ebenezer, Ebenezer, Elisha); m. at Kent Nov 1, 1871, Ellen, b there April 30, 1850, dau. of Putnam and Eunice M (Smith) Light Both living at Danbury. Children:

+936 George Light, b Aug 28, 1872, at Kent
+937 Thomas Edgar, b Aug. 2, 1874, at Kent
938 James A, b at Danbury Nov 2, 1888

626

THERON (Edwin, James, Ebenezer, Elisha), m at Pawling, N. Y, Dec. 15, 1875, Huldah Victoria, b there Sept 10, 1854, dau of Carl Shaw and Huldah (Silleck) Booth Both living at Holmes, N Y He a farmer. Children.

939 Edwin Carl, b Jan 12, 1877.
940 Huldah Booth, b Dec 16, 1879
941 Abel B, b Dec 16, 1885.
942 Child, b and d in 1889
943 Clinton Harold, b Aug 27, 1891.
944 James Riley, b Nov 14, 1893

628

EBENEZER (Edwin, James, Ebenezer, Elisha); m at Pawling Feb 1, 1888, Mary Amelia, b West Petterson, N. Y., Aug. 9, 1869, dau of George W and ——— (Merritt) Carey. He a farmer Both living at Holmes, N Y Child

945 Catharine Beatrice, b Nov 29, 1895.

636

EUGENE (Ebenezer, James, Ebenezer, Elisha); m at Haviland Hollow Oct 15, 1882, Henrietta, b at Reynoldsville, N. Y., dau of George P. and Maria (White) Ballard He was a farmer, and d at Holmes, N. Y., Oct 2, 1898 Children:

946 Jennie W, b Aug. 5, 1885.
947 George C, b Dec 25, 1888
948 Rixford, b Feb 22, 1892.
949 Howard, b May 27, 1894
950 Ethel, b March 21, 1896
951 Eugenia, b Oct 4, 1898

637

ALBERT G (Ebenezer, James, Ebenezer, Elisha), m at Kent Dec 24, 1885, Euphemia, b there Sept 26, 1865, dau of John and Chloe (Russell) Lee He is a cattle dealer, and they live at Shenandoah, Dutchess County, N Y Children

952 Sepha, b Jan 10, 1889
953 Mildred, b. Feb 10, 1907

THE DESCENDANTS OF ELISHA COLE

638

FERRIS E (Ebenezer, James, Ebenezer, Elisha), m at Ludingtonville, N. Y, Dec 4, 1887, Mary A, b at Pawling, N Y, 1873, dau of Warren and Mary (Turner) White They live at Holmes, N. Y Children

    954 Ada M, b Jan 22, 1889
    955 Ella M b Dec 25, 1890
    956 Gracie B, b Oct 14, 1892
    957 Everett F., b May 2, 1895.

643

OTIS (Amos R, Lewis, John, Elisha), m at Rochester, N Y., Nov. 29, 1855, Jennie Frances, b at Duxbury, Mass, Oct 3, 1832, dau of William and Eunice (Phelps) Knapp They lived at Rochester He was a Grand Army man, having served in the 33rd Regt, N Y State Vols, was also a 33rd degree Mason. He d at Bath, N Y, June 16, 1903 She d at Rochester, N. Y, July 24, 1892 Children·

  +958 Wray Lincoln, b at Adrian, Mich, July 21, 1858
    959 Clara Mabel, b at Rochester, N Y, July 13 1867; m there Nov 7, 1894, Maynard Hosmer, b there Nov 1, 1867, son of John M and Mary (Armstrong) Chase Both living No issue

645

LEWIS W (Darius, Lewis, John, Elisha), m Nov 15, 1866, Diana, dau of William and Ann (Pierson) Jackson She d May 22, 1890, and he m (2) Dec 31, 1903, Clara Bell Dronyor, of Rawlin, Mich He is a farmer. Children

    960 Allen, b June 28, 1870, m Angeline Clark
    961 Fred. b Dec 6, 1872; m Maine Kirkup
    962 Elsie b Dec 19, 1879, m Marvin Rhodes
    963 Darius, b Sept 6, 1883, m Myrtie Stafford.

647

AMOS ROGERS TUNISON (Elvin C., Lewis, John, Elisha), m. at Rollin, Mich, Nov. 9, 1864, Elmira, b. there July 11, 1842, dau. of Porter and Susan (Brownell) Blade. He a farmer living at Rollin She d ———. Children (born at Rollin):

- 964 Susan Lydia, b. Aug. 27, 1865; m. March 4, 1885, Lewellyn, b. Feb. 26, 1864, son of John U and Charity (Comstock) Harkness. Both living at Rollin. Children
  Edna Lou, b ———.
  Elizabeth Pauline, b. ———.
- 965 Celia Octavia, b. Feb. 20, 1867, m at Rollin Dec. 23, 1887, Ed, b. there March 11, 1864, son of Henry and Mary J (Cornelius) Rawson. Both living They have·
  Olive, b ———.
  Amos P., b ———.
- 966 Elvira Rosanna, b. Sept. 9, 1872; m. Abram Knowles. They have:
  Cole Clinton, b. ———.
  Milton, b. ———.
  Nathan, b ———.
  Elmira, b. ———.
- 967 De Witt Clinton, b. Jan. 7, 1874; m. Mabel, dau. of John DeLong He is dead.

650

ELVIN DAYTON (Elvin C, Lewis, John, Elisha); m. at Clayton, Mich, March 9, 1881, Alice Edna, b. there June 13, 1858, dau of Freeman and Lucretia (Van Voorhies) Rice He was a farmer, and d. July 18, 1905. She living at Addison, Mich. Children (born at Rollin)

- 968 Nellie Lucretia, b. Aug 31, 1882; d Sept 7, 1882.
- 969 Ray Freeman, b Sept. 13, 1885.

651

OGDEN (Elmer C, Lewis, John, Elisha), m at Rollin Oct 10, 1863, Hannah H, b May 14, 1845, dau of John R and Hannah T. (Hayward) Hawkins. He was a cattle raiser and lived at Rollin, Mich. Children:

    970 Elmer Elkanah, b April 9, 1865; m Oct 17, 1889, Lizzie E. Gardner.
    971 Rose Althea, b Aug 22, 1876; m July 15, 1900, Fred W. Breunig
    972 Mina Elizabeth, b March 6, 1883

652

JOHN ROGERS (Elmer C, Lewis, John, Elisha), m ———, Elizabeth Mary, b. Rochester, N Y, ———, dau of William M and Mary Geraldine (Scott) Hawkins. He a photographer Both living at Richmond, Va Children·

    973 William Elmer, b June 25, 1870, m Aug 14, 1902, Lucie S Blount
    974 Ida Lucretia, b Nov 6, 1875; m April 22, 1897, Harry T. Jones.
    975 Kate Geraldine, b. Jan 30, 1888.
    976 Frank Ogden, b Dec. 31, 1890

679

CHESTER GLENN (Chester S, Abner B, David, Elisha, Elisha); m at Corning, N. Y., Dec. 2, 1889, Harriet Ellen, b there Sept. 3, 1861, dau of Charles C B and Maria D (Townsend) Walker. Both living at Corning

He is president of the Corning Building Company. At the time his father, Chester Scott Cole, was chairman of the Republican State Committee, his father-in-law, Charles C. B. Walker, was chairman of the Democratic State Committee Children:

    977 Sidney Townsend, b. Feb 22, 1892
    978 Glen Walker, b May 14, 1895.
    979 Dorothy Drake, b Jan 29, 1901.

682

ARTHUR (James, Nathan, David, Elisha, Elisha), m at Moscow, Idaho, February, 1898, Jennie, b Jan 11, 1877, dau of ——— Parks and wid of Walter Hanna Living at Pullman, Wash Children.

    980 Dwight, b July 4, 1899
    981 Horace, b. ———
    982 Ralph, b. ———.

711

CLAYTON (Norman S , David, Elisha, Elisha, Elisha); m at Matteawan, N Y , June 7, 1883, Idaho, b there March 16, 1863, dau of Sylvester and Almira (Cornwell) Mase Living at Matteawan Children

    983 Irving Preston, b March, 1884, d November 20, 1886
    984 Norma, b Jan 20, 1888.

746

ARTHUR (John Roberts, Hyman, John, Elisha, Elisha), m New York City Oct 23, 1895, Albertine, b there Jan 29, 1870, dau of Benjamin and Mary (———) Fogle. Living at Orange, N J He in the trucking business in New York City. Children

    985 Helen, b July 10, 1896
    986 Muriel, b Sept 1, 1902

747

GEORGE EDWARD (John R , Hyman, John, Elisha, Elisha); m New York City, 1898, Edith, b there in 1875, dau of Samuel and Elizabeth (Luscott) Cool He m (2) Aug 24, 1907, at Waterbury, Conn , Florence Emma, b there in 1880, dau of Charles and Lucy Emma (Frost) Chatfield They live in Connecticut Child·

    987 Marjorie, b ———

749

WALTER BAILEY (Addison, Hyman, John, Elisha, Elisha), m at Rockaway Beach April 25, 1894, Margaret Jane, b New York City Oct 17, 1870, dau of Jeremiah and Anna Leslie (Gracie) Charde He d June 1, 1901. Children (born at Mahopac).

    988 Lester Stanley, b. April 22, 1896
    989 Velma Bailey, b Nov 20, 1897

752

ABNER BANGS (John P, Abner B, Nathan, Nathan, Elisha); m at Aurora, Ore, January, 1897, Glorinda Neil Child

    990 Maple Lucille, b Nov 2, 1897.

753

JOHN REASONER (John P, Abner B, Nathan, Nathan, Elisha), m. Feb 15, 1886, Ida F Smith Living at Aurora, Ore Children:

    991 Benjamin Otto, b April 24, 1888
    992 Roxie Lura, b. Oct 11, 1895
    993 Barrel Ellis, b April 22, 1896
    994 Vida Beatrice, b. May 1, 1900.
    995 Ivy Annita, b. Sept 1, 1904

754

NATHAN EDWARD (John P, Abner B., Nathan, Nathan, Elisha); m at Aurora, Ore, Nov 1, 1893, Frances Beck. Children

    996 Ruby Beatrice, b Oct 10, 1895
    997 Hazel Eunice, b Jan 6, 1901.
    998 Lester Abner, b Sept 16, 1903.

756

CHRISTOPHER OLIVER (John P., Abner B, Nathan, Nathan, Elisha), m at Bellingham, Wash, Sept 22, 1904, Dagmer Beck Living at Aurora, Ore Child:

    999 Olive O, b Aug 8, 1907

765

AUSTIN (Zachary T., Hermon C, Nathan, Nathan, Elisha), m. at Brooklyn, N Y, Aug. 31, 1898, Ivy, b at Baltimore, Md., May 21, 1875, dau of Prentiss and Rosa (Langley) Ingraham. Living at St. Louis Children.

1000 Austin, b at Los Angeles, Cal., Jan 26, 1902.
1001 Prentiss Ingraham, b. at Chicago Aug 16, 1904.

778

JOHN JACKSON (Amedee B, Nathan, Nathan, Nathan, Elisha); m at Joplin, Mo, July 4, 1905, Dorothy Walker, b. May 24, 1888. Child:

1002 Amedee Jackson, b June 8, 1906

797

JAMES STANLEY (Harvey T, Charles G, Joseph, Joseph, Elisha); m at Anderson, Ind, Aug 10, 1892, Cora May, b at Columbus, Ind., July 30, 1875, dau. of William Alfred and Narcy (Sullivan) Doyle He is a glass blower. They live at Fostoria, Ohio. Children (born at Alexandria, Ind):

1003 Victoria, b Aug 8, 1895.
1004 Ralph Leroy, b. March 20, 1900.
1005 J Stanley, b March 23, 1905

798

HARVEY TOWNSEND (Harvey T, Charles G., Joseph, Joseph, Elisha); m. at Corning, N Y., June 8, 1898, Anna Louise, b. Aug 26, 1871, at Avoca, N. Y, dau. of Alfred Cleveland and Louise Malvina (Parker) Olds He is a bookkeeper in the First National Bank at Corning, where they both live. Child:

1006 Howard F. Victor, b. Sept 21, 1899

799

OTTO PARIS (Harvey T, Charles G, Joseph, Joseph, Elisha); m. at Corning, N. Y, Oct 9, 1901, Grace, b. at Elmira, N. Y.,

April 26, 1876, dau of Elmer Ezekiel and Eliza (Brown) Johnson He is a stenographer Both living at Corning Child.

 1007 Dorothy Lucille, b Sept 20, 1907

801

NATHAN THOMPSON (Harvey T., Charles G, Joseph, Joseph, Elisha); m at Hornby, N Y, Aug 20, 1903, Idalia, b. there June 26, 1884, dau. of Robert O'Hara and Sarah Jane (Cutler) Sly He is a freight agent, N Y. C & H R R Both living at Corning. Child

 1008 Robert Sly, b July 9, 1906

809

ALBERT GEORGE (George F, Ira, Joseph, Joseph, Elisha), m at Zanesfield, Ohio, Sept 25, 1901, Leota, b there July 9, 1881, dau. of George and Elizabeth (Shoots) Peters He is a railroad conductor Both living at Springfield, Ohio Children:

 1009 Edward Cammon, b. at Bellefonte, Ohio, Dec 24 1903
 1010 Lucille Ruth, b at Springfield, Ohio, Dec. 25, 1906

813

FRANK (Charles L., Ira, Joseph, Joseph, Elisha), m. ———, Rose Kimmick, b ———. Children:

 1011 Ira, b ———.
 1012 Ruth, b. ———.
 1013 Charles, b. ———.
 1014 Stuart, b. ———.

815

IRA WOODRUFF (Charles L, Ira, Joseph, Joseph, Elisha); m. at Watkins, N Y, Oct. 26, 1898, Fannie Ames, b. there July

28, 1875, dau of John Spafford and Sarah (Ames) Budd
Both living at Watkins. He is a druggist. Children

    1015   Frank Ames, b April 14, 1900
    1016   Amy Budd, b Oct 6, 1906

820

MORTIMER (Harlem, Asahel, Joseph, Joseph, Elisha); m. at Corning N. Y, Dec 27, 1888, Nellie, b there April 15, 1868, dau of Frank and Mary Elizabeth (Wormley) Veith Both living at Youngstown, Ohio He is a printer and has the Joseph Cole family record Children:

    1017   Howard, b at Corning Sept 7, 1889
    1018   Norman b at Youngstown June 28, 1891.
    1019   Helen, b at Youngstown Sept. 29 1893
    1020   Margaret, b at Youngstown July 3, 1896

827

JAY C (Yates T, Joseph, Samuel, Joseph, Elisha); m. Nov 11, 1886, Minnie, b at Hartland, Mich, April 24, 1866, dau. of George and Anna (Kershner) Lemen Both living at Durand, Mich. Children:

    1021   Crystal J, b June 4, 1890
    1022   Anna Ruth, b. April 14, 1893
    1023   Dorothy M, b Jan 8, 1900

836

ELMER ELLSWORTH (Delevan S, Enos, Samuel, Joseph, Elisha); m in Kansas Ella C, b Nov 4, 1858, dau of Daniel and Mary Etta (Pratt) Cass He is a farmer and has 320 acres of land at Ft Laramie, Wyo, where they both live. Children:

    1024   Bessie Laura, b March 30, 1884
    1025   Daniel Delevan Pratt, b July 26, 1886
    1026   Elmer Emery Cass b July 26, 1889, d June 1, 1890

837

EUGENE ENOS (Delevan S , Enos, Samuel, Joseph, Elisha), m at Grand Island, Neb , Nov 28, 1885, Harriet Jane, b in Michigan Feb 18, 1870, dau of Charles H and Harriet (Devall) Morgan. He is a machinist Both living at Miller, Neb Children

- 1027 Laura Jane, b April 17, 1887, at Hastings, Neb , m. April 17, 1905, John W Sterns
- 1028 Viola May, b at Stockholm, Neb , March 6, 1890, m Feb 18, 1908, Oliver P Rammer
- 1029 Ada Lulu, b March 9, 1892
- 1030 Vera Daisy, b April 18, 1894 , d April 20, 1907
- 1031 Charles Eugene, b March 14, 1898 , d. Jan 25, 1907.
- 1032 Fannie Belle, b Sept 5, 1900
- 1033 Elmer Archie, b at Miller, Neb , Nov 14, 1903
- 1034 Albert Levi, b Jan 30, 1906

838

JASON HAVEN (Delevan S , Enos, Samuel, Joseph, Elisha) ; m. April 17, 1889, Sarah McAuley, b at Chicago March 17, 1872 He d Aug 16, 1894, and she m (2) May 28, 1898, Harry Venton Downing Children

- 1035 Delevan Jason, b. in Cherry County, Neb., Feb 24, 1890
- 1036 Raymond Wiltsie, b Feb 20, 1892

839

ROBERT WALKER (Delevan S , Enos, Samuel, Joseph, Elisha) ; m at Hastings, Neb Aug 10, 1889, Mary, b in Russia April 3, 1871, dau of Jacob and Mary Lena (Hoop) Gettman He is a bricklayer Both live at Hastings. Children (born at Hastings) :

- 1037 Grace Lena, b Feb 1, 1890
- 1038 Louis Jacob, b Sept. 1, 1891
- 1039 Joseph George, b June 26, 1893

849

ORVILLE WEBSTER (Arthur E, Enos, Samuel, Joseph, Elisha);
m March 21, 1894, Gay, b at Conway, Mich., Aug. 15, 1873,
dau of Covert S. and Alice L (Copeland) Sherwood   Children:

    1040 Rollin Elwood, b May 9, 1895
    1041 Ruth Alva, b Jan. 23, 1897
    1042 Roger Garwood, b March 23, 1899.
    1043 Enos Covert, b Feb 5, 1901
    1044 Alice Fidelia, b. Dec 28, 1902.

864

HARRY PUTNAM (Hascall M, Edwin W, Nathan, Joseph,
Elisha), m at Adrian, Mich, Nov 25, 1891, Julia Viletta, b.
at Rome, Mich, July 4, 1871, dau of Daniel Porter and Emily
A (Sterns) Bates Both living at Cleveland, Ohio Children:

    1045 Harold Bates, b at Adrian, Mich, Jan 26, 1893
    1046 Lowell Vincent, b at Adrian Jan 20, 1898.

866

ARTHUR VINCENT (Hascall M., Edwin W, Nathan, Joseph,
Elisha), m at Sandwich, Cal, Oct 26, 1899, Daisy Ellen, b.
at Adrian, Mich., July 2, 1879, dau. of Frederick J and Elizabeth (Pratt) Buck Both living at Adrian Children (born there):

    1047 Francis Vincent, b March 25, 1901.
    1048 Frederick Lisle, b Oct 10, 1903.
    1049 Florence Helen, b March 28, 1907.

904

DE WITT CLINTON (Henry C, Allen, Jesse, Daniel, Elisha);
m at Lake Mahopac, N Y, Oct. 22, 1902, Gertrude Catharine,
b there Oct. 18, 1879, dau of Leonard Sloat and Emma Jane
(Van Loon) Wright They live on the old Elisha Cole farm
and he is in the livery business at Lake Mahopac. Children:

    1050 Doris Emma, b July 4, 1903.
    1051 Henry Leonard, b June 27, 1904

907

CHARLES PHILIP (Theodore F., Ogden, Daniel H, Daniel, Elisha); m. at Carmel, N. Y, Oct 20, 1897, Estelle Jane, b. March 12, 1878, dau. of Benjamin and Adeline (Hopkins) Secord. Both living at Carmel.

(Secord—a corruption of Secour The earliest tombstone in Putnam County bearing this name is in a Presbyterian cemetery at Mahopac Falls, to Elizabeth, wife of John Secor, who died in 1791 The first of the name in records was James Sycar, Sr., living, aged 75 years, in New Rochelle, N. Y, on Sept. 9, 1710 The name is found on records as Se Cord, Seacord, and Secord They were French Protestants.) Children:

    1052   Raymond Lamont, b July 29, 1898
    1053   Olive Secord, b Dec 15, 1899
    1054   Haywood P, b. June 13, 1902, d in July, 1903
    1055   Charles Homer, b Dec 4, 1903.
    1056   Emma Estelle, b Oct 17, 1906
    1057   Esther Adeline, twin of above.

908

DANIEL H. (Theodore F, Ogden, Daniel H, Daniel, Elisha); m. at Carmel in January, 1896, Matilda, b. there in 1873, dau. of John Wesley and Matilda (Morley) Forshay Child

    1058   Paul Forshay, b Sept. 5, 1906.

935

EDWARD JAMES (Peter J, James, Ebenezer, Ebenezer, Elisha); m at Peekskill Aug 12, 1900, Kittie, b. there May 18, 1876, dau of Samuel and Harriet Amelia (Ferris)) Tate. He is in the fur business Both living at Peekskill. Children:

    1059   Edward Earl, b March 4, 1901.
    1060   Helen Margaret, b. Dec. 2, 1902.
    1061   George Peter, b July 3, 1905

936

GEORGE LIGHT (James H , Thomas, James, Ebenezer, Elisha);
m. at Ludingtonville Sept 18, 1895, Carrie M , b. at East Fishkill Oct 12, 1868, dau of George W and Hannah E (Northrup) Merritt. Both living at Jersey City, N. J Children:

    1062 Ellen Marian, b at Poughkeepsie, N Y , Aug 15, 1896
    1063 Donald Merritt, b Westville, Conn , Nov 6, 1898
    1064 James Vernon, b West Haven, Conn , July 7, 1901.
    1065 Frances Nelson, b at Yonkers, N Y., Jan 19, 1903.

937

THOMAS EDGAR (James H., Thomas, James, Ebenezer, Elisha);
m at Ludingtonville, N Y , Oct 2, 1895, Mary M , b at South East, N Y , Sept 13 1872, dau of Thomas and Mary (Keyes) Brien She d at Kent, Dec 5, 1905, and he m (2) at Lake Mahopac, April 19, 1908, Wilhelmina, b New York City, April 2, 1885, dau of Jacob and Wilhelmina (Faatz) Karl Both living at Carmel Children:

    1066 Florence B , b. Patterson, N. Y., Nov. 21, 1896
    1067 Edith M , b Kent, April 23, 1898.
    1068 Cordelia L., b Sept. 13, 1900
    1069 Thomas Edgar, b Oct 8, 1904.

958

WRAY LINCOLN (Otis, Amos R., Lewis, John, Elisha); m at Rochester, N Y., Jan 31, 1884, Julia Hill, b there March 16, 1857, dau. of Homer G and Helen (Woodward) Robinson She d June 29, 1897, and he m (2) at Bath, N. Y., Oct 31, 1900, Mrs Mary A Bird, b Bath, Oct. 31, 1858, dau. of Burrage and Mary Fowler (Smith) Rice He is a contractor and also in the real estate business, and lives at Rochester, N. Y. Child

    1070 Donald Robinson, b Oct 17, 1885

OTHER COLES OF PUTNAM COUNTY

While collecting the descendants of Elisha Cole the name was frequently encountered in Eastern Putnam County, and research brought out the fact that they were of different descent. It is thought best to give here a short genealogical sketch of this family in order to avoid confusion at some future date

Timothy, b at Norwalk, Conn, 1784, the third child of Thomas and Mary (Ressequie) Cole

Samuel, b Norwalk, 1791, sixth child of Thomas and Mary

Timothy settled in South East, Dutchess Co., N Y., and m Elizabeth Sterling of Amenia He d 1866, aged 82 years She d 1867, aged 76 years Buried in Milltown Cemetery Children:

+1 Emery, b April 19, 1811
 2 Edwin, b ———, m ——— Clarissa Fowler
 3 Mary, b 1816; d March 20, 1838
 4 Minerva, b 1821, d April 19, 1849.
+5 George, b 1813-14.
 6 Elisa Ann, m William Colmore She d and he m (2) his sister-in-law Sallie Cole Lived at Wilton, Conn.
 7 Sallie, b. ———.

1

EMERY (Timothy), m Ann Sutton She d and he m. (2) at South Dover, May 9, 1860, Mary Frances, b there April 3, 1832, dau. of David W and Nancy Ann (Giddings) Stevens He d. March 18, 1904 She living at Pawling, N Y. Children:

 8 George, b 1844
 9 Frank, b ———.
10 Edwin Charles, b ———
11 Mary, b ———, m Augustus Pendley She m. (2) Myron Andrews She m (3) Marshall Smith Lived at Skaneateles, N Y

By second marriage.

+12 Albert Stevens, b. May 21, 1863
13 William Wallace, b Sept. 15, 1864, m Laura Dennis.
14 Eliza Belle, b Jan 27, 1870.

5

GEORGE (Timothy); m Malissa B., b. South East, Oct. 22, 1821, dau. of Charles and Phebe (Crosby) Townsend. They lived at South East He d. in 1898 She d. Danbury, Oct. 24, 1907. Children:

15 Frank, b ———; living at Brewster
16 Estelle J, b. ———; m. ———, Brush.

12

ALBERT S (Emery, Timothy); m Clarie Belle Thomas. Children:

17 Lavenia Stevens, b. May 8, 1885
18 Howard Thomas, b Dec. 5, 1886.
19 Bulah Virginia, b July 7, 1888.
20 Vera Giddings, b. June 30, 1889
21 Edwin Russell, b Sept. 7, 1892
22 Clarie Belle, b Jan 23, 1899

Samuel (son of Thomas and Mary Cole) m Deborah Egleston. They lived at Patterson and South East Children:

23 William, b ——— 1817
24 Olonzo, b 1819
25 Henry, b ———.
26 Augustus, b 1830
27 Charles, b 1834.

First Generation of Collateral Branches

[CHILDREN NOT ALWAYS IN ORDER OF BIRTH]

5

Hackaliah Merritt—Eunice Cole.

Children:

Elisha, b 1768, d Aug. 17, 1841, m Desiah Fuller
Mary, m. (1) Jonathan Washburn, (2) John Griffin.
Hannah, m John Merrick.
Nemehiah; m ———— Wait, lived Canada.

Second marriage:

Nathan Crosby—Eunice (Cole) Merritt

Children:

Enoch, b. 1782; m Jane Kelley; b. 1784, d Nov. 10, 1862.
Eunice, d. Sept 4, 1862; m James Randall.
Stephen; m Hannah ————.

7

Freeman Hopkins—Hannah Cole.

Children.

Enos, d. unm.
Freeman

8

Jesse Smith—Naomi Cole.

Children

Anna, b April 10, 1785, m Nov 10, 1801, Thomas Hazen,
  b April 6, 1775, d April 15, 1853.
Charles G., b. Feb 13, 1789, m Margaret Cole.
Nathaniel.
Sophia, d. y
Freeman, d unm.

10

James Townsend—Priscilla A Cole

Children:

Naomi, m (1) Robert Weeks, (2) Judah Kelley
Hannah; m. Barnabas Craver.
Susannah, m (1) Stephen Waring, (2) Noah H. Crane
Almira, d aged 13 years
Charles, m Sarah Frost
Alvey, d. unm.
Adalia; m Neurissa Cole
Mercy, m Issacher Merrick
Priscilla; m Levi Bailey.
James; m Betsey Lawrence.
Naomi was second wife of Robert Weeks and also of Judah Kelley
Hannah was first wife of Barnaba Carver. He m. (2) Sarah, dau. of Elisha Cole, Jr

11

Tracy Ballard—Mercy Cole

Children:

Joseph, m Rachel Wood
Benjamin, m Naomi Hopkins
Selah, m Melvina Cole
Zeba; m. Alyada Cole
Fannie, m. (1) Jesse Wilson, (2) Jerry Wilson.
Jane, m. Joseph Hopkins

18

William Agor—Elizabeth Cole

Children·

Charles, m. Eliza Banker, Nov 13, 1816
Naomi; m Samuel Hart
Orrin, m. Adah Austin
Orson, m Abagail Barrett

Hannah, m George Curry.
Arvilla, m William Sloat
Eliza; m John Todd
Sarah, d. unm

20

Thaddeus Baxter—Hannah Cole.

Children:

Jedidah; m Joshua or John Purdy.
Elisha C ; m. (1) Elizabeth Nelson, (2) Jane Warren, (3) Frances Wright
Beulah, m. Miles Bunnell.
Sarah H ; m James Nelson.
Thomas, m Uretta Cole
Oran, d unm.
Osmond M , m (1) Sarah Ann Merrick, (2) Jane Horton Armstrong

30

Henry Nichols—Susannah Cole.

Children

Joseph Cole, m Lorietta Northrup
Perry G , m (1) Phebe Colwell, (2) Viola Cavinder
Lewis, m. Adah Cole
Henry B., m Julia Haines
Daniel R , b 1806, m Sarah Hughson
Ruth, b Jan 21, 1809. d Sept 20, 1886, m Horace Smith, b Dec 16, 1793
Elizabeth, m Jeremy Hopkins
Susan, d y

31

Charles Green—Anna Cole

Children

Susan, Rebecca, Collins

35

Alvin Chase—Ruth Cole.

Children:

Cyrus; m. Zillah Colwell
Naomi; m. Clark Beardsley.
Darius, m Phebe Smith.
Susan; m. Hiram Smith.
Lyman; m. Elizabeth Evans.
Sarah Ann, m (1) Joseph Smith, (2) Daniel Brown
Hiram; m Ellen Lewis.
Henry Nichols; m (1) Mary Walker, (2) Jane ———.
Cynthia; m. Gilbert Knapp.
Mary W ; m. Stephen Hawley.
Frank, m. Sarah Tompkins.
John; m. Caroline Terrell.

37

Enos Hopkins—Cynthia Cole

Children:

Eliza Ann, b. Aug 10, 1810, m. Ansel Hazen.
Ruth, b May 8, 1812, m. Horace Cole
Antha Jane, b April 17, 1814; m. Thos. O. Cole.
Rebecca, b May 21, 1816; d unm
William A., b Dec. 5, 1818, m April 10, 1845, Hannah E. Sunderlin
Erastus, b. Jan 17, 1821, m Theda Cole.
Almira, b. April 10, 1825, m Dec. 15, 1847, Leonard Yeamans.

41

Rev Levi Hall—Margaret Cole.

Children:

Hannah, b Oct. 1, 1795; m ———.
Daniel, b Dec. 22, 1796, m Ann Newman
Susan, b Oct 27, 1798, m. Dec. 20, 1823, James Adams.

Ann, b Nov. 10, 1800, m March 24, 1821, Morris R. McCoy
Asa Thompson, b July 30, 1802
Adah, b. March 10, 1804, m Emsley Adams.
Zillah, b. Sept. 9, 1805, m David Edsall
Golda, b Aug. 30, 1808; d y
Jane, b Nov 16, 1809; m Levi B. Russell.
Elizabeth, b July 14, 1811, m. Isaiah Adams.

Second Marriage.

Asa Wilson—Margaret (Cole) Hall.

No record of issue

42

George Frost—Mary Cole.

Children:

Orville C ; m Sarah A. Smalley.
Morris, m Adeline Cole
Laura, m Caleb Hazen
Julia, m. (1) Coleman Crawford, (2) Hiram Hastings.
Harrison, d y.
Sarah J ; m Luman Sprague

43

Elmer Chase—Eunice Cole

Children·

Sophia, m Lewis Propeo (?)
Obed; m Maria Mack
Daniel, m Sarah Hamel
Robert, m Anna Cramer.
Iva, m David Lyon.
Henah; m Malon White.
Betsey; m. Elihu Reynolds
Lydia, m Bradley Burr
Maria, m. Alson Guthrie.

44

Nathan Hall—Sarah Cole

Children.

Daniel, m ——— Porter.
Annis, m. ——— Tunison.
Maria; m. ——— Tunison
Levi

47

Hosea Townsend—Ivah Cole.

Children:

Coleman, m Carrie Hotchkiss

48

Sylvanus Townsend—Henah Cole

Children.

Hannah, m Anson Hazen
Thomas, m Angeline Kingsley.
Hosea, m. Margarte Plate (?).
Susan, m Reuben Hyatt
Rachel, m. Elijah Austin.
Zillah, m William Pierson
George, m. Lucy Wolworth.
Frank, m Mary Johnson

50

Charles B Norton—Havilah Cole

Children:

Emily C, b Jan 26, 1826 m March 21, 1854, Rev. Henry C Hazen
Charles C, m Cerepta Noble
Alfred, m Dora Norton
Mary Jane, d. unm

52

Silas Selleck—Azubah Cole.

Children.

Joseph, m. ——— Horton.
Charles; m Lucretia Cole

53

William Farrington—Vashti Cole.

Children:

Ebenezer.
Charles.
Mary, m ——— Brower.
Jane; m ———.
——— m ——— Diamond

54

Ezra Kelley—Eliza Cole.

Children:

Ebenezer; m a widow and d in California.
Antoinette; m. George Merrick
Joseph.
Horton G
Vashti Jane
Margaret, m. ——— Washburn.
Sarah B ; m George Knapp

55

Ira Kelley—Annis Cole

Children·

Mary Jane; m Rev William B. Knapp
Austin; d. unm.
William F.; m ——— Cooper.
Albert; m. Fanny C. Tevis.
John; m. ——— Leonard.

Sarah E.; m. Clark Townsend
Alanson C.
Almira M , m Samuel B. Tuttle

60

John Odel—Naomi Cole.

Children.

James; m. (1) ——— Christian, (2) ———,
Charles, m. Martha A. Lickley.
William, d. y.
Mary, m. Leonard Cummings
Susan M.; m. James Hopkins

61

John Lickley—Mary Cole.

Children:

*Martha A., b Jan 28, 1810; d. unm. May 15, 1834.
Mary, b. Sept 25, 1811; m. Dr John G. Tompkins.
Margaret; m Thomas Utter
William C, b March 28, 1814; d Nov. 20, 1855; m. Julia Smith
James B , m. (1) Mary Bunnell, (2) Fayette Owen
Adelia, m James Romer.
John M , b. May 8, 1826, m. Emeline Horton
Ebenezer, b. Jan 6, 1830, d. unm.
Sarah Emeline, b. March 20, 1834; d Nov. 4, 1865; m. Robert Buckbee

*It is also said she m Charles Odel.

76

Eleazer II Baldwin—Hannah Cole

Children:

Reuben D ; m. Calista Hopkins.
Eliza; m. Henry S Baldwin.

77

Frederick Knox—Sarah Cole

Children:

Zillah, m Jerome La Due
Frederick H., m. Abby J. Reynolds.
Emily, m. Owen Sherrow.
John; m Martha T Baker.
Hannah, m. William Lyons
Charles; went to California
Reuben; m. (?).

81

Lewis Nichols—Adah Cole

Children·

Zillah, m Tillott Cole.
Chauncey; m. Emily Cole.
Edgar.
Edwin; m Naomi J Kelley
Henrietta; m. James Madison Newman.

92

William McKinstry—Sarah M. Cole.

Children·

Mary Elizabeth, m Sept 4, 1870, Cyrus A Rollins.
Betsey Amelia, b April 23, 1839, d unm. May 29, 1876.
Hannah Maria, m July 18, 1864, Charles P Wilcox.
Harriet Amanda, m June 28, 1870, Horace P Sheldon
William Paul, m Jan. 5, 1884, Stella D. Hart.
Lester Cole

96

John Reynolds—Naomi Cole

Children:

Emily.
Sarah; m (1) —— Hawkins, (2) ——.
Floyd.
Louisa.

101

Jesse Hughson—Sarah Jane Cole.

Children:

Harriet, m. William G. Hurlburt.
Le Grand; m Emma B Moss.
Julia, m. John S. Wheeler.
Harmon, d. unm.
Almond, d unm.
Mary, d. unm.
Jane, m John J Fisher.
Ann, d. unm.
Frances R., d. unm
James, d. unm.

105

Erastus Hopkins—Theda Cole.

Children:

Alice Augusta, b Feb. 13, 1851, m. March 20, 1879, Isaac L Barrett

Theron Cole, b Oct. 29, 1854; d. May 8, 1889; m. Sept 20, 1887, Emma Wilson

Chauncey Ambrose, b Feb. 22, 1870; m June 3, 1891, Antoinette Barrett

107

Mentor W Hazen—Rachel Cole

Children:

Rev. Henry C., b July 29, 1818, m (1) Sept 26, 1838, Frances A Ballard, (2) March 31, 1854, Emily L Norton.

Orson, m. Phebe Carver.

109

Bailey Howes—Mary Cole

Children:

Oscar, b April 30, 1831; m. Aug 8, 1858, Adelaide Hazen.

Byron, b. March 9, 1833, m. June, 1854, Mary Ketcham.
Felix, b May 15, 1838, m. 1866, Clara Getchell.

112

Edson Sloat—Eliza Cole.

Children:

Lydia Ann, m George Seaman.
Stanley, d. unm.

113

William Clauson—Minerva A. Cole

Children.

Olan, b. Oct 5, 1849, d unm. Feb. 24, 1879

Second Marriage.

James M. Brown—Minerva A (Cole) Clauson.
(No issue.)

116

Floyd Bailey—Eliza Cole.

Children.

Orville, m Hannah S Norton.
Thomas, m Elizabeth Fowler
Albro, d. unm.
Erastus, m Emma Robinson
Herbert, b Feb. 24, 1838; m. Jan 24, 1871, Lucy A. McMahan
Augusta, m Dr Elias Clark
Sarah; m Lewis H Durland.

122

Harry Hanford—Huldah Cole.

Children

Sarah, b Feb. 8, 1838, d Feb 10, 1838
Helen, b Feb 28, 1839, d March 24, 1854.

Hobart, b Feb 15, 1841, d Dec 16, 1845
Henry Clay, b Feb 2, 1844, m 1865, Jane Whitbeck
Heber H, b. Sept 13, 1846; m. October, 1874, Sarah Osborn.
H Byron, b Dec 15, 1851, m. Oct 13, 1880, Hattie E. Cortrite
Rufus, b May 12, 1854; d July 21, 1854
Hopkins J, b Oct 1, 1856, m. Feb 12, 1879, Mayme O'Connor
Erastus, b Sept 9, 1860; d. 1862

123

Isaac Kelley—Antoinette Cole

Children:

Lydia, b Oct 11, 1841, d Jan 28, 1883, m Jan 31, 1860, James H Nichols
Jessie, b May 10, 1843, d unm Nov. 26, 1860
Henrietta F, b July 9, 1845, d Aug 31, 1894, m Jan 30, 1875, Peter Z. Kirkham
Chauncey Ragan, b Jan 29, 1849, d Dec 15, 1883, m Oct. 8, 1874, Mary M Bell
Byronette Cole, b Feb 25, 1851, m Dec 28, 1869, William D Northrup
Nellie F b Sept 22, 1856, d. unm April 28, 1876
A daughter, d y

126

William Tunison—Julia Cole.

Children:

Eliza, m Theron Hamilton
Lydia Jane, m William McMillan
Charles, m. Ruth Crissey
Philip, m Lenora Trayer
Sarah L

127

Thomas Tunison—Anna Cole

Children:

Elizabeth, m. Caleb Crissey.
Sarah, m. William Conklin.
Ezra, m Harriet Knox.
Daniel Cole, m Lucy Hodge.
Susan, m. Henry Williams
John, m Helen Tenbrook

130

John Terry—Elizabeth Cole

Children:

Ann Elizabeth, b Oct. 13, 1832, d May 14, 1893, m Feb. 23, 1854, Vinton Cherry, he d May 24, 1894
John McClure, b Oct 18, 1835, m Dec 4, 1856, Mary Eliza Howe.
Ira Cole, b Feb 6, 1838; m Jan 21, 1873, Georgia Copley.
Cecelia Oselton, b Sept 20, 1841, m. Feb 6, 1868, Hiram Towne, d Jan. 28, 1894
Sarah Louise, b Aug 22, 1844, d March 16, 1881, m June 25, 1867, George H. Sauer

134

John C Hall—Adelia Cole

Children:

Augusta.
Ira C, b Oct. 9, 1846, m Carrie F Cole
Louise.

135

Pierpont Bassett—Sarah R Cole

Children:

Sarah L, m Eli Morehouse
John, m Helen Timerson
Frank, m Geneveve Jackson

136

James H Denison—Louisa Cole

Children (born at Sheboygan Falls, Wis)

Mary, b. Aug 2, 1847, m. Jan 11, 1872, Fred Leavens.
Gertrude, b Aug. 28, 1849, m May 29, 1872, Frank T. Bemis.
George H., b Dec 17, 1853, d. Feb 12, 1861.
Charles B , b July 27, 1855, d Feb 23, 1861
Frank H , b Feb 8, 1862, m Aug 8 1897, Agnes Cooper.
James Floyd, b Dec 12, 1866, unm

137

Morris Frost—Adeline Cole.

Children:

Susan, m Floyd Higgins
Laura, m. Emory Higgins.

145

Elah Ballard—Lydia Cole.

Children ·

Eliza A , m Elah B Hopkins
Susan, d. unm
Marietta, d. unm

158

Selah Ballard—Melinda Cole

Children

Amanda, b Feb 18, 1815, m Nov 6, 1831, Aaron Ganong
Frances A b ———; m Sept 27 1838, Henry C Hazen
Osman b Nov 24, 1817, m Jan 8, 1840, Augusta J Ganong
Abiathar R , b Sept 29, 1825 m Nov 6, 1850, Sarah Hederick

160

Stephen Wood—Rebecca Cole

Children:

Adelia Ann, m Augustus J Monroe

Berry Cole, b. Oct. 16, 1818, m Mary Ann Feigles, he d March 14, 1902.

Eliza Jane, b Sept 28, 1819, d Oct 20, 1891, m John G Lozier, b March, 1815, d Aug 23, 1887.

Jeremiah V, b. 1830, d May 30, 1864, in Union Army near Dalton, Ga.; m Elizabeth Vanderhoff He enlisted July 9, 1862, was a Sergeant, Company F, 107th N Y Infantry

161

Zeba Ballard—Alzada Cole.

Children:

Jane Ann; m Elam Hopkins.

Juliette, m Steven W Carver.

Hannah, m Jeremiah L Green

162

Ardalia Townsend—Neurissa Cole.

Children

Alveyson, m Phebe Jane Smith

Harriet, m George Weston

Lewis, m. (1) Emeline Whitney, (2) Julia Reynolds

Second Marriage

*William Smith—Neurissa (Cole) Townsend.

*William Smith was of a cheerful disposition and made it a rule never to cross a bridge until he came to it He possessed a fund of real wit He was a great reader and was well posted on current events When a young man he joined the Baptist Church at Carmel, N Y, and for many years was an active worker in the church

Children:

Ormond J , d unm
Hannah J.
Samuel B., m Nancy Smith
Ann Jeanette, m. James Losee

165

Jonet Ganong—Clarinda Cole

Children:

Emily; m. (1) Samuel Wright, (2) ―――― Barnum.
Oscar; m. Deborah Travis

166

Thomas Baxter—Uretta Cole.

Children

Oran, m Elizabeth Morgan (no issue).
Thomas C., d unm.

168

Hosea Carver—Hannah Jane Cole

Children:

James H , b June 19, 1841, d May 31, 1843
Delicy S , b. June 2, 1844, m Dec. 9, 1875. Saxton E Smith
Sarietta, b. Feb 20, 1848; m. June 16, 1869, John H. Hodgson.
Ida, b Aug 28, 1850, d April 1, 1880, m April 26, 1870, Hayward Smith

179

Uriah R Patchen—Minerva Ruth Cole

Children:

George Henry, b Sept 26, 1845; m October, 1876, Laura Spencer

Antha Minerva, b. Feb. 6, 1852, m July 23, 1878, Almon K
Virgil (Divorced 1900 and she m (2) Oct 19, 1903,
Amos Cole Bergman)

180

Benjamin Jefferson—Elizabeth Cole.

Children:

Sandford
Clinton
Theodore, d unm
Marvin, d. unm.

182

Abram Hendrickson—Anna Cole

Children:

Cornelia A , b 1825, d 1850, m Peter Reese
G W , b. Oct. 10, 1827, m Aug 29, 1852, Mary E. Parks
He living

Second Marriage

William Sherborne—Anna (Cole) Hendrickson.

Children:

William O , living at Soldiers' Home, Grand Rapids, Mich
Samuel, d. in the Army

184

George Lawrence—Zillah Cole

Children:

Nathan, d aged 7 years
George, 5th Mich Inf , killed at Gettysburg
Elvira, m. Edward Wesley.
Phebe, m (1) Porter Bristol, (2) Thomas Walker
James, m Emma Van Cott.
Luzina, m John Swart
Clinton, d unm

185

John A Van Camp—Catharine Cole

Children:

Mary Jane b Oct 16, 1829; m Dec 6, 1846, David B Mason. She d. Feb 11, 1908

Prudence, b. May 29, 1833; m May 4, 1850, Daniel Townley

Nancy, b March 22, 1836, d July 30 1904; m Dec 24, 1861, George Dodds

Marcia, b Dec 19, 1838, m Jan 1, 1856, Benjamin R. Townley.

Martin P, b Feb 20, 1841; m Dec 31, 1861, Emily Coder

Catharine, b April 8, 1846, m April 22, 1866, Warren Cornell.

192

John Beach—Louisa Cole

Children·

Edward; m Mary ———.
Cynthia. m Jerry Murray.
George.
Charles
Martha, m. William Harrold

193

Riley Earle—Ada Jane Cole

Children:

Olivia, m. Thomas Conely (no issue).
George, m Ida J Rupert
Marcus, m Florence Adele Rumsey (no issue).

196

Walker Bennett—Cynthia Cole.

Children:

Porteous, d. unm

Ann Eliza, d. unm
Maria, b Oct 2, 1830, d March 10, 1880; m George J. Fenn

197

Benjamin Arrowsmith—Ursula Cole

Children (born in Seneca County, N Y):

James, b 1826, d May 6 1870, m. Kate Dayton.
Mary Ann, b. Sept 11, 1828, d. unm. 1865.
Edwin C., b Jan. 21, 1836, d. unm Sept. 8, 1860.
Myron.

198

Sylvester King—Sarah A Cole

Children (born at Covert, N. Y):

Louise, b. Dec. 12, 1822; m Sept 11, 1844, John C. Porter.
Phebe, b. Oct. 30, 1826, d Aug 21, 1869; m Jan 2, 1849, Nestor Woodworth
Harvey F, b Dec 13, 1828, m Harriet Porter
Susan B, b Feb 26, 1832, m George B Denison
Cynthia A, b Aug 16, 18—, d June 6, 1864, m Nicholas Johnson
George, b. May 6, 1842 (killed at Gettysburg, July 8 1863).

203

Ezra Colwell—Hannah Cole.

Children:

Asahel Cole, b Dec 9, 1834, m. Feb 27, 1868, Phebe Holmes, b May 12, 1844, d June 30, 1894
Eliza Jane, b Oct 29, 1836; unm
Editha, b June 8, 1839; d unm July 30, 1892
Martha Augusta, b Oct 2, 1841; unm

206

Isaac Barrett—Mary Ann Cole.

Children:

Levi Cole, b Aug. 5, 1838; d. July 16, 1847.

Antha Jane, b. Aug 21, 1840; m. Oct. 16, 1884, Theron Cole, d. Dec 16, 1907.

Ermina Townly, b Dec 24, 1841, m Jan 10, 1872, William John Charlton.

Elon Galusha, b Feb 21, 1844, m Oct 23, 1866, Margaret Ann Wixsom.

Emma Saphronia, b Apr 25, 1846, d. August, 1893, m May 21, 1865, Theodore Fielinghuysen Cole, d Dec. 6, 1907.

Helen Cerena, b Jan 10, 1849, m Nov 4, 1869, James K. Smalley.

Adoniram Judson, b. March 29, 1851, m June 17, 1891, Adaline May Agor.

Alonzo Cole, b. Sept 20, 1853.

Marcus Moran, b Nov 17, 1857, m Nov 16, 1881, Minnie O. Agor.

209

Sidney B Tompkins—Caroline Cole

Children:

Eva, m. Frank Caywood
Willis H.
Coleman, d y
Carrie, d y.

212

Amos L Austin—Cynthia Cole.

Children·

Sarah E, b Aug 26, 1856, d Jan. 6, 1859

Sarah E, b Dec. 9, 1857, m (1) La Fayette Pinckney, (2) Dec 9, 1878, Hall B. Waring.

Silas, b March 9, 1859, m March 17, 1880, Abigail Barrett

Levi Cole, b April 9, 1861; m. Jan 1, 1883, Susan Smith

Nelson, b Jan 8, 1864
Mila, b Nov 30, 1866
Theodore, b Feb 13, 1871

213

Ira T. Horton—Adaline M Cole.

Children:

Ramahette, b April 1, 1858.
Anna.
Spencer
Carrie
Elias.
Samuel
Arthur.
William

226

Marcus Barrett—Viola Cole

Children (born in Steuben County, N Y):

Osman, b. March 26, 1835; m Susan McIntyre.
Warren, b Jan. 2, 1837; m Amy J Tompkins.
Eliza, b 1840, m Frank Longwell
Newman, b Sept 19, 1842, m Mary E Carpenter.
Ann, b July 7, 1847, m Frank A Mead.
Emma, b 1849, m Charles W Cole.
Sarah, b 1852, d unm. 1882

244

Alanson Adams—Mary Margaret Cole.

Children:

Nathaniel Alanson, b Sept 14, 1835; d May 2, 1895 He was Major in the 11th Kans Cavalry in the Civil War. He m Dec. 27, 1859, Clarissa Amanda Macomber

Second Marriage

Ephriam Hoyt—Mary Margaret (Cole) Adams.

Children:

Hannah Ann Elizabeth, b Oct. 6, 1843; m. Oct 8, 1870, Edward Benton Purcell
Frank, b. Nov. 14, 1845; d unm April 23, 1879.
Margaret, b. April 9, 1848, m. May 15, 1876, Thomas Jefferson Jenkins.

247

Washington W. Mead—Catharine Ann Cole

Children:

Chloretta, b Oct 25, 1841, d March 30, 1906.
Charles Wiloby, b. Oct 8, 1844
George Watson, b. Jan 21, 1847.
Edwin, b June 19, 1851.
Alice Levisa, b. July 24, 1854.
Vashti A , b. March 10, 1858
Nathaniel, b. Sept 23, 1862

252

George Washington Depew—Vashti Cole

Children:

George W , b July 29, 1837, m Julia Pentreath
William Willoby, b May 20, 1840
Annie Louisa, b Aug. 4, 1843, m Henry Thomas Wooster.
Vashti Susie, b Nov. 9, 1847, m Charles Worth Folger. He d Feb 3, 1895

Second Marriage

George Washington Depew—Elmira Cole.

Child.

Rodney H , b Feb 2, 1853; d y

258

Charles Selleck—Lucretia Cole.

Children:

Esther M., b. Aug 30, 1838, living unm.
Lorana, b June 1, 1840, m Charles C Crowther
Elizabeth, b. April 4, 1842, m Frank Carlton
Ophelia, b. April 25, 1844, m. Marcellus Emlitch
Ebenezer, b April 24 1850, m. Emma D. Austin.

293

Jermiah Hine—Zillah Cole

(No issue)

Second Marriage

William Howes—Zillah (Cole) Hine.

Children:

Josephine, m Edward C. Weeks.
Lydia; m. Bryant S Palmer

300

Benjamin Fowler—Mary Ann Cole

Children·

John W., d unm.
Eli, m Sarah Doty (no issue)
Irene, m Mills Reynolds

Second Marriage

George Doughty—Mary Ann (Cole) Fowler

(No issue)

307

Daniel L Hart—Mary E Cole

Children

Edgar D., m Rose Webster

Stella D.; m. William P. McKinstry.
Allen M.
Nellie M.

309

Effingham Bower—Caroline D Cole.

Children.

Katie.
Bertram.
Carroll.
Theron.
Homer.
Ferry.
Frank.

321

Henry L Haight—Juliette Cole

Children

Alice E, b July 6, 1864, unm.
Adelbert S, b Dec 16, 1865, m July 26, 1906, Emma Carley.
Fannie A, b Jan. 13, 1868, m June 30, 1892, Fred M. Brooks.
Benjamin D, b. July 5, 1875; unm

323

Herbert W Hills—Augusta Cole

Children:

James A, b May 15, 1871, m Jan 23, 1901, Catharine Hunter.
Florence C., b Aug. 28, 1876, m March 16, 1903, Henry Edelmann.
Clarence A, b Oct 6, 1882, m May 2, 1906, Pearl May Harrington

326

William Ward—Charlotte Eva Cole

Children:

William Berton, b May 30, 1881.
Walter Rutherford, b. Sept. 21, 1883.
Alice Almira, b May 2, 1885
Charlotte Cole, b Dec. 27, 1893

327

John Rutherford—Adelia Cole

Children·

Paul, b. Feb 25, 1889
Margaret, b Oct 30, 1891.

347

Thomas H Brown—Mary Ann Cole.

Children:

Laura Eliza, d unm.
Ida May.
Stella Loella

351

Henry A Saliers—Ann Amanda Cole

Children.

Cora M , m Charles Williams
Fred A
Nettie M
Earl A

352

Ira George Labounty—Harriet E Cole.

Children:

Lettie Leonel
Bertha Bessie

359

Theodore F. Kelley—Antoinette K. Cole.

Children:

Jessie, b Aug. 4, 1862, m. Dec 31, 1884, Willard J. Dykeman

Seth Foster, b Aug 23, 1864, m Jan. 20, 1874, Sarah Eleanor Cooper.

Paul Vincent, b Sept. 9, 1866, d Feb. 7, 1889.

Frederick Cole, b Nov 7, 1868, m. Sept. 21, 1892, Sadie E. Bloomer

361

Irwin Thomas—Minerva Cole.

Children:

Agnes.
Jessie

375

Charles Frank Sullaway—Ella Ann Cole.

Children:

Fred Willard, b Aug 2, 1882
Bert Cole, b Feb 7, 1884
Ruby Edna, b. Oct 14, 1885
Roy Parker, b Oct 14, 1887
Earl Foster, b April 9, 1890
Pearl Hazel, b Dec 26, 1891.
Fay Inez, b Nov. 28, 1896
Earl Knox, b. May 5, 1898
Chloe Maude, b Feb 21, 1900

386

Cornelius Quick—Samantha Cole.

Children:

Angeline
Lydia.

George
Mary Ann
Frank, m Carrie Mead.
Florence.
Myron
Samantha

387

George Holden—Lydia Cole

Children·

Mary, m. Sidney Rathfon
John
Nellie.

388

George Price—Lois S Cole.
(No issue.)
Second Marriage.
George Acker—Lois Cole Price
(No issue)

389

David Holden—Harriet Cole

Children:

Belle, m Charles Mead
Jennie, m Marion Southworth
Charles
George.
Frank.

392

William Tenbrook—Jane Cole.

Children:

John.
Ezra

George
Anna
Andrew.
Lois.

398

Howard B Taft—Harriet C Cole

Children:

Minor Cole, b. July 19, 1862
George Wheaton, b July 17, 1865.

406

Matthew L Bennett—Adelaide Cole

Children:

Matthew W
Arthur C
Irving C

425

Morris C. Crissey—Mary Cole

Children.

Mary Alice, b Sept 17, 1867, unm
John Waterbury, b Oct 6, 1869; m. Oct 10, 1899, Grace Calhoun
Frederick, b Jan 8, 1872, d July 15, 1873
Nancy Ethel, b Feb 16, 1874, m Dec 25, 1901, Raymond Hardy
Susan Agnes, b June 2, 1876, m April 16, 1902 Ralph Edwin McLean
Ruth Elizabeth, b Jan 20, 1879, m Willis Aylbuyton Thorne
William Morris, b March 5, 1881

453

Joseph L Hebert—Hallie R Cole

Children:

Thomas Richardson, b June 9, 1889
Nathan Cole, b May 6, 1892

475

Lovett La Fever—Susan Cole

Children

Wilmer, b May 25, 1857; m Dec 15, 1886, Mary E. Wickham
Eldora, b Dec 22, 1862, m Dec 10, 1884, Hiram Lockwood
Austin, b Nov 14, 1864, m. Sept 27, 1892, Nettie M Durand
Agnes, b Jan 16, 1867, m Sept 4, 1895, Joseph H Bong.
Ophelia, b April 3, 1869, d Oct 17, 1875
Dana. b July 25, 1874, m Feb 27, 1902, Elsie Smith

481

Israel Parshall—Minerva Cole

Children:

Lemira, b July 3, 1840, d Aug 18, 1906, m Jan. 1, 1857, William H Niver.
Merritt, b April 1, 1844, m July 28, 1867, Addie Fuller.
Ursula, b Jan 20, 1847, m July 4, 1868, Ranson N Parshall
Milton Chatman, b Jan 23, 1850, m July 3, 1870, Charlotte Ismon.
Alvira Elizabeth, b April 25, 1852; m Feb 6, 1870, Stewart Lindaburg
Cynthia Cordelia, b Dec. 9, 1855, d July 24, 1859
Millis Lincoln, b Dec. 25, 1864; m Sept. 12, 1887, Delaphine Judd

483

Jesse Parshall—Prudence Cole

Children:

Lenora A, b Sept 12, 1866, m Jan 28, 1890, Walter Van Camp

Milan G, b June 5, 1869, m April 13, 1893, Mattie Wolverton

Edgar J, b April 30, 1851, d July 11, 1858

Almond, b July 26, 1865, d. Sept 21, 1865

Also two d. y

484

Aaron Huff—Elizabeth Cole.

Children:

Phebe, m Thomas Peck
Charles, m Harriet Bedell
Minnie, m ——— Peck
Alida; m ——— Peck
Rolla J, unm

489

Robert W Walker—Fidelia E Cole

Children·

Laura Phebe, b. July 15, 1855, m. Oct 14, 1873, William Blake Eager

Lyman Enos, b Nov 22, 1857, m March 9, 1880, Harriet Alice McMillan

Mason Erastus, b Aug 18, 1859, m May 1, 1880, Jessie Rumsey.

Thomas Webster b Sept 19, 1862, m Jan 30, 1884, Etta Hardy.

491

Aaron B Durfee—Sarah A Cole

Children

Frank E

IRA C. HALL
No. 531

Myron W, b March 28, 1862, d Sept 6, 1865
Robert W, b July 2, 1867, d Sept 25, 1868
Hope, b 1877, d y.

492

Edgar L Rathbun—Ada O Cole.

Children:

Laura Eunice, b Nov 8, 1866, m Feb 16, 1888, Chester B Dean
Fred Arthur, b May 8, 1872, m Nov 7, 1894, Grace Olds.

497

Frederick Roat—Adah Cole

Children

Mina C, b Dec 7, 1867, m Feb 9, 1886, Willard Marks
Bessie E, b Dec 17, 1870, d Jan 1, 1871
Milton D, b Dec 17, 1871, m Jan 10, 1894, Cora A Lord
Daisy E, b Jan 4, 1874, d Oct 5, 1883
George A, b July 31, 1875
Winifred M, b Aug 18, 1877, m Dec 26, 1900, Clark E Woodley
Lewis F, b Dec 11, 1879
Harry N, b May 5, 1882, m Oct 5, 1904, Lena M Kline
Edith A, b July 19, 1887, d April 13, 1901.

499

Robert Clendening—Hannah Cole

Children:

Mary E, b April 26, 1867, m Dec 28, 1892, Daniel P. Christian
Pearl B, b Jan 12, 1869
Grace J, b Dec 29, 1870, d Feb 5, 1892
Nathan A, b Sept 27, 1872, d same day.
Lillian J, b Aug 13, 1874.
Roberta, b April 5, 1877

505

Edward Townsend—Laura Cole

Children:

Charles A.
Millie M.
Lydia M.
Frank J
Ernest E

512

Thomas Judson Hopkins—Mary Louise Cole.

Children:

Clinton Henry, b Feb 20, 1857, m Dec. 10, 1885 Amelia Gordon McHattie

Harriet Eliza, b Nov 18, 1859, m. July 27, 1883 Benjamin Stamp Ackels

Carrie Louise, b March 11, 1864, d April 12, 1864

Arvah Cole, b Sept 14, 1867, d May 11, 1870.

Edla May, b May 26, 1871, m Jan 1, 1901, Roy Cameron Blackburn.

Ada Bertha, b Sept 13, 1873, m Jan. 11, 1900, M Seward Doty.

518

Charles S. Hopkins—Julia F Cole.

Children:

Florence A, b. Sept 22, 1878, m March 26, 1891, Theodore Rahn.

Fannie A., b. July 20, 1881; m. July 15, 1908, Frank Pardeaux

519

Edmund C. Woodworth—Ada F Cole

Children:

Chester N, b Dec. 15, 1874

Edna, b April 24, 1877.
Harvey K , b April 16, 1880
Irwin C , twin of above
Leon E , b Dec 15, 1881
Mabel, b. Aug 27, 1884
Lida May, b Aug 1, 1886.
Herbert, b April 1, 1891

521

Arthur Bates—Anna Sarah Cole.

Children·

Arthur Lee, b Aug 15, 1888
Ada C , b Feb 6, 1893

528

William H Parker—Rachel Emily Cole

Children

Hervey Nathan
Amanda W.
Lulu

531

Ira C Hall—Carrie F Cole.

Children:

Wallace Stowell, b May 19, 1872, d y
Alice Louise, b Nov 2, 1876, m Dec 25, 1903, Walter D Hopkins
John Wilbur, b Oct 9, 1879, m Sept 1, 1906, Mrs Edith Lewis Penn

541

Harry W. Doremus—Ella E. Cole.

Children.

Robert Child, b May 31, 1890
Helen Marguerite, b April 20, 1892

Dorothy Carl, b July 11, 1895
Jeannette Claire, b March 27, 1897

544

Millard F. Agor—Jennie A Cole.

Children.

Alonzo Cole, b Sept 16, 1886
Muriel, b Aug 23, 1889

554

Sidney C Davis—Belle F Cole

Children:

Edith Sedina, b Feb 15, 1885; m Sept 24, 1907, Paul Laverents
Grace Muriel, b Feb 19, 1887.
Paul Judson, b June 8, 1891
Reginald Sidney, b Oct 24, 1892

644

Albert Case—Lydia H Cole

Children

Mary Frances, b Jan 17, 1862, m July 23, 1897, Albert Philipps.
Minnie Adelaide, b Sept 11, 1863, m Nov. 5, 1884, Oscar Longyear.
Nathan Amos, b Feb 10, 1871; m September, 1896, Gertrude Maule
Hannah Gannett, b. Sept 22, 1874, m. Jan. 21, 1896, George Brown.
George Valentine, b Feb 14, 1877, m May 10, 1905, Mrs. Ida Stoutenberg

649

J C Schneider—Emma C Cole

Children

Cecile Elvira, b. Genoa, O., Aug 9, 1874
Katharine M, b Rollin, Mich, Nov 17, 1876
Leroy F, b Rollin, Mich, Feb 16, 1880

653

Frank B Johnson—Belle Cole.

Child:

Samuel B

Second Marriage

Edgar D Johnson—Belle (Cole) Johnson

Children.

Ruth W
Paul, d y

656

Charles B Gregory—Ida Cole

Children.

Jessie E
Clara V
Georgia A

677

Charles E Winters—Alice B Cole

Children (born at Brooklyn, N Y)

Katherine, b Oct 19, 1890
Charles Evans, b June 25, 1892
Evelyn, b Oct 5, 1894

680

George T. Hawley—MaBelle Cole.

Children:

Chester Cole, b June 9, 1891.
Alan Wayne, b. March 14, 1897.

814

Walter Colgrove—Florence E Cole

Children:

Katharine, b. Burdett, N Y, July 8, 1889.
Olive Cole, b. Burdett, N. Y., Oct. 25, 1891
Mary Wood, b Burdett, N. Y, Sept. 15, 1893, d Oct 11, 1899.

Second Marriage.

Edward C Cooper—Florence E (Cole) Colegrove

Child:

Marion Sarah, b. Waverly, N Y, Jan 25, 1908

INDEX

INDEX

[Certain names, viz Abigail, Abby, Betsey, Elizabeth, Polly, Mary, Sally, Sarah, Dolly, Dorothy, will be found indexed under their different spellings]

Abbott, Frederick, 55
Ackels, Benjamin Stamp, 194
    Harriet Eliza, 194
Acker, Geo, 73, 189
Ackley, Lucinda, 137
Adams, Adah, 167
    Alanson, 57, 183
    Clarissa Amanda, 183
    Elizabeth, 167
    Emsley, 167
    Isaiah, 167
    James, 166
    John, 57
    Mary Margaret, 57
    Nathaniel Alanson, 183
    Susan, 33, 166
Agor, Abigail, 164
    Adah, 164
    Adaline May, 182
    Alonzo Cole, 196
    Arvilla, 165
    Charles, 29, 164
    Elisha Cole, 95
    Eliza, 164, 165
    Elizabeth, 29
    Hannah, 165
    Jennie Augusta, 95
    Kelsie, 95
    Millard Fillmore, 95, 196
    Minnie O, 182
    Muriel, 196
    Naomi, 164
    Orrin, 164
    Orson, 164
    Sarah, 165
    William, 29, 164
Alderdice, Margaret, 124
Alexander, John, 113
    Maude, 113
    William, 113
Allen, Anna, 50
    Lovica, 133
    Mary Ann, 107
    Spencer, 107, 108
Ames, Sarah, 156

Andrews, Benjamin, 134
    Benjamin F, 134
    Carrie Amelia, 134
    Cynthia L, 133
    Morris Gilbert, 133
    Myron, 161
Armstrong, Alexander, 104
    Cassie Belle, 143
    Emma B, 104
    Harriet R, 104
    Jane Horton, 165
    John, 143
    Margaret, 104
    Mary, 119
    Selah, 104
    William Henry, 143
Arnold, Clinton Sears, 99
    Cornelia Minor, 99
    James, 99
    Matilda, 88
Arrowsmith, Benjamin, 51, 181
    Edwin G, 181
    James, 181
    Kate, 181
    Mary Ann, 181
    Myron, 181
    Ursula, 51
Ash, Margaret W, 116
Atherton, Rachel, 130
Auble, Elizabeth, 52
Austin, Abigail, 182
    Adah, 164
    Amos Lane, 53, 182
    Carrie Augusta, 96
    Cynthia, 53
    David Campbell, 96
    Elijah, 168
    Emma D, 185
    Levi Cole, 182
    Mila, 183
    Nelson, 183
    Rachel, 168
    Sarah E, 182
    Silas, 53, 182
    Susan, 182

Austin, Theodore, 183
　Viola, 147
Axtell, Hannah Maria, 96

Babcock, Roxie B., 64
Backer, Elmer Ross, 122
　Nelle Emeline, 122
Badgley, Sarah Ann, 145
Bailey, Albro, 173
　Anna, 109
　Augusta, 173
　Eliza, 41
　Elizabeth, 173
　Emma, 173
　Erastus, 173
　Floyd, 41, 173
　Gilbert, 41
　Hannah S, 173
　Herbert, 173
　Julia A., 124
　Levi, 164
　Lucy A., 173
　Mary, 84
　Nancy, 85
　Orville, 173
　Priscilla, 164
　Samuel, 84, 85
　Sarah, 74, 173
　Susan C., 63
　Thomas, 173
Baker, Edmond, 7, 30
　Joseph, 7
　Josiah, 7, 30
　Martha T., 171
　Mary, 108
　Mary Elizabeth, 107
Baldwin, Anna, 61
　Calista, 170
　Eleazer Henry, 37, 170
　Eliza, 170
　Eva Jane, 117
　Hannah, 37, 40
　Henry, 37, 39
　Henry S., 170
　Lydia, 39
　Reuben D., 170
　Robert, 117
　Sarah, 87
Ballard, Abel Evans, 105
　Abiather R., 95, 176
　Alyada, 164
　Alzada, 17
　Amanda, 176
　Augusta J., 176
　Benjamin, 164
　Elah, 45, 176
　Eliza Ann, 45, 67, 176
　Fanny, 67, 164

Ballard, Frances A., 172, 176
　George P., 148
　Hannah, 177
　Henrietta, 148
　Jane, 164
　Jane Ann, 177
　Joseph, 45, 164
　Juliette, 143, 177
　Lavenia, 105
　Lydia, 45
　Mariette, 45, 176
　Melinda, 47
　Melvina, 164
　Mercy, 28
　Naomi, 4, 164
　Osman, 176
　Rachel, 164
　Sarah, 176
　Selah, 47, 84, 164, 176
　Susan, 45, 176
　Tracy, 28, 47, 67, 164
　William, 105
　Zeba, 47, 164, 177
Bangs, Abner, 12
　Edward, 22
　Hannah, 37
　Jonathan, 22
Banker, Eliza, 164
Barber, Eunice, 7
　Joseph, 7
Barbour, ———, 26
　Adaline, Mrs., 89
　Charles N., 89
　Giles, 89
　Zuba, 89
Barnes, Deborah Jane, 110
Barnum, Emily, 178
Barrett, Abigail, 164, 182
　Adaline May, 182
　Adoniram Judson, 182
　Alice Augusta, 182
　Alonzo Cole, 182
　Amy J., 183
　Ann, 183
　Antha Jane, 67, 182
　Antoinette, 172
　Coleman Robinson, 100
　Eliza, 183
　Elon Galusba, 182
　Emma, 183
　Emma Frances, 143
　Emma Jane, 100
　Emma Safronia, 144, 182
　Ermina Townly, 182
　Fanny, 98
　Helen Cerena, 182
　Isaac, 53, 67, 144, 182
　Isaac L., 172

INDEX 203

Barrett, John, 98
  John, Mrs, 129
  Marcus, 53, 55, 143, 183
  Marcus Moran, 182
  Margaret Ann, 182
  Martha, 35
  Mary, 53
  Mary E , 183
  Mary Jane, 53
  Minnie O , 182
  Newman, 183
  Osman, 183
  Prudence, 50
  Rachel, 55, 56
  Samuel, 55
  Sarah, 183
  Solomon, Mrs , 99
  Steven R , 100
  Susan, 183
  Viola, 55
  Warren, 183
Barton, Sarah, 142
Bassett, Frank, 175
  Geneveve, 175
  Helen, 175
  John, 175
  Lemuel, 44
  Pierpont, 44, 175
  Sarah L , 175
  Sarah R , 44
Bates, Ada C , 195
  Anna Sarah, 92
  Arthur, 92, 195
  Arthur Lee, 195
  Daniel Porter, 158
  Julia Viletta, 158
Baxter, Beulah, 165
  Clara L , 115
  Elisha Cole, 165
  Elizabeth, 165, 178
  Frances, 165
  Hannah, 29
  Jane, 165
  Jane Horton, 165
  Jedidah, 165
  John B G , 115
  Oran, 165, 178
  Osmond M , 165
  Sarah Ann, 165
  Sarah H , 165
  Thaddeus, 29, 48, 165
  Thomas, 29, 48, 165, 178
  Thomas C , 178
  Uretta, 48, 165
Beach, Agnes Olympia, 81
  Charles, 180
  Cynthia, 180
  Esther M , 89

Beach, Edmond, 51, 89
  Edward, 180
  George, 180
  Harney H , 81
  Jarvis Varnel, 81
  John, 51, 180
  Leonard D , 106
  Louisa M., 51
  Martha, 180
  Mary, 180
  Orson, 106
  Varnal Douglas, 81
Beadle, Mary, 42
Beardsley, Clara W , 101
  Clark, 166
  Naomi, 166
Beck, Dagmer, 153
  Frances, 153
Bedell, Clara, 97
  Frank, 97
  George Washington, 97
  Grace Emma, 97
  Harriet, 192
  Lula Bell, 97
  Paul, 97
  Verge, 97
Beebe, Olive, 114
  Samuel, 7
Beers, Lillie, 71
  Stephen, 71
Bellyet, Mary Jane, 115
Belshaw, Elizabeth Ann, 146
  James, 146
  Jane, 146
Bemis, Frank T , 176
  Gertrude, 176
Benjamin, Charles, 89
Bennett, Adelaide, 79
  Alma Ann, 143
  Ann Eliza, 181
  Charles, 87
  Cynthia, 51
  Elizabeth A , 126
  Geo Hunber, 143
  Green, Col , 87
  Henry A , 79
  Irving C , 190
  John, 145
  Julia, 44
  Lois, 116
  Maria, 181
  Matthew L , D1 , 79, 190
  Matthew W , 190
  Melissa, 87
  Porteous, 180
  Sarah, 115
  Walker, 51, 180
Bergman, Amos Cole, 179

204 INDEX

Berry, Jabez, 31
    Lemuel, 30
    Lydia, 30
    Mary or Mercy, 12
    Mehitable, 30
    Rebecca, 31
    Susan, 32, 34
Besson, Frances Ellen, 72
    Welborn, 72
Bird, Mary A, Mrs, 160
Birdsall, Archibald, 49
    Elizabeth, 49
Bixby, Genevieve, 146
    Henry Merrill, 146
    Willard G, 146
Black, Ada Eleanor, 112
    George, 112
    Melville, 112
Blackburn, Edla May, 194
    Roy Cameron, 194
Blade, Elmira, 150
    Portor, 150
Blaine, Electra, 79
Blair, Catharine, 130
    Flora Linda, 130
    John, 130
    Walter Joseph, 130
Bloomer, Sadie E, 188
Blount, Lucie S, 151
Boardman, Herbert, 92
    Truman, 92
    Ursula, 92
Bobbett, Obediance, 7
Bolton, Maria, 69
Bong, Agnes, 191
    Joseph H, 191
Booth, Carl Shaw, 147
    Huldah Victoria, 147
Borodel, Ann, 16
Bourbon, Mary, 99
Bouton, Elizabeth, 32
Bower, Bertram, 186
    Caroline De F, 63
    Carroll, 186
    Effingham, 63, 186
    Ferry, 186
    Frank, 186
    Homer, 186
    Katie, 186
    Theron, 186
Bowman, Ella, 115
    Samuel W, 115
Boyd, Althea, 67
    James, 67
    Nellie, 67
Boynton, Nancy, 70
Bradbury, Sarah, 82
Bradford, Almira, 64

Bradford, Perese, 64
Bradstreet, Mercy, 14
    Simon, 14
Brayton, Almeda Maria, 139
Brazin, Catharine, 94
Breunig, Fred W, 151
    Rose Althea, 151
Brewster family, 9
    Love, 21
    Mary, 9
    Patience, 9
    William, 9
Brien, Mary M, 160
    Thomas, 160
Brigham, Emma F, 74
Bristol, Lydia, 90
    Phebe, 179
    Porter, 179
Bronson, Jemima, 14
Brooks, Fannie A, 186
    Fred M, 186
    Leora, 141
Brophy, Mary Catharine, 72
Brower, Mary, 169
Brown, ———, 56
    Charles, Dr, 143
    Cora Electa, 142
    Daniel, 166
    Eliza, 155
    George, 14, 196
    Harriet Esther, 143
    Hannah Gannett, 196
    Ida May, 187
    James M, 40, 173
    Katharine, 57
    Laura Eliza, 187
    Mary Ann, 66
    Milan Marcellus, 142
    Minerva Ann, 40
    Sarah Ann, 166
    Stella Lovella, 187
    Thomas H, 66, 187
Brownell, Eunice, 7
    Mary, 104
    Morgan, 104
    Susan, 150
Browner, Emma Matilda, 95
    Jacob, 95
Brundage, Harriet, 98
Brundell, Anna, 134
Brush, ———, 162
Bryan, Ida May, 131
    John Wilson, 131
    William, 131
Bryant, Loraine, 91
Buck, Daisy Ellen, 158
    Frederick J., 158
Buckbee, Robert, 170

INDEX 205

Buckbee, Sarah Emeline, 170
Buckingham, Esther, 34
Budd, Fannie Ames, 156
    James, 101
    Jane Ann, 101
    John Spafford, 156
Buell, Charles, 117
    Helen, 117
Bunnell, Beulah, 165
    Mary, 170
    Miles, 165
Burch, Susannah, 7
Burnett Helen Gertrude, 123
    William Hiram, 123
Burr, Bradley, 167
    Lydia, 167
Bushnell, Hortense, 134
Button, Dency E., 137
Byington, Elizabeth, 110

Caldwell, Abigail, 17
    Jane, 130
    Mary, 15, 60, 61
    Matthew, 17
Calhoun, Grace, 190
Calkins, Elijah, 7
    Lenora, 115
    Sarah, 7
Campbell, Augusta Malvina, 97
    Geo Washington, 142
    Nettie, 142
    Samuel Reed, 97
Carey, George W., 148
    Mary Amelia, 148
Cargill, James, 102
    Letitia, 102
Carl, Adah, 47
Carley, Emma, 186
Carlton, Elizabeth, 185
    Frank, 185
Carpenter, John, 47
    Mary E., 183
    Sarah, 47
Carr, Ida, 141
    Jesse Foster, 141
    Robert, 141
Carter, David, 7
    Hannah, 126
Cartright, Elizabeth, 36
Carver, Barnabas, 29, 164
    Charlotte, 94
    Delicy S., 178
    Hannah, 164
    Hannah Ann, 143
    Hannah Jane, 48
    Hosea, 48, 178
    Ida, 178
    James, 48, 94

Carver, John, 29
    Juliette, 177
    Phebe, 172
    Sarah, 29
    Sarietta, 178
    Stephen W., 143, 177
    Timothy, 29
Case, Albert, 107, 196
    Alice, 7
    George Valentine, 196
    Gertrude, 196
    Hannah Gannett, 196
    Ida Stoutenberg, 196
    Lydia Hathaway, 107
    Mary Frances, 196
    Minnie Adeline, 196
    Nathan, 107
    Nathan Amos, 196
Cass, Daniel, 156
    Ella C., 156
Catlin, Mary, 137
Cavender, Ada Theresa, 121
    Harriet, 120
    John Milton M., 120, 121
Cavinder, Viola, 165
Caywood, Eva, 182
    Frank, 182
Chambers, Charity, 131
Chandler, Margaret, 15
Chapman, Delia, 64
    Elizabeth, 58
    Hannah, 44
    Henry, Rev., 64
    Jeremiah, 58
    Sarah A., 104
Chard, Jeremiah, 153
    Margaret Jane, 153
Charlton, Ermina Townley, 182
    William John, 182
Chase, Alvin, 32, 166
    Anna, 167
    Betsey, 167
    Caroline, 166
    Charlotte, 100
    Clara Mabel, 149
    Cynthia, 166
    Cyrus 100, 166
    Daniel, 167
    Darius, 166
    Elizabeth, 166
    Ellen, 166
    Elmer, 31, 167
    Eunice, 34
    Frank, 166
    Henah, 167
    Henry Nichols, 166
    Hiram, 166
    Iva, 167

INDEX

Chase, Jane, 166
    John, 166
    John M , 149
    Lydia 167
    Lyman, 166
    Maria, 167
    Mary, 166
    Mary W , 166
    Maynard Hosmer, 149
    Naomi, 166
    Obed, 167
    Obediah, 32, 34
    Phebe, 166
    Robert, 167
    Ruth, 32
    Sarah, 166, 167
    Sarah Ann, 166
    Sophia, 167
    Susan, 166
    Zillah, 166
Chatfield, Chas , 152
    Florence Emma, 152
Cherry, Ann Elizabeth, 175
    Vinton, 175
Chester, Ruth, 22
Chichester, Sarah, 7
Christ, Elizabeth, 138
Christian, ———, 170
    Daniel P., 193
    Mary E , 193
Clark, Angeline, 149
    Augusta, 173
    Elias, Dr , 173
    Harriet Calista, 120
    Herbert Ralph, 120
    John C , 81
    Ralph Jerome, 120
Clary, Ellen, 70
    John, 70
Clausen, Minerva Ann, 40
    Olan, 40, 173
    William, 40, 173
Clement, Eleanor, 82
Clements, Henry Clay, 92
    Maria, 92
Clendening, Edward, 89
    Grace J , 193
    Hannah, 89
    Lillian J , 193
    Mary F , 193
    Pearl B , 193
    Robert, 89, 193
    Roberta, 193
Close, Reuben, 7
Coburn, Mary, 140
    Miner T , 140
    Samantha L , 136
Cochrane, Nancy R , 80

Cocks, Emily, 81
    Mary, 80
Coder, Emily, 180
Cole, Aaron Hazen, 43, 73
    Abel B , 148
    Abiatha, 48
    Abigail, 98
    Abner Bangs, 38, 46, 63, 80, 124, 153
    Abner Sweetland, 63, 110
    Abraham, 3
    Adah, 37, 59, 89, 165
    Ada Blanche, 137
    Ada Eleanor, 112
    Ada Elvira, 135
    Ada Esther, 137
    Ada Frances, 91
    Ada Isadore, 136
    Ada Jane, 51
    Ada Louise, 121
    Ada Lulu, 157
    Ada M , 149
    Ada Olive, 88
    Ada Theresa, 121
    Addie, 118
    Addie Belle, 136
    Addie J , 131
    Addie May, 110
    Addison, 79, 124
    Adelbert, 90, 137
    Adele M , 111
    Adelia, 44, 64
    Adelia Tidd, 61
    Adeline, 44, 49, 60, 79, 130
    Adeline Eleanor, 112
    Adeline Minerva, 54
    Adoniram Judson, 55, 74, 97, 101
    Agnes Eleanor, 82
    Agnes Maria, 140
    Agnes Olympia, 81
    Aileen, 71
    Alaida, 139
    Alanson, 40
    Albert, 80
    Albert G , 106, 148
    Albert George, 115, 131
    Albert Levi, 157
    Albert Stevens, 162
    Albertine, 152
    Alexander Hamilton, 90, 137
    Alfred, 40, 67
    Alice, 71, 97, 111, 125, 141
    Alice Bertha, 112
    Alice Edna, 150
    Alice Emily, 81
    Alice Fidelia, 158
    Alice Jane, 101, 125
    Allen, 45, 56, 99, 108, 149

INDEX

Cole, Allen M., 111
  Alma Ann, 143
  Alma R., 90
  Almeda, 45
  Almeran Horace, 143
  Almira, 64
  Almon, 38
  Alonzo, 38, 66
  Alonzo E., 111
  Alonzo Ojida, 53, 84, 95
  Alta Belle, 138
  Althea, 67
  Alvah, 44, 60, 106
  Alveyson, 47
  Alyada, 164
  Alzada, 45, 47
  Amanda, 48, 53, 67, 69, 79
  Amedee Berthold, 83, 127
  Amedee Jackson, 154
  Amos Rogers, 60, 107
  Amos Rogers Tunison, 108, 150
  Amy Budd, 156
  Anadella C., 111
  Angeline, 72, 149
  Angeline Mary, 111
  Angevine, 102
  Ann, 68, 161
  Ann Amanda, 67
  Ann Elizabeth, 57, 61, 103
  Ann W., 96
  Anna, 32, 43, 50, 61
  Anna Eliza, 66
  Anna Louise, 154
  Anna Mary, 94, 127
  Anna Ruth, 156
  Anna Sarah, 92
  Anne, 21
  Anne Amelia, 129
  Annie, 101, 136
  Annie Augusta, 98
  Annie C., 117
  Annie E., 144
  Annie Jackson, 128
  Annie Louise, 96
  Annie Orlinda, 114
  Annis, 35, 45
  Ansel, 44
  Antha Jane, 67, 100
  Anthony Wm., 58, 101, 102
  Antoinette, 41, 54, 57, 68, 145
  Antoinette Kelley, 68
  Arnet Judson, 142
  Arthur, 113, 124, 152
  Arthur B., 111
  Arthur Bliss, 136
  Arthur Enos, 89, 137
  Arthur Lawrence, 111
  Arthur Vincent, 139, 158

Cole, Arvah Hopkins, 94, 140
  Asahel, 32, 50, 52, 86
  Augusta, 64
  Augusta Malvina, 97
  Augustus, 162
  Aurelia, 85
  Aurelia Celestine, 113
  Austin, 126, 154
  Azmon Wood, 52
  Azubah, 34
  Barnum, 66
  Barret Ellis, 153
  Belle Frances, 97
  Benjamin Otto, 153
  Bernice, 142
  Berry, 32, 47
  Bertha, 110, 114
  Bertha Marguerite, 118
  Bertha May, 145
  Bertine, 142
  Bessie, 136, 139
  Bessie Jane, 142
  Bessie Laura, 156
  Bethia, 37
  Betsey, 45, 62, 89
  Betsey A., 102
  Blanche, 126
  Blanche Owens, 126
  Bulah Virginia, 162
  Burr Marion, 131
  Burt, 125
  Burt Scott, 46
  Byron, 42, 71
  Byron Hopkins, 72
  Caroline, 53, 85
  Caroline C., 120
  Calista Jane, 67
  Calvin, 115
  Carrie Amelia, 134
  Carrie Anna, 140
  Carrie Augusta, 96
  Carrie Frances, 93
  Carrie L., 107
  Carrie Louise, 140
  Carrie M., 160
  Carrie Moore, 140
  Cassie Belle, 113
  Catharine, 50, 60, 88, 105, 125
  Catharine Beatrice, 148
  Cecelia Almira, 138
  Cecil Aurelia, 113
  Celia Octavia, 150
  Cepha Hortense, 115
  Charity, 28
  Charles, 37, 58, 60, 62, 97, 102, 103, 106, 130, 142, 155, 162
  Chas Alland, 114
  Chas Briggs, 46, 81, 125

208 INDEX

Cole, Chas E, 88, 134
    Chas Cavender, 120
    Charles E, 100, 105, 106
    Chas Green, 50, 84
    Chas Henry, 65, 114
    Chas Herbert, 138
    Chas Homer, 159
    Chas Lewis, 86, 131
    Chas Norton, 57, 101
    Chas Ogden, 101, 103, 147
    Chas Philip, 144, 159
    Chas Wm, 98, 113
    Charlotte, 60, 94, 100, 105
    Charlotte Angeline, 111
    Charlotte Caroline, 121
    Charlotte De Forest, 63
    Charlotte Eva, 64
    Charlotte Louise, 141
    Chester, 38
    Chester David, 114
    Chester Enos, 98, 142
    Chester Glenn, 113, 151
    Chester S, 65
    Chester Scott, 63, 112
    Chloe, 61, 108
    Chloe Ann, 41, 71
    Christopher Oliver, 125, 153
    Circassia Jenette, 80
    Clara Bell, 149
    Clara C, 129
    Clara L, 115
    Clara Lucretia, 118
    Clara Mabel, 149
    Clara W, 101
    Clarissa, 161
    Clarie Belle, 162
    Clarence, 142
    Clarinda, 48, 61
    Clarissa Malissa, 63
    Claude, 97, 142
    Claude Burton, 133
    Clayton, 116, 152
    Clementina, 82
    Clemina, 63
    Clinton Harold, 148
    Clyde, 98, 142
    Cora Electa, 142
    Cora Lillian, 127
    Cora M, 140
    Cora May, 154
    Cora Verna, 81
    Cordelia L, 160
    Cornelia A, 117
    Cornelia Minor, 99
    Crystal J, 156
    Cynthia, 13, 32, 51, 53, 54
    Cynthia L, 133
    Cynthia M, 137

Cole, Cyrus, 36, 60, 98
    Cyrus E, 106
    Dagmer, 153
    Daisy Ellen, 158
    Daniel, 3, 11, 12, 18, 19, 21, 22, 24, 27, 30, 33, 42, 115
    Daniel Delevan Pratt, 156
    Daniel H, 34, 56, 144, 159
    Daniel Harrison, 73
    Daniel Webster, 54
    Darius, 60, 107, 108, 149
    David, 24, 29, 37, 41, 64, 69
    David B, 38
    David Elliott, 70, 116
    David Orlando, 63, 111
    Dean Jervis, 133
    Deborah, 162
    Delephine, 131
    Delevan Samuel, 88, 135, 157
    Delia, 64
    Della Mason, 136
    DeWitt Clinton, 60, 144, 150, 158
    Diana, 149
    Don Samuel, 133
    Donald Merritt, 160
    Donald Robinson, 160
    Doris Emma, 158
    Dorothea, 126
    Dorothy, 154
    Dorothy Drake, 151
    Dorothy Elizabeth, 141
    Dorothy Lucille, 155
    Dorothy M, 156
    Druzilla, 92
    Dunbar, 127
    Dwight, 152
    Dwight H, 64, 114
    Ebenezer, 27, 28, 33–35, 37, 51, 57, 58, 60, 63, 102, 105, 106, 148
    Edgar Thomas, 91, 138
    Edith, 71, 102, 141, 142, 152
    Edith Leonard, 133
    Edith M, 160
    Edith Z, 145
    Edmund, 62, 109
    Edna, 126, 130
    Edward Cammon, 155
    Edward Earle, 131, 159
    Edward Eleazer, 66, 115
    Edward Everett, 81, 126
    Edward Hanford, 127
    Edward James, 147, 159
    Edward Judson, 97, 142
    Edwin, 59, 62, 91, 105, 106, 110, 161
    Edwin Carl, 148
    Edwin Charles, 161
    Edwin Russell, 162
    Edwin Wildman, 52, 92

Cole, Effie Elizabeth, 134
　Elbert, 79
　Eleanor, 82, 113
　Eleanor Florence, 124
　Eleanor Louise, 138
　Eleazer, 29, 38
　Eleazer H , 38, 56, 66
　Eli, 37, 46, 51, 62, 73, 91
　Eli Kelley, 70, 117
　Elisha, 3, 7, 11, 12, 15, 24, 26–29, 38, 41, 64
　Elisha J , 34, 57
　Elisha, Jr , 25
　Elisha Kelley, 69, 115
　Eliza, 35, 36, 41, 52, 55, 61, 62, 102
　Eliza Ann, 161
　Eliza Belle, 162
　Eliza Corson, 117
　Eliza L , 65
　Elizabeth, 29, 40, 43, 49, 50, 52, 58, 59, 87, 88, 107, 109, 130, 161
　Elizabeth Ann, 146
　Elmira, 58, 160
　Ella, 115
　Ella Ann, 71
　Ella C , 156
　Ella Euphemia, 95
　Ella Lillian, 127
　Ella Louise, 94
　Ella M , 149
　Ella Victoria, 115
　Ellen, 62, 70, 147
　Ellen Marion, 160
　Elmer, 104
　Elmer Archie, 157
　Elmer C , 60, 109
　Elmer Elkanah, 151
　Elmer Ellsworth, 135, 156
　Elmer Hopkins, 122
　Elsie, 146, 149
　Elvin Clayton, 108
　Elvin Clinton, 60
　Elvin Dayton, 108, 150
　Elvira Laura, 108
　Elvira Rosanna, 150
　Elwin Samuel, 135
　Emeline, 102
　Emery, 161
　Emily, 56, 70, 81
　Emily Augusta, 95, 124
　Emily Augusta Frost, 146
　Emily De Russy, 117
　Emily Preston, 69
　Emma, 92, 144
　Emma Agnes, 125
　Emma Celia, 108
　Emma Eliza, 100
　Emma Estelle, 124, 159

Cole, Emma Frances, 80, 143
　Emma Jane, 69, 71
　Emma L , 114
　Emma Louisa, 91, 103, 140
　Emma Matilda, 95
　Emma Safronia, 144
　Enos, 50, 88
　Enos Covert, 158
　Ernest Jackson, 128
　Ersula, 132
　Estelle, 82, 105, 106
　Estelle J , 162
　Estelle Jane, 159
　Esther, 45, 54, 68
　Esther Adeline, 159
　Esther Ann, 102
　Esther M , 89
　Ethel, 148
　Eugene, 106, 148
　Eugene Enos, 135, 157
　Eugenia, 148
　Eunice, 24, 27, 31, 105
　Eunice Elizabeth, 81
　Eunice Lucy, 136
　Euphemia, 148
　Eva Isabel, 124
　Eva Jane, 117
　Evalena Hall, 94
　Evangeline, 141
　Evangeline Virginie, 141
　Everett F , 149
　Ezra, 43, 72, 138
　Faith Adelaide, 121
　Fannie Ames, 155
　Fannie Belle, 157
　Fannie Fern, 131
　Fanny, 60, 98
　Fanny Estelle, 96
　Fanny Hazen, 61
　Ferris E , 106, 149
　Fidelia Elizabeth, 88
　Flora, 111
　Flora Linda, 130
　Florence, 139
　Florence Adelaide, 139
　Florence B , 160
　Florence Elizabeth, 132
　Florence Emma, 152
　Florence Helen, 158
　Florence Marion, 120
　Florence Nightingale, 80
　Florence Viola, 114
　Francelia, 102
　Frances, 91, 102, 137, 153
　Frances Augusta, 138
　Frances Eliza, 65
　Frances Ellen, 72
　Frances Louise, 120

INDEX

Cole, Frances Nelson, 160
    Francis Vincent, 158
    Francis Wayland, 67, 115
    Frank, 132, 146, 155, 161, 162
    Frank Ames, 156
    Frank Elsworth, 114
    Frank Josiah, 94, 141
    Frank M , 118
    Frank Marion, 74, 120
    Frank Nathaniel, 101
    Frank Ogden, 151
    Fred, 149
    Frederick Lisle, 158
    Frederick Tripler, 141
    Freeborn, 54
    Fremont, 79, 121
    Gay, 158
    Genevieve, 146
    George, 101, 102, 161, 162
    George C , 148
    George Edward, 152
    George Edwin, 124
    George Eugene, 145
    George Frost, 49, 86, 131
    George Harrison, 57, 100
    George Herbert, 79
    George Henry, 101
    George Ide, 74, 124
    George Light, 147, 150
    George Peter, 159
    George Richardson, 100, 144
    George Samuel, 137
    George Tillott, 144
    George Washington, 91, 138
    Georgia Imogene, 121
    Georgiania Irene, 107
    Gertrude Catharine, 158
    Gertrude O , 101
    Gilbert, 105
    Gladys Colestin, 72
    Glen Walker, 151
    Glorinda, 153
    Goolda Ruth, 98
    Grace, 81, 130, 154
    Grace Elizabeth, 71
    Grace Emma, 97
    Grace Lena, 157
    Grace Manchester, 141
    Gracie B , 149
    Green, 66
    Grover, 115
    Grover C , 129
    Guy A , 90
    Hallie Rachel, 83
    Hannah, 11, 23, 24, 26, 27, 29, 34, 37, 47, 50, 52, 53, 60, 79, 89
    Hannah Ann, 143
    Hannah Elizabeth, 145

Cole, Hannah Gannett, 107
    Hannah H , 151
    Hannah Jane, 48, 109
    Hannah Maria, 63
    Harlem, 50, 87, 133
    Harley Lynn, 120
    Harly, 139
    Harmon, 39, 56
    Harold Bates, 158
    Harold Marion, 120
    Harriet, 120, 126, 136
    Harriet B , 90
    Harriet Calista, 73, 120
    Harriet E , 101
    Harriet Eliza, 67
    Harriet Ellen, 151
    Harriet Esther, 143
    Harriet Jane, 157
    Harriet L , 99
    Harriet Newell, 69
    Harriet Pixley, 73
    Harriet Rebecca, 91
    Harrison, 39, 66, 115
    Harry, 49
    Harry Putnam, 139, 158
    Harvey, 36, 61, 113
    Harvey Townsend, 85, 130, 154
    Hascall Myron, 92, 139
    Hattie C , 118
    Hattie Isabel, 96
    Havilah, 34, 143
    Hazel Dorothy, 120
    Hazel Eunice, 153
    Helen, 115, 117, 133, 152, 156
    Helen Gertrude, 123
    Helen Margaret, 159
    Heman, 36, 61
    Heman Hopkins, 62, 109
    Henah, 34
    Henrietta, 65, 148
    Henry, 39, 45, 57, 102, 162
    Henry B , 67
    Henry B , Dr , 115
    Henry Ballard, 143
    Henry Clay, 46, 66, 72, 81, 99, 114, 126, 143
    Henry Denison, 123
    Henry Ernest, 83
    Henry Leonard, 158
    Henry Newton, 116
    Hepzebiah, 22, 23
    Herbert, 103
    Herbert B , 115
    Herbert Bailey, 72
    Herbert Milton, 95, 141
    Herman, 127
    Hermon C , 127
    Hermon Camp, 46, 81, 82, 83

INDEX 211

Cole, Hervey Denison, 79
  Hester Amelia, 95
  Hettie Maria, 104
  Hiram, 38, 55, 66, 98
  Hiram Mason, 89, 136
  Horace, 55, 64, 98, 113, 152
  Horace Wellington, 142
  Horton Sherwood, 102, 145
  Howard, 148, 156
  Howard F Victor, 154
  Howard Loud, 71
  Howard Thomas, 162
  Hugh Clifford, 114
  Hugh Franklin, 71
  Huldah, 41
  Huldah Booth, 148
  Huldah Victoria, 147
  Hymen, 45, 79
  Ida, 110, 135, 141
  Ida Belle 110
  Ida Elizabeth, 109
  Ida Elmira, 146
  Ida F, 153
  Ida Lucretia, 151
  Ida May, 131
  Idalia, 155
  Idaho, 152
  Inez Elvira, 137
  Ira, 50, 61, 84, 85, 155
  Ira Hazen, 18, 44, 74
  Ira Joseph, 123
  Ira Savory, 87, 133
  Ira T, 90
  Ira Woodruff, 132, 155
  Irine, 146
  Irma, 127
  Irma Estelle, 70
  Irving Washington, 79, 122
  Isaac, 3
  Isaac Thompson, 51, 90
  Isabel, 71
  Isabella, 109
  Israel, 22, 23
  Ivah, 34, 55
  Ivy, 154
  Ivy Annista, 153
  Ivy Louise, 111
  J Stanley, 154
  Jacob, 41, 68
  Jacob Edwin, 145
  James, 3, 22, 24, 35, 58, 59, 64, 103, 113
  James A, 147
  James Garfield, 139
  James Henry, 105, 147
  James Kelley, 80, 124
  James Madison, 47, 82
  James Monroe, 46

Cole, James Ogden, 58
  James Riley, 148
  James Stanley, 130, 154
  James Vernon, 160
  James W, 98
  James Wood, 60, 107
  Jane, 24, 68, 101
  Jane Ann, 85, 101, 110
  Jane Bradley, 140
  Jane Elizabeth, 137
  Jane Thursey, 73
  Jarvis Asaheh, 85, 130
  Jarvis Washburn, 45, 79
  Jason Haven, 135, 157
  Jasper, 54, 68
  Jay C, 134, 156
  Jeannette, 80
  Jennie, 101, 102, 152
  Jennie Antoinette, 145
  Jennie Augusta, 95
  Jennie Frances, 149
  Jennie Louise, 109
  Jennie W, 148
  Jeremiah, 59, 147
  Jerome, 67
  Jesse, 34, 55, 56
  Jessie Edith, 72
  Jessie Fremont, 100
  Jessie Lena, 96
  Jewett, 126
  Job, 3, 21
  John, 3, 21-24, 28, 30, 33, 35, 37, 38, 45, 55, 62, 65, 103, 110
  John Benjamin, 58
  John Berry, 53, 94
  John Elkanah, 61
  John Emory, 102
  John Hall, 73
  John Jackson, 128, 154
  John Peck, 80, 124
  John Reasoner, 124, 153
  John Roberts, 79, 123, 144
  John Rogers, 109, 151
  John Tyler, 65
  John Wood, 85
  Jonathan, 24, 41, 70
  Jordan J, 49
  Joseph, 13, 23, 24, 27, 31, 32, 35, 49, 50, 59, 87
  Joseph Bailey, 85, 129
  Joseph Ganong, 84, 125, 129
  Joseph George, 157
  Joseph W, 88, 134
  Joseph Watson, 54, 96
  Josephine Howes, 116
  Joshua, 12, 24-27, 30, 44
  Jules Francis, 71
  Julia, 39, 43, 56, 66, 118

Cole, Julia Augusta, 68
    Julia Fenn, 91
    Julia Frances, 104
    Julia Hill, 160
    Julia Viletta, 158
    Juliette, 64
    Kate Geraldine, 151
    Katharine, 115
    Katharine Ann, 58
    Kenneth Besson, 72
    Kittie, 159
    Laban, 41, 60
    Laura, 39, 88, 135, 162
    Laura Amelia, 125
    Laura J., 66, 90
    Laura Jane, 157
    Laura May, 135
    Lavenia, 105
    Lavenia Stevens, 162
    Le Grand, 62
    Leander, 64, 114
    Lelia Floyd, 127
    Leon Edwin, 67
    Leon Jacob, 116
    Leota, 155
    Lester Abner, 153
    Lester Stanley, 153
    Letitia, 102
    Levi, 55, 68, 98
    Levi H, 67
    Levi Hall, 33, 34, 53
    Lewis, 36, 60
    Lewis Edgar, 100, 145
    Lewis Gregory, 129
    Lewis Porter, 92
    Lewis W., 108, 149
    Libbeus, 36
    Lillie, 71, 111
    Lizzie E, 151
    Loella Augusta, 97
    Lois S, 73
    Louis Jacob, 157
    Louisa, 63, 66, 106
    Louisa Jane, 66
    Louisa M, 51
    Louise, 18, 44, 46, 105
    Louise Laura, 129
    Lovisa, 55
    Lowell Vincent, 158
    Lucena Catharine, 128
    Lucie S, 151
    Lucie Ruth, 155
    Lucretia, 59, 109
    Lucy, 54, 63, 130
    Lucy Harriet, 129
    Luella Jane, 130
    Luke Salathiel, 135
    Lulu, 111

Cole, Lurana, 59, 104
    Lurana Elizabeth, 147
    Lydia, 31, 43, 45, 57, 73, 108
    Lydia Bloomer, 73
    Lydia Hathaway, 107
    Lyman Mason, 63, 111
    Mabel, 150
    Mae, 83
    Maine, 149
    Malissa B, 162
    Malvina, 101
    Maple Lucille, 153
    Marcus, 50
    Margaret, 27, 33, 35, 103, 104, 156, 163
    Margaret Ann, 102
    Margaret Jane, 153
    Margaret Lavinia, 147
    Maria, 89, 92
    Maria Elizabeth, 101
    Marie Antoinette, 100, 144
    Marie Louise, 141
    Marinda, 86
    Marion, 123, 126
    Marion E, 129
    Marion Lucena, 129
    Marjorie, 152
    Marjorie Jackson, 128
    Martha, 51, 85, 94, 106, 126
    Marvin, 61
    Mary, 3, 11, 22-24, 26, 33, 35, 40, 55, 58-60, 65, 79, 80, 83, 84, 90, 98, 102, 104, 115, 116, 123, 129, 133, 140, 157, 161
    Mary A, 72, 124, 149, 160
    Mary Ann, 53, 62, 66, 67, 92, 107
    Mary Ann (Allen), Mrs, 108
    Mary Ann Ball, 86
    Mary Almira, 131
    Mary Amelia, 148
    Mary Caroline, 74
    Mary Constance, 116
    Mary Cynthia, 98
    Mary Downes, 144
    Mary Elizabeth, 63, 70, 96, 102, 130, 146, 151
    Mary Ellen, 101, 125, 128
    Mary Fayette, 84, 95
    Mary Frances, 103, 161
    Mary Gladys, 128
    Mary Horton, 88
    Mary Jane, 55, 80, 103, 112, 115, 119
    Mary Lillian, 139
    Mary Louisa, 91
    Mary Luella, 114
    Mary Lydia, 118
    Mary M, 160

Cole, Mary Margaret, 57
  Mary Taylor 120
  Mary Washburn, 61
  Matilda, 159
  Matilda Louisa, 73, 138
  Maude, 113, 135
  Maude Evelyn, 123
  Maxwell, 117
  May, 146
  May Belle, 113, 145
  Medora Jane, 110
  Mehitable, 7, 30, 31
  Melinda, 47, 50, 62, 114
  Melissa, 87, 103, 116
  Melvena, 164
  Mercy, 28, 47
  Merrick L, 65
  Milan Jedediah, 52
  Mildred, 148
  Millie, 114
  Millie M, 134
  Milo, 51
  Milo Van Duzen, 52, 92, 139
  Mina Elizabeth, 151
  Miner Coburn, 140
  Miner Thomas, 44, 74, 118
  Minerva, 69, 86, 87, 161
  Minerva Ann, 40
  Minerva Ruth, 50
  Minnie, 67, 73, 126, 156
  Minnie May, 112
  Minnie Rachel, 134
  Mortimer, 133, 156
  Mortimer Belding, 101, 145
  Moses, 24
  Moses Hazen, 60
  Muriel, 152
  Myron Rowland, 52
  Myrtie, 149
  Nancy, 44, 85, 90, 91
  Nancy R, 80
  Naomi, 27, 30, 35, 38
  Nathalie Rachel, 128
  Nathan, 7, 8, 24, 27, 30-32, 35, 38, 45, 47, 51, 57, 63, 82, 83, 89, 101, 128
  Nathan Edward, 125, 153
  Nathan Thompson, 91, 130, 155
  Nathan W, 92, 140
  Nellie, 138, 156
  Nellie B, 147
  Nellie Belle, 65
  Nellie Emeline, 122
  Nellie Josephine, 107
  Nellie Louise, 96
  Nellie Walker, 117
  Nelson, 62
  Nettie, 142

Cole, Newissa, 48, 164
  Newell, 82
  Norma, 138, 152
  Norman, 56, 156
  Norman Sheldon, 69, 116
  Norvin Green, 144
  Obed, 29, 39
  Ogden, 36, 56, 61, 99, 102, 109, 151
  Olive, 114
  Olive O, 153
  Olive Secord, 159
  Oliver C, 46
  Oliver Garrison, 80, 125
  Oliver Kenneth, 125
  Olonzo, 162
  Onken Willard, 70, 117
  Ormond Hayes, 18, 83
  Orson, 109
  Orville Porter, 73
  Orville Seymour, 131
  Orville Webster, 137, 158
  Oscar Gregory, 139
  Otis, 4, 107, 149
  Otis Hazen, 129
  Otto Paris, 130, 154
  Paul Forshay, 159
  Peninnah Owen, 145
  Percival Victor, 83
  Peter James, 103, 147
  Phebe, 24, 36, 49
  Phebe Ann, 86
  Phebe J, 56
  Phebe Jane, 79
  Philip, 115
  Polly, 38
  Prentiss Ingraham, 154
  Priscilla, 25, 103
  Priscilla Ann, 28
  Prudence, 88
  Rachel, 39, 56, 57, 66, 115, 136
  Rachel Adelia, 134
  Rachel Emily, 92
  Rachel Jane, 106
  Ralph, 152
  Ralph Dana, 121
  Ralph Leroy, 154
  Ralph Tichenor, 140
  Ralph Tunis, 74, 120
  Rama Milan, 142
  Ramah, 33, 53, 54, 94
  Ramah Elliot, 141
  Ray Freeman, 150
  Raymond Lamont, 159
  Raymond Wiltsie, 157
  Rebecca, 21, 47, 128
  Rebecca Augustine, 125
  Rebecca Fagan, 128
  Rebecca Lane, 82, 83

Cole, Reuben, 29, 36, 56, 99
   Richard Barton, 142
   Richard Hood, 83
   Rixford, 148
   Robert Frank, 118
   Robert Sly, 155
   Robert Walker, 135, 157
   Roena, 110
   Roger Garwood, 158
   Rollin Elwood, 158
   Rollo M, 111
   Romaine Harvey, 61
   Rose, 155
   Rose Althea, 151
   Roxie Lura, 153
   Roy Edgar, 139
   Ruby Beatrice, 153
   Rudy, 127
   Rufus, 42, 70
   Rufus Jay, 70
   Ruth, 22, 23, 32, 155
   Ruth Alva, 158
   Ruth Esther, 137
   Ruth Payne, 96
   Ruth Violet, 142
   Sallie, 161
   Samantha, 73
   Samantha L, 136
   Samuel, 32, 50, 161, 162
   Samuel Bailey, 86, 132
   Sarah, 3, 23, 29, 34, 37, 45, 56, 58, 99, 101, 103, 142, 145, 157
   Sarah A, 88
   Sarah Almira, 131
   Sarah Anna, 51
   Sarah C, 95
   Sarah H, 73
   Sarah Jane, 39, 81, 106
   Sarah Louisa, 79
   Sarah Maria, 38
   Sarah Roxanna, 44
   Saxon, 126
   Selema, 147
   Sepha, 148
   Seraphina, 133
   Sidney Townsend, 151
   Spencer Houghton, 67
   Stanley Sands, 145
   States G, 49
   Stuart, 155
   Susan, 45, 52, 69, 70, 84, 86, 99
   Susan C, 63
   Susan Elizabeth, 105, 110
   Susan Jane, 104, 111
   Susan Lydia, 150
   Susannah, 32
   Thaddeus, 80
   Thaddeus Lincoln, 124
   Cole, Thankful, 24
   Theda, 39
   Theodore Frelinghuysen, 99, 104
   Theron, 39, 53 67, 105, 147
   Theron Hopkins, 67
   Thomas, 59, 104, 161
   Thomas Edgar, 147, 160
   Thomas Owen, 57, 100
   Thurza, 36
   Tillie Grant, 115
   Tillott 56, 100
   Timothy, 22, 161
   Trenton Leland, 117
   Una, 126
   Uretta, 48, 165
   Ursula, 51, 92
   Van Renselaer, 115
   Vashti, 35
   Vashti Susan, 58
   Velma Bailey, 153
   Vera Giddings, 162
   Victor Leroy, 130
   Victoria, 154
   Vida Beatrice, 153
   Vincent Peter, 147
   Viola, 55, 147
   Viola May, 157
   Virtue Elvira, 65
   Walter, 101
   Walter Bailey, 124, 153
   Walter Hascall, 139
   Walter Henry, 114
   Walter Sinclair, 66
   Walter Todd, 66
   Wallace Henry, 94, 140
   Warren, 65
   Warren Ramah, 87, 88
   Washburn Ogden, 61
   Watson, 51, 90
   Webster Knapp, 89, 136
   Wilbur, 110
   Wilbur Milton, 92
   Wilhelmina, 160
   Willard Harvey, 71
   Willard Leonard, 71
   William, 22, 23, 32, 35, 58-60, 104, 105, 146, 162
   William Denison, 79
   William Elmer, 151
   William Gregory, 129
   William H, 102, 110
   William Henry, 73, 91, 138
   William Ide, 118
   William J, 147
   William Jay, 133
   William John, 103, 146
   William L, 111
   William Martin, 55, 97

Cole, William R , 104
   William Rappleye, 74, 117
   William Sylvester, 96
   William Walker, 115
   William Wallace, 63, 112, 162
   William Van Zant, 80
   Willie, 113
   Wray Lincoln, 149, 160
   Yates Thompson, 88, 133
   Zachariah, 98
   Zachary Taylor, 81, 126
   Zella Alice, 125
   Zellah Celeno, 128
   Zillah, 37, 50, 61, 98, 100
   Zora Belle, 97
   Zuba, 89
Colgrove, Florence E , 132
   Katharine, 198
   Olive Cole, 198
   Silas C , 132
   Walter, 132, 198
Collier, Elizabeth, 21
   Mary, 9, 21
   Rebecca, 21
   Sarah, 21
   William, 9, 21
Colmore, Eliza Ann, 161
   Sallie, 161
   William, 161
Colwell, Adah, 59
   Asahel Cole, 181
   Editha, 181
   Eliza Jane, 181
   Ezra, 52, 181
   Hannah, 52, 98
   Martha Augusta, 181
   Mary, 80
   Phebe, 165, 181
   Thomas, 52, 59
   Zillah, 100, 166
Comstock, Charity, 150
Condit, Mary A , Mrs , 124
Conely, Olivia, 180
   Thomas, 180
Conklin, Sarah, 175
   William, 175
Cool, Edith, 152
   Samuel, 152
Cooper, ——, 169
   Agnes, 176
   Edward Clarence, 132, 198
   Ezekiel, Capt , 5
   Frank L , 115
   Marion Sarah, 198
   Rachel, 115
   Sarah Eleanor, 188
   William, 132
Copeland, Alice L , 158

Copley, Georgia, 175
Corbet, Mary Ellen, 128
   William Zachary, 128
Corbitt, Almira Ann, 120
Cordill, Eleanor, 113
   Hiram, 113
Cornelius, Mary J , 150
Cornell, Catharine, 180
   Warren, 180
Cornwell, Almira, 152
Corson, Mary, 117
   Mary M , 119
Cortrite, Hattie E , 174
Covert, Magdalena, 108
   Rynear, Col , 108
Cramer, Anna, 167
Crane, Jared, 84
   Noah H , 164
   Susannah, 164
Crawford, Coleman, 167
   Esther, 133
   Frances, 137
   John, 137
   Julia, 167
Crisp, George, 22
Crissey, Caleb, 175
   Elizabeth, 175
   Frederick, 80
   Grace, 190
   John W , 190
   Mary, 80
   Mary Alice, 190
   Morris C , 80, 190
   Nancy Ethel, 190
   Ruth, 174
   Ruth Elizabeth, 190
   Susan Agnes, 190
   William Morris, 190
Crocker, Margaret, 94
Cronk, Susan, 35
Crosby, Clara, 62
   Elizabeth, 12
   Enoch, 41, 163
   Eunice, 27, 163
   Hannah, 163
   Jane, 163
   Lydia, 31
   Nathan, 27, 31, 163
   Phebe, 162
   Stephen, 163
Cross, Maria, 85
   Sarah Emma, 95
Crowther, Charles C., 185
   Lorena, 185
Cummings, Leonard, 170
   Martha A , 128
   Mary, 170
Cunningham, Mary, 117

216 INDEX

Curry, Ann, 102
  George, 165
  Hannah, 165
  Peter B , 95
  Sarah Amanda, 95
Cutler, Sarah Jane, 155

Dakin, Emma, 144
  James J , 144
  Joshua, 7
  Rebecca, 7
  Simon, 6, 7
Dargavel, Rachel, 96
Darrow, Lydia, 91
Dart, Daniel, 14
  Elizabeth, 14
Davenport, Clarissa, 90
Davis, Belle Frances, 97
  Edith Sedina, 196
  Grace Muriel, 196
  Loella Augusta, 97
  Paul Judson, 196
  Philip Judson, 97
  Reginald Sidney, 196
  Sarah, 105
  Sidney Cornish, 97, 196
  Tillie Grant, 115
  William, 97
  William Henry, 97
  William Howard, 97
Daw, Elizabeth, 97
Day, Annie, 136
  Maria L , 98
Dayton, Asa 108
  Elvira Laura, 108
  Kate, 181
Dean, Chester B , 193
  Elizabeth, 84
  Ersula, 132
  Jervis, 132
  Julia, 70
  Laura Eunice, 193
Deane, Stephen, 23
Debar, Harriet B , 90
  Jacob, 90
De Groot, Eliza, 91
Delaney, Frances, 91
De Long, John, 150
  Mabel, 150
Denison family, 15
  Agnes, 176
  Beckwith, 16, 18, 44, 74
  Christopher, 16
  Daniel, 15
  Edward 16
  Frank H , 176
  George, 16
  George B , 181

Denison, Gertrude, 176
  Louise, 44
  Mary, 176
  Mary Caroline, 17, 18, 74
  Mercy, 16
  Samuel, 16
  Susan B , 181
  William, 15
  James Floyd, 176
  James Henry, 44, 176
  James Hervey, 18, 19
  John, 16
Dennis, Laura, 162
Depew, Annie Louisa, 184
  Elmira, 58
  George Washington, 58, 184
  Julia, 184
  Vashti Susan, 58, 184
  William Willoby, 184
De Vall, Harriet, 157
Dexter, Harriet, 134
Diamond, ———, 169
Dingee, Charlotte, 57
  David, 32
  Martha Elizabeth, 32
Doane, Daniel, 22
  Hepzeibah, 22
  John, 22
Dodds, George, 180
  Nancy, 180
Dolbee, Blanche Owens, 126
  Shadrack R , 126
Donk, Flora, 111
Doolittle, Alma R., 90
  Alonzo, 90
Doran, David, 145
  Hannah Elizabeth, 145
Doremus, Andrew J , 95
  Dorothy Carl, 196
  Ella Euphemia, 95
  Harry Whitehouse, 95, 195
  Helen Marguerite, 195
  Jeannette Claire, 196
  Robert Child, 195
Doty, Ada Bertha, 194
  M Seward, 194
  Sarah, 185
Douglas, James, 80
  Jeanetie, 80
Douglass, Hattie C , 118
  Rawlins, 118
Doughty, George, 62, 185
  Maria, 97
  Mary Ann (Fowler), 62
Downer, Martha, 51
Downing, Harry Venton, 157
Doyle, Cora May, 154
  Sarah Clarkson, 109

INDEX 217

Doyle, William Alfred, 154
Drew, Sarah, 98
Dronyor, Clara Bell, 149
Dudley, Anna, 14
Durand, Nettie M., 191
Durfee, Aaron B., 88, 192
    Borden, 88
    Frank, 192
    Sarah A., 88
Durland, Lewis H., 173
    Sarah, 173
Durrand, Hannah M., 51
Dykeman, Jessie, 188
    Willard J., 188

Eager, Laura Phebe, 192
    William Blake, 192
Eames, Anna Matilda, 128
Earle, Ada Jane, 51
    Florence Adele, 180
    George, 180
    Ida J., 180
    Marcus, 180
    Olivia, 180
    Riley, 51, 180
    William, 51
Eastman, Hezekiah, 7
    Joseph D., 7
Eastwood, Alvin, 107
    Elizabeth, 107
Ebelmesser, Caroline, 120
Edelmann, Florence C., 186
    Henry, 186
Edmonds, Charles Oscar, 141
    Chauncey Brooks, 141
    Edith, 141
Edsall, David, 167
    Zillah, 167
Edson, Fanny, Mrs., 65
Edwards, Betsey, 51, 89
Egleston, Deborah, 162
Ellis, Betsey, 62
Elmer, Martin, 7
Emlitch, Marcellus, 185
    Ophelia, 185
Emmons, Eliza, 52
    Isaac, 52
English, John, 98
    Zillah, 98
Estrange, Mary L., 93
Evans, Elizabeth, 71, 166
Everett, Charles, 106
    Louisa, 106
    Mary, 92
Everts, Phebe, 133

Faatz, Wilhelmina, 160
Fagin, Aaron W., 82

Fagin, Rebecca Lane, 82
Fairchild, Clarissa, 48
Farnham, Adelbert Marcillus, 134
    John, 134
    Millie M., 134
Farrington, Charles, 169
    Ebenezer, 169
    Jane, 169
    Mary, 169
    Vashti, 35
    William, 35, 169
Feigles, Mary Ann, 177
Fenn, Maria, 181
    George J., 181
Fero, Nancy, 91
    Peter, 91
Ferro, Jane Ann, 85
Ferris, Amanda, 69
    Andrew, 69
    David Augustus, 124
    Deborah, 51
    Emily Augusta, 124
    Harriet Amelia, 159
    Lurana, 58
Field, Sarah, 41
Finch, Mary, 104
    Tremaine, 104
Fisher, Bertha, 106
    Edwin, 106
    Elizabeth, 10
    Freeman, 106
    Jane, 172
    John J., 172
    Martha, 106
Fitch, Catharine, 131
Flagg, James M., 97
    Zora Belle, 97
Flanagin, Joseph S., 81
Fogle, Albertine, 152
    Benjamin, 152
Folger, Charles Worth, 184
    Vashti Susie, 184
Ford, Catharine, 83
Forshay, Matilda, 159
    John Wesley, 159
Foster, Eleanor, 42, 68, 70
    Huldah, 52
Fowler, Benjamin, 62, 185
    Clarissa, 161
    Eli, 185
    Elizabeth, 173
    Esther, 68
    Irine, 185
    John W., 185
    Major, 62
    Mary, 79
    Mary Ann, 62
    Sarah, 185

Fowler, William, 68
Francis, Lucinda, 134
   Lucinda H , 134
French, Alta Belle, 138
   Edward Ernest, 138
   William, 138
Freeman, John, 9
   Joseph, 10
   Mary, 10
   Nathaniel, 10
   Rebecca, 10, 11, 27
   Thomas, 10
Fritcher, Elizabeth Maria, 85
Frost, Adeline, 44, 130
   David, 49
   Emily Augusta, 146
   George, 33, 44
   Jacob, 130
   Julia, 167
   Laura, 167, 176
   Lucy Emma, 152
   Lydia, 57
   Mary, 33
   Morris, 44, 167, 176
   Orville C , 167
   Phebe, 49
   Sarah, 164
   Sarah A , 167
   Sarah J , 167
   Susan, 176
   Underhill, 84
Fuller, Addie, 191
   Desire, 163
   Lillie, 111
   Mercy, 22
   Robert, 7, 30
   Samuel, Rev , 22

Gadbury, Hannah, 128
Gainey, Julia, 134
Galloway, Jane, 101
Ganong family, 48
   Aaron, 176
   Abigail, 47, 52
   Adah, 48
   Alexander, 83
   Amanda, 176
   Augusta J , 176
   Calista, 40
   Clarinda, 48
   Daniel, 48
   Deborah, 178
   Emily, 178
   Isaac, 48
   Jacob, 48
   John, 48
   Jonet, 48, 178
   Joseph, 40
   Martha, 40, 48

Ganong, Mary, 83
   Oscar, 178
   Reuben, 48
Ga Nunn, Lewis, 144
   Mary Downes, 144
Gardner, James Lion, 86
   John Lion, 86
   Lizzie E , 151
   Marinda, 86
Gay, Rebecca, 85
Genung, John, 48
Getchell, Clara, 173
Gettman, Jacob, 157
   Mary, 157
Gibbs, Mary, 112
Giddings, Rowland, 125
   Nancy Ann, 151
   Zella Alice, 125
Gilbert, Julia Ann, 104
   Mary Frances, 103
   Reuben Burr, 103
Gildersleeve, Mary, 116
Gillett, Emma L , 114
   Mary Jane, 103
   Thomas, 103
Gillhan, Daniel Brown, 127
   Ella Lilian, 127
Glover, Margueritte, 136
Godsey, Addie, 118
   George, 118
Goewey, David, 129
   Lucy Harriet, 129
Gold, John, 94
Gorham, John, 16
   Mercy, 16
Gouverneur, Mary, 41
Gracie, Anna Leslie, 153
Graham, Harriet, 142
   James Stewart, 112
   Jane, 92
   Mary Jane, 112
Grant, Hannah, 14
Gray, Alice, 117
Green, Annie, 97
   Charles, 32, 165
   Collins, 165
   Hannah, 177
   Jeremiah L., 84, 177
   Nellie, 138
   Rebecca, 165
   Sarah, 81
   Susan, 165
   Thomas, 139
Greenleaf, Bethia, 38
   Israel, 37
   William, 37
Gregory, Charles Byington, 110, 197
   Clara V , 197

INDEX

Gregory, George Washington, 110
  Georgia A , 197
  Ida, 110
  Jessie L , 197
  Lewis H , 128
  Lucena Catharine, 128
Griffin, Eliza, 53
  John, 163
  Mary, 163
Griswold, ———, 19
  Evalina Hall, 94
  Frank, 94
  Frank Lorin, 94
  Mary, 18
Guenon, Jean, 48
  John, 48
Guthrie, Alson, 167
  Maria, 167
  Virginia, 127
Guy, Evangeline Virginie, 141
  Marie Louise, 141
  Samuel Smith, Dr , 141

Hackett, Abigail, 63, 65
  Josiah, 65
Haight, ———, 66
  Adelbert S , 186
  Alice E , 186
  Benjamin, 64
  Benjamin D , 185
  Elizabeth, 103
  Emma, 186
  Fannie A , 186
  Henry, 64
  Henry L , 186
  Juliette, 64
  Mary, 147
Haines, Edmond, 39
  Esther, 39
  Julia, 165
Hall, Adah, 167
  Adelia, 44
  Adelia Cole, 93
  Alice Louise, 195
  Ann, 166, 167
  Annis, 168
  Asa Thompson, 167
  Augusta, 175
  Caleb, 33, 34
  Carrie F , 175
  Carrie Frances, 93
  Daniel, 165, 168
  Edith L Penn, 195
  Elizabeth, 167
  Hannah, 166
  Ira Cole, 93, 175, 195
  Jane, 167
  John, 44

Hall, John C , 175
  John Chapman, 44, 93
  John Wilbur, 195
  Levi, 33, 34, 166, 168
  Louise, 175
  Margaret, 33
  Maria, 168
  Nathan, 34, 168
  Sarah, 34
  Susan, 166
  Zillah, 167
Hamblin, Eleazer, 15
  Sarah, 15, 28
Hambridge, Eliza, 141
Hamel, Sarah, 167
Hamilton, Eliza, 174
  Sarah E , 115
  Theron, 174
Hammersley, Annie, 101
Hanchet, Amos, 7
Hand, Eleanor, 113
  Harvey, 113
Hanford, H Byron, 174
  Harry, 41, 173
  Hattie E , 174
  Heber H , 174
  Henry Clay, 174
  Hopkins J , 174
  Huldah, 41
  Jane, 174
  Lewis, 41
  Mayme, 174
  Sarah, 174
Hanna, Jennie, 152
  Walter, 152
Hardy, Etta, 192
  Nancy Ethel, 190
  Raymond, 190
Harkness, Edna Lou, 150
  Elizabeth Pauline, 150
  John U , 150
  Lewellyn, 150
  Susan Lydia, 150
Harrington, Pearl May, 186
Harrison, Virginia Narcissa, 127
Harrold, Martha, 180
  William, 180
Harsha, Ida, 125
Hart, Allen M , 186
  Daniel L , 63, 185
  Edgar D , 185
  James, 94
  Martha, 94
  Mary Elizabeth, 63
  Naomi, 164
  Nellie M , 186
  Rose, 185
  Samuel, 164

Hart, Stella D., 171, 186
Harvey, Alice, 71
   Mary, 131
   Mercy, 7
   Obed, 7
   Obed, Jr, 7
   Thaddeus F, 71
Harwood, Andrew, 130
   Edna, 130
   Wm Stevenson, 130
Haslet, Mary A, 88
Hastings, Hiram, 167
   Julia, 167
Hawkins, Hannah H, 151
   John R, 151
   Margaret, Mrs, 103
   Mary Elizabeth, 151
   Sarah, 171
   William M, 151
Hawley, Alan Wayne, 198
   Chester Cole, 198
   Chester W, 113
   George T, 198
   Geo Thompson, Dr, 113
   Mary C, 90
   Mary W, 166
   May Belle, 113
   Stephen, 166
Hayes, Eunice, 7
   Jonathan, 7
Hayward, Hannah T, 151
Hazen, Abigail, 15
   Adeline, 172
   Anna, 61, 163
   Annie Augusta, 98
   Ansel, 128, 166
   Ansel E, 98
   Anson, 168
   Byron E, 98
   Caleb, 15, 28, 40, 167
   Charity, 15, 28
   Edward, 14
   Eleazer, 15
   Eliza Ann, 166
   Elizabeth, 14
   Emily C, 168
   Emily L, 172
   Fanny, 60
   Frances A, 172, 176
   Hannah, 168
   Henry C., 168, 172, 176
   Jerome B, 52
   John, 14
   Laura, 167
   Mentor W, 39, 172
   Mercy, 15
   Moses, 15, 60, 61
   Orson, 172

Hazen, Phebe, 172
   Rachel, 39
   Richard, 14
   Sarah, 15
   Thomas, 14, 163
   Zillah, 98
   Zellah Celeno, 128
Heacock, Mary, 60
Hebert, Hallie Rachel, 83
   Joseph Louis, 83, 191
   Nathan Cole, 191
   Thomas Richardson, 191
Hederick, Frederick, 95
   Sarah, 176
   Sarah C, 95
Henderson, James, 63
   Louisa, 63
Hendricks, Jacob, 133
   Mary, 133
Hendrickson, Abram, 50, 179
   Anna, 50
   Cornelia A, 179
   G W, 179
   Mary E, 179
Henion, Hannah, 71
Henry, Eleanor Isabella, 81
Henshaw, Mary Luella, 114
Herr, Henry, 138
   John, 138
   Norma, 138
Herrick, Roena, 110
Herring, Marion E, 129
   William H, 129
Hersey, Edward Payson, 139
   Mary Lillian, 139
Hetchler, John, 134
   Rachel Adelia, 134
Hewlet, Mary, 14
   Thomas, 14
Hicks, Harry Clark, 110
   Ida Belle, 110
   Jean, 110
Higgins, Emory, 176
   Floyd, 176
   H J, 135
   Ida, 135
   Laura, 176
   Susan, 176
Hilliker, Charles A, 96
Hills, Albert W, 64
   Augusta, 64
   Catharine, 186
   Clarence A, 186
   Florence C, 186
   Herbert Walker, 64, 186
   James A, 186
   Pearl May, 186
Hine, Charles, 61

INDEX 221

Hine, Jeremiah, 61, 185
  Zillah, 61
Hinkley, Mercy, 23
Hitchcock, Sarah, 38
Hodge, James, 146
  Lavina, 63
  Lucy, 175
  Mary Elizabeth, 146
  Robert, 146
Hodgson, John H., 178
  Sarietta, 178
Hoffman, Selema, 147
  William J., 147
Holden, Addie May, 110
  Belle, 189
  Charles, 189
  David, 73, 189
  Elizabeth Brown, 82
  Frank, 189
  George, 73, 189
  Harriet Pixley, 73
  Jennie, 189
  John, 189
  Lafayette, 110
  Lydia, 73
  Mary, 189
  Nellie, 189
Holledge, Rebecca, 96
Holmes, Phebe, 181
Hoop, Mary Lena, 157
Hopkins family, 10
  Abraham, 13
  Ada Bertha, 194
  Adeline, 159
  Adilla, 12
  Alice Augusta, 172
  Alice Louise, 195
  Almira, 166
  Alvah, 12
  Amelia Gordon, 194
  Antha Jane, 100, 166
  Antoinette, 172
  Asenath, 12
  Benjamin, 14
  Berry, 12
  Bethia, 13
  Calista, 170
  Carrie Moore, 140
  Charles S., 194
  Charles Samuel, 91
  Chauncey Ambrose, 172
  Chloe, 12, 61
  Clinton Henry, 194
  Constance, 10
  Cynthia, 32
  Deborah, 11
  Don A., 140
  Druzilla, 92

Hopkins, Edla May, 194
  Edmund, 11, 93
  Edward, 12
  Elah, 45
  Elah B., 67, 176
  Elam, 177
  Eli, 12
  Eliza A., 98, 128, 176
  Eliza Ann, 166
  Elizabeth, 13, 165
  Emma, 172
  Enos, 32, 39, 98, 100, 163, 166
  Erastus, 39, 166, 172
  Fannie A., 194
  Florence A., 194
  Freeman, 11, 27, 33, 163
  Giles, 10, 22
  Goolda Ruth, 98
  Hannah, 12, 13, 27
  Hannah E., 166
  Harriet Eliza, 194
  Isaiah, 12
  James, 170
  Jane, 12, 30, 164
  Jane Ann, 177
  Jemina, 13
  Jeremiah, 13, 32, 165
  Jonathan, 10, 11, 12, 27, 42
  Joseph, 11, 12, 13, 30, 41, 42, 44, 61, 164
  Joshua, 11, 22
  Julia Fenn, 91
  Leonard, 12
  Lizzie, 12
  Lydia, 11
  Marion, 106
  Mary, 11–13, 22
  Mary Louisa, 91
  Michal, 13
  Minnie, 67
  Muah, 13
  Noah, 13
  Nancy, 12
  Naomi, 13, 164
  Nathaniel, 13
  Rebecca, 12, 41, 166
  Reuben, 13, 14, 107
  Roswell, 13
  Ruth, 166
  Sarah, 13, 42
  Sarah Jane, 106
  Soloman, 12, 13
  Stephen, 10, 11, 13, 14
  Susan M., 170
  Thatcher, 11
  Theda, 39
  Theron Cole, 172
  Thomas, 12, 13

222 INDEX

Hopkins, Thomas Anson, 91
    Thomas Judson, 91, 194
    Walter D , 195
    William A , 166
    Wright, 14
Horton, ———, 169
    Adaline Minerva, 54
    Agnes Ann, 95
    Anna, 183
    Arthur, 183
    Carrie, 183
    Cyrus, 102
    Elias, 183
    Elijah, 54
    Eliza, 102
    Emeline, 170
    Harriet Rebecca, 73, 91
    Ira T , 54, 183
    Jesse, 91
    Mary, 102
    Ramahette, 183
    Samuel, 183
    Spencer, 183
    William, 183
Hotchkiss, Carrie, 168
Houch, Amanda, 67
    Andrew, 67
Howe, Mary Eliza, 175
Howes, Adeline, 172
    Bailey, 40, 172
    Byron, 173
    Clara, 173
    Felix, 173
    Hannah Jane, 109
    Jacob Orson, 109
    Josephine, 185
    Lydia, 185
    Mary, 40, 173
    Nathan Alva, 62
    Oscar, 172
    William, 185
    William Edgar, 61
    Zillah (Hine), 62
Howland, Desire, 16
    John, 16
Hoyt, Elizabeth, 106
    Ephraim, 57, 184
    Frank, 184
    Gates, 68
    Hannah Ann Elizabeth, 184
    Julia Augusta, 68
    Margaret, 184
    Mary Margaret, 57
    Thaddeus, 57
Htzenbuchler, J , 118
    Mary Lydia, 118
Hubbard, Abel, 90
    Daniel, 17

Hubbard, George W , 89
    Maria, 89
    Mary, 17, 18
Huff, Aaron, 88, 192
    Alida, 192
    Bertha May, 145
    Catharine, 88
    Charles, 192
    Dorothy May, 145
    Elizabeth, 88
    John N., 88
    Minnie, 192
    Oliver, 145
    Oliver David, 145
    Phebe, 192
    Rolla J., 192
Hughson, Almond, 172
    Ann, 172
    Emma B , 172
    Esther, 39
    Frances R , 172
    George M , 39
    Harmon, 172
    Harriet, 172
    James, 39, 79, 172
    Jane, 172
    Jesse, 39, 172
    Julia, 172
    Laura, 39
    Le Grand, 172
    Mary, 79, 172
    Minerva, 107
    Russell, 39
    Sarah, 165
    Sarah Jane, 39
Hulbert, Esther, 143
Humphrey, Elizabeth, 130
    James Burton, 130
Hunt, Lelia Floyd, 127
    Thomas Winn, 127
Hunter, Catharine, 186
Hunting, Betsey, 131
Hurd, Aaron, 19
    Achilles, 18
    Artemus Bodman, 133
    Caleb Leete, 16, 18
    Daniel, 18
    Dolly, 19
    Dorothy, 18
    Ebenezer, 18
    Edith Leonard, 133
    Elias, 18, 19
    Ethlinda, 19
    George W , 133
    Laura, 19
    Laura Ann, 19
    Leete, 18, 19
    Mary, 16, 18, 44, 74

INDEX 223

Hurd, Samuel, 19
  William, 18, 19
Hurlburt, Harriet, 172
  William G , 172
Hurley, Minerva, 86
  Thomas K , 86
  William, 86
Hyatt, Reuben, 168
  Sarah, 49
  Susan, 168

Ingraham, Ivy, 154
  Prentiss, 154
Ismon, Charlotta, 191

Jackson, Anna Mary, 127
  Diana, 149
  Frances Augusta, 138
  Geneveve, 175
  John, 127
  Oliver Herman, 138
  William, 149
Jacobs, ———, 104
  Deborah, 58
  Lurana, 104
Jahns, Anneke, 108
January, Jeannette, 127
Jefferson, Benjamin, 50, 179
  Clinton, 179
  Elizabeth, 50
  Lena, 88
  Marvin, 179
  Sandford, 179
  Theodore, 179
Jenells, Alice Amelia, 120
Jenkins, ———, 101, 102
  Margaret, 184
  Mary Elizabeth, 102
  Sarah, 101
  Thomas Jefferson, 184
Jessup, Jane, 95
Johnson, Augustus (Gus), 136
  Cynthia A , 181
  Della Mason, 136
  Edgar Doyle, 109, 197
  Elmer Ezekiel, 155
  Franklin Burbank, 109, 197
  Grace, 154
  Isabella, 109
  Mary, 168
  Nicholas, 181
  Ruth W , 197
  Samuel Burbank, 109, 197
  William Dewey, 136
Jones, Harry T , 151
  Ida Lucretia, 151
  Jay, 131
  Prosser, 131

Jordan, Elizabeth, 17, 18
  Thomas, 17
Judd, Delaphine, 191

Karl, Jacob, 160
  Wilhelmina, 160
Kealer, Mary B , 117
Keiler, Elizabeth, 21
Kelley, Alanson C , 170
  Albert, 167
  Almira M , 170
  Annis, 35
  Antoinette, 41, 169
  Antoinette Kelley, 68
  Austin, 169
  Byronette Cole 174
  Charlotte, 52, 59
  Chauncey Ragan, 174
  Clara N , 32
  Ebenezer, 52, 169
  Eliza, 35
  Elizabeth, 16
  Ezra, 35, 169
  Fanny C , 169
  Frederick Cole, 188
  Hannah, 36
  Henrietta F , 174
  Horton G , 169
  Ira, 35, 169
  Isaac, 42, 174
  Jane, 68, 163
  Jesse, 42, 68, 70, 188
  John, 35, 40, 68, 169
  Joseph, 169
  Judah, 164
  Levi, 80
  Lydia, 174
  Margaret, 169
  Mary Jane, 169
  Mary M , 174
  Naomi, 40, 164
  Naomi J , 171
  Nellie F , 174
  Paul Vincent, 188
  Phebe Jane, 79
  Sadie E , 188
  Sarah B , 169
  Sarah E , 170
  Sarah Eleanor, 188
  Seth Foster, 188
  Sophia, 107
  Susan, 52, 70
  Theodore F , 68, 188
  Vashti Jane, 169
  William F , 169
Kellogg, Melinda, 50
Kendall, Alice, 81
  Eugene, 81

Kendall, Eunice Elizabeth, 81
  George J, 81
  Henry C, 81
Kendrick, Catharine, 125
  Justin Smith, 125
Kennedy, Alexander S, 126
  Martha, 126
Kent, Elisha, Rev, 12
  Josephine, 147
  Sarah, 39
  William, 147
Kershner, Anna, 156
Ketcham, Hannah, 105
  Mary, 173
Keyes, Charles B, 39
  Mary, 160
Kimbel, Melissa, 103
Kimmick, Rose, 155
King, Asaph, 51
  Barzillai, 7, 30
  Cynthia A, 181
  Elizabeth, 36
  George, 181
  Harriet,' 181
  Harvey F, 181
  Heman, 7, 30, 36
  Louise, 181
  Mary Ann, 79
  Phebe, 91, 181
  Samantha, 36, 92
  Samuel, 11
  Sarah Anna, 51
  Susan B, 181
  Sylvester, 51, 181
Kingsley, Angeline, 168
Kinney, Susan, 87
Kinsman, Ebenezer, 96
  Fanny Estelle, 96
  William Ross, 96
Kirkham, Charity, 104
  Henrietta F, 174
  Peter Z, 174
Kirkup, Maine, 149
Kline, Lena M, 193
Knapp, Cynthia, 166
  George, 169
  Gilbert, 166
  Henry, 70
  James Alonzo, 70
  Jennie Frances, 149
  Mary Elizabeth, 70
  Mary Jane, 169
  Sarah B, 169
  Thomas, 7
  William B, 149, 169
Kniffen, "Anor," 69
Knowles, Abram, 150
  Cole Clinton, 150

Knowles, Elmira, 150
  Elvira Rosanna, 150
  Milton, 150
  Nathan, 150
Knox, Abby J, 171
  Charles, 171
  Chloe Ann, 71
  Edmond, 71
  Emily, 171
  Frederick, 37, 171
  Frederick H, 171
  Hannah, 171
  Harriet, 175
  John, 171
  Martha T, 171
  Reuben, 171
  Sarah, 37
  Zillah, 171
Kohler, Mary E, 95
Kool, Jacob, 3
Koons, Aurelia, 85
  Francis L, 85
  Jacob, 85
Kraft, Abigail, 129

Labounty, Bertha Bessie, 187
  Harriet Eliza, 67
  Ira George, 67, 187
  Lettie Leonel, 187
La Due, Jerome, 171
  Zillah, 171
Laethum, John V, 80
  Mary Jane, 80
La Fever, Agnes, 191
  Austin, 191
  Dana, 191
  Eldora, 191
  Elsie, 191
  Lovett, 86, 191
  Mary E, 191
  Minard, 86
  Nettie M, 191
  Susan, 86
  Wilmur, 191
Lance, Sarah, 18
Langley, Rosa, 154
Laverents, Edith Sedina, 196
  Paul, 196
Larzalest, ——, 98
Lawrence, Betsey, 164
  Charles S, 82
  Clinton, 179
  Elvira, 179
  Emma, 179
  Estelle, 82
  Geo, 50, 179
  James, 179
  John, 8

INDEX

Lawrence, Luzina, 179
    Phebe, 179
    Zillah, 50
Layman, Laura Amelia, 125
Leavens, Fred, 176
    Mary, 176
Lee, Euphemia, 148
    John, 148
Leete, Andrew, 17
    Caleb, 17
    Dorothy, 18
    John, 17
    Thomas, 17
    William, 17
Lemen, Geo , 156
    Minnie, 156
Lent, Benson Oakley, 104
    Hettie A , 104
    Susan Jane, 104
    Thos Stockton, 104
    William Benson, 104
Leonard, ———, 169
    Helen, 133
    Seth Gregory, 133
Lewis, Ellen, 166
    Hannah, 47
    Joseph, 47
    Louisa, 66
    Nellie B , 147
Light, Ellen, 147
    Putnam, 147
Likely, Absalom, 58
Lickley, Adelia, 170
    Ebenezer, 170
    Emeline, 170
    Fayette, 170
    James B , 170
    John, 35, 170
    John M , 170
    Julia, 170
    Lucy, 103
    Margaret, 170
    Martha A , 170
    Mary, 35, 170
    Sarah Emeline, 170
    William C , 170
Lindaburg, Alvira E , 191
    Stewart, 191
Little, Annie C , 117
"Lo," Jeannette, 80
Lockhart, Christiana, 85
Lockwood, Eldora, 191
    Hiram, 191
Longwell, Amanda, 67
    Eliza, 183
    Frank, 183
    Hosea, 98
    Mary Cynthia, 98

Longwell, Zillah, 143
Longyear, Minnie Adeline, 196
    Oscar, 196
Loomer, Maria, 94
Loomis, Harrison, 86
    Phebe Ann, 86
    William, 86
Lord, Cora A , 193
Losee, Ann Jeanette, 178
    James, 178
Lounsbury, Mary, 39
Lozier, Eliza Jane, 177
    John G , 177
Ludenton, Henry, Col , 28
Luscott, Elizabeth, 152
Lusk, Sylvester J , Rev , 143
Luther, Elipheanet, 133
    Seraphina, 133
Lyon, David, 167
    Iva, 167
Lyons, Elizabeth, 83
    Hannah, 171
    William, 171

McAllister, Eliza, 136
McAuley, Sarah, 157
McCall, Mrs , 63
McCann, Anne Eliza, 141
McClintock, Andrew, 124
    Andrew James, 124
    Emma Estelle, 124
    Eva Isabel, 124
McClure, Cynthia, 87
    Irine, 43
McCollum, Elizabeth, 140
McCoy, Ann, 167
    Morris R , 167
McCrea, John, 128
    Rebecca Fagan, 128
    Roscoe Lorenzo, 128
McCulloch, Addie Belle, 136
    Mason Wm , 136
    Thomas, 136
McGregor, ———, 29
McHattie, Amelia Gordon, 194
McIntire, Susan, 183
McKeel, Margaret Lavinia, 147
    Reuben, 147
McKinstry, Betsey Amelia, 171
    Harriet Amanda, 171
    Hannah Maria, 171
    Lester Cole, 171
    Mary E , 171
    Sarah Maria, 38
    Stella D , 171, 186
    William, 38, 171
    William Paul, 171, 186
McLean, Edwin, 190

McLean, Susan Agnes, 190
McMahan, Lucy A, 173
McMillan, Harriet Alice, 192
    Lydia Jane, 174
    William, 174
McNeal, Jane Hannah, 142
McNemor, Mary Jane, 145
McOmber, Hannah S, 69
Mabie, Phebe, 29
Mack, Maria, 167
Macomber, Clarissa Amanda, 183
Maidment, Charlotte Louise, 141
    William, 141
Mapes, Mary, 86
Marks, Mina C, 193
    Willard, 193
Marsh, May, 65
Marston, Emma Louisa, 140
    Samuel Wyatt, 141
Mart, Elizabeth Jane, 125
Martin, Cynthia, 54
    Mary, 132
Mase, Idaho, 152
    Sylvester, 152
Mason, David B, 180
    Edith, 142
    Fanny, 65
    Hiram, 88
    Laura, 88
    Mary Jane, 180
    William, 142
Masters, Martha, 85
    Silas M, 85
    Charles N, 85
Matson, Amanda, 108
Maule, Gertrude, 196
Maxwell, Emily De Russy, 117
    John William C, 117
Mayo, Mary, 11
Mead, Abner, 15
    Alice Levisa, 184
    Ann, 183
    Belle, 189
    Carrie, 189
    Charles, 189
    Charles Wiloby, 184
    Chloretta, 184
    Edwin, 184
    Frank A, 183
    George Watson, 184
    Henry Axtel, 112
    Katharine Ann, 58
    Lucy Alice, 112
    Minnie May, 112
    Nathaniel, 184
    Robert Carson, 112
    Vashti A, 184
    Washington W, 184

Mead, Wiloby, 58
Mekeel, Peter, 103
    Sarah, 103
Mekeer, ———, 103
Melville, Louisa Jane, 112
Merrett, Desire, 163
    Elisha, 163
Merrick, Antoinette, 169
    David, 79
    Elizabeth, 49
    George, 169
    Hannah, 79, 163
    Isaac, 15
    Issacher, 164
    John, 163
    Mercy, 164
    Sarah Ann, 165
Merritt, ———, 148
    Carrie M, 160
    Eunice, 27
    George W, 160
    Hackaliah, 27, 45, 163
    Hannah, 163
    Joseph, 27
    Mary, 45, 163
    Nehemiah, 163
    Phebe, 100
Mercereau, David Lyman, 124
    Eleanor F, 124
Metcalf, Charlotte, 60
    Edward, 60
    John, 60
Michael, Ada Elvira, 135
    Geo Emmons, 135
    Thaddeus Delos, 135
Miles, Harriet E, 101
Miller, Edward G, 125
    Eliza, 134
    Eliza Jane, 147
    Elizabeth, 34, 43
    Mary, 132
    Nancy, Mrs, 91
    Pulaski, 91
    Rebecca Augustine, 125
    Samuel, 40
Millington, Annie Louise, 96
    Edwin H, 96
    William Fenton, 96
Mills, Esther, 54
    Mary Jane, 135
Minor, Harriet L., 99
    Mary, 16
    Sherman, 99
Minto, Rachel, 136
    Thomas, 136
Mohr (Moore), Anna Mary, 94
    John George, 94
    William C, 94

Monroe, Adelia Ann, 177
    Augustus J, 177
Moore, Priscilla, 103
Moorehouse, Eli, 175
    Sarah L, 175
Morgan, Charles H, 157
    Elizabeth, 95, 178
    Harriet Jane, 157
Morley, Matilda, 159
Morris, Roger, 26
Morse, Agnes Eleanor, 82
    Albert Stephen, 82
    Edwin, 82
    Kendall P, 82
Morton, Esther, 99
    Harriet, 139
    Mary, 129
Moss, Emma B., 172
Moulton, Miriam, 125
Mourtland, Jane, 89
Mowe, Annie Marie, 71
Mudge, Esther Marie, 88
    Sarah, 90
Munsell, Margaret E, 135
Murphy, Emma Louisa, 91
    Fred, 91
    Lena May, 91
    Mary, 72
    William R, 91
Murray, Alexander S, 135
    Cynthia, 180
    Jay Nellis, 116
    Jerry, 180
    Mary Constance, 116
    Robert Maynard, 117
    William, 135
Myer, Bertha, 114
    N Lemuel, 114
    Noah, 114
Myrick, Mary, 11

Nash, Susan Jane, 111
Naylor, Clara C, 129
    Joseph L, 129
Neil, Glorinda, 153
Nelson, Elizabeth, 165
    James, 165
    Sarah H, 165
Nesper, Caroline C., 120
    Gustav Henry, 120
Newbury, Sarah, 7
    Zeruiah, 7
Newell, Isaac D, Rev, 81
    Sarah Jane, 81
Newkirk, Ella Victoria, 115
Newman, Ann, 166
    Henrietta, 171
    James Madison, 171

Newton, Helen, 115
    Ivah, 55
    Jesse, 115
    Lauren, 55
    Louisa, 55
    Rebecca, 111
Niblo, Rev Mr, 11
Nichols, Adah, 37, 165
    Chauncey, 56, 171
    Cynthia M, 137
    Daniel R, 165
    Edgar, 171
    Edward, 56
    Edwin, 171
    Elizabeth, 165
    Emily, 56
    Henrietta, 171
    Henry, 32, 37, 165
    Henry B, 165
    James H, 174
    Jessie Fremont, 100
    John Francis, 100
    Joseph, 100
    Joseph Cole, 165
    Josiah, 32
    Julia, 165
    Lewis, 37, 56, 100, 165, 171
    Loretta, 165
    Lydia, 174
    Naomi J, 171
    Nathan S, 137
    Perry G, 165
    Phebe, 165
    Ruth, 165
    Sarah, 165
    Susannah, 32
    Viola, 165
    Zillah, 100
Nickerson, Mary, 64
Niver, Lemira, 191
    William H, 191
Noble, Cerepta, 168
North, Mary, 132
Northrup, Byronette Cole, 174
    Esther, 45
    Hannah E, 160
    Loretta, 100, 165
    William D, 174
Norton, Alfred, 168
    Cerepta, 168
    Charles, 34
    Chas B, 168
    Chas C, 168
    Dora, 168
    Emily C, 168
    Emily L, 172
    Hannah S, 173
    Havilah, 34

Norton, Issacher, 34
    Jennie, 102
    Mary Jane, 168
Nosler, Claude H , 125
    Emma Agnes, 125
    Lynde Claude, 125
Nunn, Emma Jane, 69
    George, 69
    Henry, 69
Nurse, Ethel, 146
    Harriet, 146
    Ida Elmira, 146
    Walter, 146
    Walter George, 146

O'Connor, Mayme, 174
O'Neill, John, 72
    Mary A , 72
Obert, Caroline, 85
    Leroy Deven, 85
    Margaret, 86
    Peter, 85
Odel, Charles, 170
    James, 170
    John, 170
    Martha A , 170
    Mary, 170
    Susan M , 170
Odell, Betsey, 59
    John, 35, 58
    Naomi, 35
    Sarah, 58
Ogden, ———, 35
    Charles, 43
    Joseph, 34
    Lydia, 43
    Mary, 34
    Samuel, 43
    Susannah, 33
Olds, Alfred Cleveland, 154
    Anna Louise, 154
    Grace, 193
Oliver, Elspeth, 64
Olmstead, Ida Elizabeth, 109
    Linus, 109
Onderdunk, Hannah M , 96
Organ, Cornelias, 55, 56, 66
    Jesse, 66
    Mary, 55, 66
    Rachel, 66
Orton, Jane, 112
Osborn, Mary, 42
    Sarah, 174
Owen, Bertha, 110
    Elizabeth, 109
    Fayette, 170
    John, 109
    Ruth, 56, 57

Owens, Temperance, 130
Paddock, Geo W , Dr , 68
Paine, Anne, 17
Palmer, Alonzo, 110
    Alonzo Augustus, 110
    Bryant S , 185
    Carrie Anna, 140
    Josiah C , 125
    Lydia, 185
    Mary Ellen, 125
    Mary Horton, 88
    Medora Jane, 110
    Matthew, 88
    Philip, 140
Pardeaux, Fannie A , 194
    Frank, 194
Paris, Isaac, Col , 85
    James, Jr , 85
    Jane Ann, 85
    Otto Marshall, 85
Park, Alexander, 72
    Frank Lane, 71
    Gertrude Celia, 72
    Grace Elizabeth, 71
    Jessie Cecil, 72
    Lloyd Clayton, 72
    Percy Cole, 72
Parks, Jennie, 152
    Mary E , 179
Parker, Amanda W., 195
    Hervey Nathan, 195
    John, 92
    Louise Malvina, 154
    Lulu, 195
    Mary, 71, 143
    Rachel Emily, 92
    Susannah, 8
    William H , 92, 195
Parshall family, 87
    Addie, 191
    Alvira E , 191
    Asa, 87
    Charlotta, 191
    Delaphine, 191
    Israel, 87, 191
    Jesse, 88, 192
    Lemira, 191
    Lenora, 192
    Mattie, 192
    Merritt, 191
    Milan G , 192
    Millis Lincoln, 191
    Milton Chatman, 191
    Minerva, 87
    Prudence, 88
    Ranson N , 191
    Ursula, 191

Patchen, Antha Minerva, 170
  George, 50
  George Henry, 178
  Laura, 178
  Minerva Ruth, 50
  Uriah R , 50, 178
Patterson, Cecilia Almira, 138
  John James, 138
Paxton, Carrie Louisa, 140
  James, 140
  John William, 140
Pease, Charles, 102
Peck, Alida, 192
  Harriet, 192
  Katharine, 112
  Minnie, 192
  Phebe, 192
  Thomas, 192
Peebles, Alice Jane, 125
  John Cannon, 125
Pendleton, Aurelia Celestine, 113
  Joseph Thomas, 113
Pendley, Augustus, 161
Penn, Edith Lewis, Mrs , 195
Pentreath, Julia, 184
Paters, George, 155
  Leota, 155
Pettingill, Hannah Elizabeth, 126
Petty, Nancy, 86
Phelps, Eunice, 149
Philips, Anna Eliza, 66
  Albert, 196
  Lefferetta A , 123
  Mary Frances, 196
Phillipse, Frederick, 26, 41
Pierce, Catharine, 144
  Margaret, 107
Pierson, Ann, 149
  William, 168
  Zillah, 168
Pinckney, Chloe, 40
  La Fayette, 182
  Sarah E , 182
Place, Georgiana Irine, 107
  John Wildy, 107
  John J. W , 107
Plate(?), Margaret, 168
Platt, Abijah, 59
  Ebenezer, 59
  Mary, 59
  William C , 59
  William N , 59
Pomeroy, Kate, 117
Poor, Alice Mowe, 71
  Emma Jane, 71
  Fred Allen, 71
  Herbert Knox, 71
  Joseph, 71

Pope, James, 96
  Mary Elizabeth, 96
Porter, ———, 168
  Angeline, 72
  Emma, 92
  Harriet, 181
  John C , 181
  Lewis, 36, 92
  Louise, 181
  Thurza, 36
Potter, ———, 60
  Lucinda, 140
Powell, Melvina, 114
Pratt, ———, 103
  Elizabeth, 158
  Lydia, 16
  Mary Etta, 156
Price, Emily, 110
  George, 73, 189
  Lois S , 73
Propeo(?), Lewis, 167
  Sophia, 167
Prince, Mercy, 9
  Thomas, 9, 21
Purcell, Edward Benton, 184
  Hannah Ann Elizabeth, 184
Purdy, Betsey A , 102
  Jedidah, 165
  John, 165
  Joshua, 165
Putnam, Mary, 129
  Norman, 129

Quick, Angeline, 188
  Carrie, 189
  Cornelius, 73, 188
  Florence, 189
  Frank, 189
  George, 189
  Lydia, 188
  Mary Ann, 92, 189
  Myron, 189
  Peter, 92
  Samantha, 73, 189

Radcliff, Elizabeth, 146
Ragan, Eleanor, 11
Rahn, Florence A , 194
  Thodore, 194
Rammer, Oliver P , 157
  Viola May, 157
Randall, Emma, 65
  Eunice, 163
  Frances L , 65
  Frankie, 65
  Gideon, 107
  Hannah Gannett, 107
  James, 163

Randall, Julia, 66
  Nathan, 65
  Nathaniel L , 65
Rappleye, Lydia Bloomer, 73
  Minnie, 73
  William, 73
Raredon, Theodosia, 114
Rath, Mary, 189
  Sidney, 189
Rathbun, Ada Olive, 88
  Edgar Lucius, 88, 193
  Fred Arthur, 193
  Grace, 193
  James W , 89
  Laura Eunice, 193
  Valentine, 8
Rawson, Amos P , 150
  Celia Octavia, 150
  Ed , 150
  Henry, 150
  John, 83
  Mae, 83
  Olive, 150
Raymond, ———, 102
Reasoner, Mary A , 124
Rector, Wilhelmina Ann, 138
Redfield, Elizabeth, 59
Reed, Effie Elizabeth, 134
  Emily Augusta, 95
  Fred C , 134
  L Augustus, 95
  William, 134
Reese, Cornelia A., 179
  Peter, 179
Ressequie, Mary, 161
Retan, Almeran, 143
  Sarah, 143
Reniff, Caroline, 129
Reynolds, Abby J , 171
  Betsey, 167
  Elihu, 167
  Emily, 171
  Floyd, 171
  Irine, 185
  John, 38, 171
  Julia, 77
  Louise, 171
  Mary Elizabeth, 111
  Mills, 185
  Naomi, 38
  Sarah, 171
Rhodes, Elsie, 149
  Marvin, 149
Rice, Alice Edna, 150
  Burrage, 160
  Freeman, 150
  Mary A., 160
Richards, John, 59

Richards, Lurana, 59
  Melinda, 114
  Sardinia, 114
  William, 59
Richardson, Lavina, 86
Richmond, Adeline, 89
Ritchie, Sarah, 110
Roat, Adah, 89
  Betsey, 89
  Cora A , 193
  David, 89
  Frederick, 89, 193
  George A , 193
  Harry N , 193
  Lena M , 193
  Lewis F , 193
  Milton D , 193
  Mina C , 193
  Winirfed M , 193
Robbins, Harriet, 136
  Lillian F , 129
Roberts, Abigail, 39, 79
  Charlotte Caroline, 121
  Cyrus, 121
Robinson, Amai, 7
  Emma, 173
  Homer G., 160
  Isaiah, 7
  Julia Hill, 160
Rockwell, Phebe, 50
Roe, Ann, 7
Rogers, Anna, 7
  Hannah, 60
  Jane, 127
  Joseph, 23
  Mary, 23, 116
  Thomas S , 116
Rollins, Cyrus A , 171
  Mary E., 171
Romer, Adelia, 170
  James, 170
Rotherforth, Carrie, 107
  Henry, 107
Rouse, Angeline Mary, 111
  Duane, 111
Rowland, Anna, 51
Rowlee, Huldah, 15
  Matthew, 7
Rudd, Zerush, 14
Rude, Anadella C , 111
  Caleb M , 63
  Clarissa Malissa, 63
Ruland, Mary, 72
Rumsey, Florence Adele, 180
  Jessie, 192
Rundle, Ezra, 110
  Jane Ann, 110
  Mary, 7

Rundel, Joseph, 7
Rupert, Ida T , 180
Russell, Chloe, 148
    Eunice, 105, 106
    Jane, 167
    Levi B , 167
    Louise, 105
    Morris, 56
    Phebe J , 56
    Sarah, 95
Rutherford, Adelia, 64
    Henry, 17
    John, 64, 187
    Margaret, 187
    Paul, 187
    Sarah, 17
Ryer, Ann W , 96
    William T , 96

Saliers, Ann Amanda, 67
    Cora M , 187
    Earl A , 187
    Fred A , 187
    Henry A , 67, 187
    Nettie M , 187
Sands, Antoinette, 145
    Isaac G , 145
Savory Family, The, 86
    Mary Ann Ball, 86
    Ira, 86
Sauer, George H , 175
    Sarah Louise, 175
Schigler, Augustus, 98
    Mary, 98
Schneider, Cecile Elvira, 197
    Emma Celia, 108
    J C., 108, 197
    Katharine M , 197
    Leroy F , 197
    William, 108
Schoonover, Elizabeth, 138
Schutt, Alfred, 116
    Melissa, 116
Schuyler, Sarah Hodge, Mrs , 86
Scott, Chester, 63, 65
    Eliza E , 65
    George, 65
    Henrietta, 65
    Jason Haven, 135
    John Ellis, 116
    Laura, 135
    Lucy, 63
    Lyman, 65
    Mary, 65, 116
    Mary Geraldine, 151
    Nathaniel, 65
    Sarah, 45
Scranton, Ada Blanche, 137

Scranton, Ward L., 137
    Winona Cole, 137
Seaman, George, 173
    Lydia Ann, 173
Sears, Eliza, 37
    Mary, 37
    Sarah, 15
Secord-Secour-Se Cord, 159
Secord, Benjamin, 159
    Estelle Jane, 159
Seger, Geo. B McClellan, Dr , 120
    Eugene, 120
    Mary Taylor, 120
Selleck, Azubah, 34
    Charles, 59, 169, 185
    Ebenezer, 185
    Elizabeth, 105, 185
    Emma D , 185
    Esther M , 185
    Gould John, 34
    Huldah, 147
    Joseph, 169
    Lorana, 185
    Lucretia, 59
    Ophelia, 185
    Silas, 34, 59, 169
Semple, Jane, 135
Seymour, Hannah, 57
Shaffer, Lois, 112
Sharp, Dominie, 108
Shaw, ———, 102
    Mary, 90
Shears, Elizabeth, 144
Sheldon, Ann, 68
    Ebenezer, 68
    Emily Preston, 69
    Harriet Amanda, 171
    Horace P , 171
    William, 69
Shepherd, Frances, 121
Shepard, Lucy Ann, 143
Sherborne, Anna, 50
    Samuel, 179
    William, 50, 179
    William O , 179
Sherman, Chloe, 108
    Levi, 108
Sherrow, Emily, 171
    Owen, 171
Sherwood, Covert S , 158
    Francis, 102
    Gay, 158
    James, 103
    James, Capt , 102
Shoots, Elizabeth, 155
Shute, Ann, 17
    Robert, 17
Sigerson, Nancy, 64

232 INDEX

Simpson, Celia, 124
Sinclair, Bradley, 65
   Samuel, Maj, 65
   Virtue Elvira, 65
Slade, Edward, 17
   Maria, 17
Sloat, Arvilla, 165
   Elizabeth, 40
   Edson, 40, 173
   James, 40
   Lydia Ann, 173
   Stanley, 173
   Tamar, 94
   William, 165
Sly, Idalia, 155
   Robert O'Hara, 155
Smalley (Smale, Smally), Abagail, 98
   Caleb, 105
   Eunice, 105
   Freeman, 105
   Hannah, 24, 26
   Helen Cerena, 182
   James K, 182
   Joseph, 25
   Louise, 105
   Lovisa, 55
   Priscilla, 25
   Sarah A, 167
   Zachariah, 55
Smith, ———, 18, 161
   Abel, 15
   Alice Emily, 81
   Ann Jeanette, 178
   Anna, 163
   Angustus, 92
   Charles G, 27, 35, 163
   Charles Irving, 96
   Clarinda, 61
   Darius, 48
   Delicy S, 178
   Elisha, 7
   Ellen, 81
   Elsie, 191
   Eunice, 81
   Eunice M, 147
   Fannie Fern, 131
   Freeman, 163
   Hannah, 107
   Hannah J, 178
   Hayward, 178
   Hettie Maria, 104
   Hiram, 166
   Horace, 165
   Ida, 178
   Ida F, 153
   Jesse, 7, 27, 35, 41, 163
   Jessie Lena, 96
   John, 131

Smith, John H, 96
   Joseph, 166
   Julia, 170
   Lemuel, 104
   "Liddey," 7
   Lucretia, 109
   Lyman, 131
   Margaret, 35, 163
   Mary, 7, 55
   Mary Ann, 92
   Mary Fowler, 160
   Naomi, 27
   Nancy, 178
   Nathaniel, 163
   Neurissa, 48
   Ormond J, 178
   Phebe, 166
   Phebe Jane, 177
   Philip, 55
   Ruth, 64, 165
   Samuel B, 178
   Sarah, 41
   Sarah Ann, 166
   Sarah K, 95
   Saxton E, 178
   Susan, 166, 182
   William, 48, 177
   William Elliot, 81
   William Henry, 81
Sniffen, Charles Samuel, 79
   Edna Caroline, 79
   Harry, 79
   Sarah Louisa, 79
Snow, Dorothy Elizabeth, 141
   George Henry, 142
   Hannah, 23
   Joseph, 23
   Ruth, 23
   Stephen, 23
Soper, Docia, 142
Southworth, ———, 189
   Constant, 21
   Jennie, 189
   Mrs, 9
Sowber, ———, 101
Sparrow, Rebecca, 10
Spencer, Laura, 178
   Philip, 13
Sprague, Ada Esther, 137
   Catharine, 105
   Elizabeth, 144
   Emma, 144
   Freeman, 105, 106
   Luman, 167
   Pamelia, 145
   Rachel Jane, 106
   Samuel, 144
   Sarah J, 167

Sprague, Truman, 137
St Vrain, Minnie, 126
    Savimen, 127
Stafford, Myrtie, 149
Stanfield, Ruth Esther, 137
    Thomas, 137
Stanley, Lulu, 111
Steele, William, 57
Stephenson, Ann Eliza, 129
Sterling, Elizabeth, 161
Sterns, Emily A, 158
    John W, 157
    Laura Jane, 157
Stetson, Mary Cornelia, 138
Stevens, David W, 161
    Hannah Lavinia, 139
    Howard Robert, 144
    Marie Antoinette, 144
    Mary Frances, 161
    William Henry, 144
Stewart, Henry, 131
    Jemima, 7
    Mary Almira, 131
Stiles, Almira, 92
    Harry Wilson, 83
    Lewis C, 83
    Nallie C, 83
    Rebecca Lane, 83
    Susan Jane, 83
Stoddard, David Henry, 134
    Elijah, 134
Stone, Mary Kendall, 97
    Thankful, 13, 32
Stoutenberg, Ida, Mrs., 196
Stowe, Louise, 46
Stratton, Franc, 65
Street, Mary, 17
    Nicholas, 17
Stripling, Jemima, 110
Strong, Cynthia Lovicia, 120, 121
Sullaway, Bert Cole, 188
    Charles Frank, 71, 188
    Chloe Maude, 188
    Earl Foster, 188
    Earl Knox, 188
    Ella Ann, 71
    Fay Inez, 188
    Fred Willard, 188
    Pearl Hazel, 188
    Roy Parker, 188
    Ruby Edna, 188
    William, 71
Sullivan, Nancy, 154
Sunderlin, Hannah E, 166
    Rachel, 34, 40, 68
Sutphen, Sarah, 88
Sutton, Ann, 161
Swart, John, 179

Sweetland, Abner, 62
    Malinda, 62
Swick, Barbara, 73
Symonds, Eliza Shatswell, 146

Taft, Amos, Dea, 74
    Emma F, 74
    George Wheaton, 190
    Harriet Calista, 73
    Howard Bailey, Rev, 73, 190
    Miner Cole, 190
Tate, Kittie, 159
    Samuel, 159
Taylor, Eliza Corson, 117
    Mary Jane, 119
    William, 117, 119
Tenbrook, Andrew, 190
    Anna, 190
    Ezra, 189
    George, 190
    Helen, 175
    Jane Thursey, 73
    John, 189
    Lois, 190
    William, 73, 189
Terrell, Caroline, 166
Terry, Ann Elizabeth, 175
    Cecelia Oselton, 175
    Elizabeth, 43
    Georgia, 175
    Ira, 100
    Ira Cole, 175
    John, 43, 175
    John McClure, 175
    Marie Antoinette, 100
    Mary Eliza, 175
    Phebe Ann, 104
    Samual, 43
    Sarah Louise, 175
Tevis, Fanny C, 169
Thatcher, Adaline, 49
    Catharine, 109
    John, 49
    Lydia, 10
Thomas, Agnes, 188
    Anson Lawrence, 69
    Clarie Belle, 162
    David, 36
    Irving, 69
    Irwin, 188
    Jessie, 188
    Leverton, 12
    Minerva, 69
    Phebe, 36
    Recompense, 7, 30
Thompson, Alexander, 90
    Bridget, 16
    Eliza, 113

Thompson, Nancy, 90
Thorn, ———, 49
Thorne, Ruth Elizabeth, 190
    Willis A , 190
Tichenor, Cora M , 140
Tidd, Anna, 43
Tilley, Elizabeth, 16
Tillott, Josephus, 56, 57
    Rachel, 57
    Sarah, 56
Timerson, Helen, 175
Tinker, J F , 123
    Mary, 123
Todd, Eliza, 165
    John, 165
Tompkins, Amy J , 183
    Caroline, 53
    Elias Q , 53
    Elizabeth, 54
    Eva, 182
    Howard, 60
    Jane Adeline, 123
    John G , Dr , 170
    Mary, 60, 170
    Nancy, 105
    Nathaniel, 58
    Phebe Elizabeth, 144
    Sarah, 166
    Sidney Brooks, 53, 182
    Willis H , 182
Towne, Cecelia O , 175
    Hiram, 175
Townley, Benjamin R , 180
    Daniel, 180
    Marcia, 180
    Prudence, 180
Townsend, 61
    Adalia, 164
    Agnes Maria, 140
    Almira, 164
    Alvey, 164
    Alveyson, 177
    Angeline, 168
    Annie E , 144
    Ardalia, 48, 177
    Arvah C , 140
    Betsey, 164
    Carlton G , 140
    Carrie, 168
    Charles, 28, 162, 164
    Charles A , 194
    Clark, 170
    Coleman, 168
    Edward, 90, 194
    Eli, 144
    Elisha, 28
    Elizabeth, 12, 41, 42, 44
    Emeline, 177

Townsend, Emily, 100
    Ernest E , 194
    Ernest Howard, 144
    Frank, 168
    Frank J , 194
    George, 168
    Gilbert D , 140
    Hannah, 164, 168
    Harriet, 177
    Henah, 34
    Hosea, 34, 168
    Ivah, 34
    James, 28, 28, 48, 164
    Julia, 177
    Laura J., 90
    Lewis, 177
    Lucy, 168
    Lydia M , 194
    Malissa B., 162
    Margaret, 168
    Maria D , 151
    Mariette, 39
    Mary, 168
    Mercy, 164
    Millie M , 194
    Naomi, 164
    Neurissa, 48, 164
    Phebe Jane, 177
    Priscilla, 164
    Priscilla Ann, 82
    Rachel, 168
    Sally, 49
    Samuel A , 98
    Sarah, 94, 164
    Sarah E , 170
    Silvanus, 34
    Susan, 168
    Susannah, 164
    Sylvanus, 168
    Thomas, 34, 168
    Zillah, 98, 168
Tracy, Mary, 28
Traver, Lany, 131
Travis, Betsey Ann, 54
    Charles B , 103
    Deborah, 178
    Emma Louise, 103
    James Henry, 103
    Theresa, 13
Trayer, Lenora, 174
Tripler, Anne Amelia, 129
    Frederick R , 129
    John, 129
Tunison, ———, 168
    Anna, 43
    Annis, 168
    Charles, 174
    Claudius, 43

Tunison, Daniel Cole, 175
   Eliza, 174
   Elizabeth, 175
   Ezra, 175
   Harriet, 175
   Helen, 175
   John, 175
   John P., 43
   Julia, 43
   Lenora, 174
   Lucy, 175
   Lydia, 108
   Lydia Jane, 174
   Maria, 168
   Philip, 108, 174
   Ruth, 174
   Sarah, 175
   Sarah L., 174
   Susan, 175
   Thomas, 43, 175
   William, 43, 174
Turner, Albert, 105
   Charles L., 105
   Charlotte, 105
   Georgiana, 105
   Mary, 149
Tuttle, Almira M., 170
   Samuel B., 170
Twining, Ruth, 23
   William, 23
Twentymen, Martha, 113

Uhl, Jane, 140
Utter, Margaret, 170
   Thomas, 170

Van Blarcom, Maria, 109
Van Camp, Catharine, 50, 180
   Emily, 180
   John A., 50, 180
   Lenora, 192
   Marcia, 180
   Martin P., 180
   Mary Jane, 180
   Nancy, 180
   Prudence, 180
   Walter, 192
   William, 50
Van Cott, Emma, 179
Vanderhoff, Elizabeth, 177
Van Gorder, Guy, 87
   John, 87
Van Horn, Adele M., 111
   C. C., 111
   Roy C., 111
Van Loon, Alaida, 139
Van Loom, Delephine, 131
   Emma Jane, 158

Van Loom, Hepsibah, 131
   Peter, Jr., 139
   Samuel, 131
Van Voorhies, Lucretia, 150
Vany, Harriet, 107
Veech, Harry, 46
Veith, Frank, 156
   Nellie, 156
Von Deleer, Mary, 90
Vosburgh, Addie J., 131
   John, 131
Virgil, Almon K., 179
   Antha M., 179

Waddell, Fanny, 43
Wait, ———, 163
Waldo, Samuel, 8
Walker, Charles C. B., 151
   Cornelia A., 117
   Dorothy, 154
   Elihu F., 117
   Etta, 192
   Fidelia Elizabeth, 88
   Harriet Alice, 192
   Harriet Ellen, 151
   Henson, 88
   Jessie, 192
   Laura Phebe, 192
   Lyman Enos, 192
   Mary, 166
   Mason Erastus, 192
   Phebe, 179
   Robert Wesley, 88, 192
   Thomas, 179
   Thomas Webster, 192
Walkin, Charles Hyde, 131
   Sarah Almira, 131
Wall, Mary, 115
Wands, Ann, 130
Ward, Alice Almira, 187
   Charlotte Eva, 64
   Charlotte Cole, 187
   Joseph, 64
   Walter Rutherford, 187
   William, 64, 187
   William Berton, 187
Waring, Hall B., 182
   Maria, 141
   Susannah, 164
   Stephen, 164
Warren, Jane, 165
   Mehitable, 40
Washburn, Elizabeth, 38, 45
   Jonathan, 45, 163
   Margaret, 169
   Mary, 36, 163
Wasson, Lucy, 130
   David, 130

Wasson, Walter Franklin, 130
Watkins, Emeline Catharine, 122
Watson, Elkanah, 10
Watts, Martha, 62
Webb, Debra Ann, 41
Webster, Rose, 185
Weeks, Arthur, 104
  Edward Crosby, 185
  Josephine, 185
  Julia Frances, 104
  Libbie, 104
  Naomi, 164
  Robert, 164
  Steven V, 104
  William Benjamin, 104
Weld, Ivy Louise, 111
  John Newton, 111
  William, 111
Wesley, Edward, 179
  Elvira, 179
Westfall, Eliza, 82
Weston, George, 177
  Harriet, 177
Wheat, Adeline, Eleanor, 112
  George Charles, 112
Wheeler, John S, 172
  Julia, 172
Whelden, Catorne, 10
  Gabriel, 10
Whitbeck, Jane, 174
White, Anne (Fuller), 9
  Charles Erna, 134
  George Hall, 95
  Hannah, 50
  Harry, 99
  Henah, 167
  Henry Morgan, 95
  Hester Amelia, 95
  Isaac, 134
  Lydia Caroline, 133
  Malon 167
  Maria, 148
  Mary A., 149
  Minnie Rachel, 134
  Peregrine, 9
  Sarah, 99
  Warren, 149
Whitney, Aurilla C, 92
  Emeline, 177
Wickham, Mary E, 191
Wicks, Elizabeth, 87
Wilcox, Charles P., 171
  Hannah Maria, 171
Wildman, Frederick Starr, 117
  Herbert Augustus, 117
  Talbot Cole, 117
  Thomas Gregory, 117
Wilkinson, Alice Jane, 71

Williams, Alice, 97
  Charles, 187
  Cora A, 187
  Henry, 175
  Isabel, 71
  John, 97
  Mary, 72
  Susan, 175
Williamson, ———, 55
Willkon(?), Elizabeth, 7
Willoughby, Alice, 7
Wilson, Asa, 33, 167
  Calista Jane, 67
  Emma, 172
  Fannie, 164
  Jane, 131
  Jeremiah, 67, 164
  Jesse, 67, 164
  Margaret (Cole) Hall, 167
  Mary, 34
  Thomas, 34
Wiltse, Eunice, 89
  Sarah, 135
Winans, Lucy, 54
Winslow, Edward, 9
Winters, Alice Bertha, 112
  Charles Evans, 112, 197
  Evelyn, 197
  Katharine, 197
  William Schuyler, 112
Withers, Alford, 126
  Hannah, 126
  Perry Carter, 126
  Una, 126
Wixom, Amial T, 36
  Ann Thursa, 36
  Desire, 16
  Eliza, 36
Wixsom, Margaret Ann, 182
Wixson, Pelig, 105
  Robert, 105
  Shubel, 105
  Susan Elizabeth, 105
Wolverton, Mattie, 192
Wolworth, Lucy, 168
Wood, Adelia Ann, 177
  Berry Cole, 177
  Caroline L, 96
  Eliza Jane, 177
  Elizabeth, 52, 177
  Harriet N, 117
  Jedediah, 47, 52
  Jeremiah V, 177
  John, 110
  John Weeks, 96
  Mary Ann, 177
  Nehemiah, 47
  Rachel, 45, 164

INDEX

Woods, Rebecca, 47
  Ruth Payne, 96
  Stephen, 47, 177
  Susan, 84
  Susan Elizabeth, 110
  Ursula, 38
Woodley, Clark E , 193
  Winifred M , 193
Woodin, Henry, 55
Woodworth, Ada Frances, 91
  Chester N , 194
  Edmund C., 91, 194
  Edna, 195
  Harvey K , 195
  Helen, 160
  Herbert, 195
  Irwin C , 195
  Leon E , 195
  Lida May, 195
  Mabel, 195
  Nestor, 91, 181
  Phebe, 181
Woolheizer, Ann Elizabeth, 57
  Anthony, 57
  Fredrick, 57
  Jacob, 57
  John, 57
  Katharine, 57
Withers, Laura, 126
Wooster, Annie Louisa, 184
  Henry, Thomas, 184
Wormley, Mary Elizabeth, 156

Worthington, Mehitabel, 13
  William, Rev., 13
Wright, Emily, 178
  Frances, 165
  Gertrude Catharine, 158
  Hannah, 84, 85
  Jane, 40
  John, 30
  Leonard Sloat, 158
  Lewis, 40
  Mary Emeline, 113
  Ruth, 15, 40
  Samuel, 178
  Sarah Jane, 116
Wyckoff, Eliza Ann, 141

Yeamans, Almira, 166
  Leonard, 166
Yeomans, Epenitus, 68
York, Jane, 117
Young, Emma, 89
Youngs, John, 22
  Priscilla, 25
  Ruth, 22

Zent, Claude Raymond, 72
  Grace Zerelda, 72
  Isaac Chase, 72
  Isaac Weaver, 72
  Jessie Edith, 72
  Willard Clayton, 72

CPSIA information can be obtained
at www.ICGtesting.com
Printed in the USA
LVHW082106080323
741211LV00004BB/142